D0984100

Understanding the Sacred Text

Understanding the Sacred Text

Essays in honor of Morton S. Enslin on the Hebrew Bible and Christian Beginnings

Edited by John Reumann

Advisory Editorial Committee
F. W. Beare, Trinity College, Toronto, Canada
Sheldon H. Blank, Hebrew Union College — Jewish Institute
of Religion, Cincinnati
John L. McKenzie, S.J., De Paul University, Chicago

JUDSON PRESS   Valley Forge

UNDERSTANDING THE SACRED TEXT

Copyright © 1972
Judson Press, Valley Forge, Pa. 19481

International Standard Book No. 0-8170-0487-4
Library of Congress Catalog Card No. 72-165592

Printed in the U.S.A.

Introduction

March 8, 1972, marks the seventy-fifth birthday of Morton Scott Enslin. The year also marks the fiftieth anniversary of his graduation from theological school, entry into the Baptist ministry and into graduate study at Harvard, and marriage to his gracious wife. Twenty-five years ago he was in the midst of a distinguished editorship of the *Crozer Quarterly*, to be followed by a decade at the helm of the *Journal of Biblical Literature*. Throughout the years a stream of books, translations, and some ninety articles and essays has come from his pen (written sometimes in an inimitable scrawl, legible only to himself and his closest friends, yet always meticulously expressed and carefully edited), especially about the topics treated in this book by pupils, colleagues, and friends: the Bible, Jesus and the Gospels, and Christian origins. (Paul, and Dr. Enslin's interest in ethics are not reflected in our essays.) Today, after a teaching career in seminary and university, he is a professor at Dropsie University.

Late in 1967, F. W. Beare, of Toronto, suggested that a volume of essays would be appropriate to honor Dr. Enslin and his accomplishments. Dr. Maurice Jacobs, Philadelphia, Professor Virgil Rogers (New Brunswick Theological Seminary), and others encouraged the idea. Dr. Sheldon Blank (Hebrew Union College—Jewish Institute of Religion, Cincinnati) and Father John McKenzie, S. J. (then at Notre Dame, now at De Paul University, Chicago) agreed to serve with Professor Beare as an advisory committee. Plans were developed in 1968, and in 1969 arrangements made with Judson Press, of the American Baptist Board of Education and Publication, to publish the volume, and the essays were commissioned. Thirteen of the sixteen scholars approached offer the essays which follow as a tribute to Morton S. Enslin's service to biblical scholarship.

All of the contributions are by those who know Professor Enslin as both scholar and friend. One was a colleague at Crozer (James B. Pritchard), one at Bryn Mawr (Howard Kee). Two were doctoral pupils at the University of Pennsylvania (Everett

M. Harrison, John Reumann). All the others have worked with Dr. Enslin in the Society of Biblical Literature (and Exegesis) and its journal. Death prevented one old friend, S. MacLean Gilmour, from participating in the project, and age prevented others. Because of a heavy schedule of administrative and teaching duties, Franklin Young, a former pupil at Crozer and now Director of Graduate Studies in Religion at Duke University, has been unable to complete the article he desired to write. A dear friend and colleague at Dropsie, Professor Solomon Zeitlin, could not, because of ill health, prepare his promised contribution on "Justin Martyr's Monologue" in time for the deadline for this volume; he expects to publish it in the *Jewish Quarterly Review* in 1972 as his salute. A host of friends and well-wishers append their names to the Tabula Gratulatoria.

A word of thanks is due to Mr. Harold L. Twiss, of Judson Press, for his interest in the project; to the copy editors there; to Mr. Roland Tapp, who did the basic editing on our disparate manuscripts; and to the craftsmen at the press of Maurice Jacobs for setting the sections involving foreign-language type.

Any excellencies there are of contents, style, precision, or originality are appropriate tributes to the friend we honor. "No shortcuts" was the formula once ascribed to Morton S. Enslin in the *Bulletin* of Crozer Theological Seminary (60,3 [July, 1968], p. 15). We are in his debt, each one, for high standards of honest workmanship. This volume is public token of our praise for one who could move from learned but lively essays on the church fathers or the Synoptic problem to analyses and reminiscences about Horatio Alger, Jr. (Dr. Enslin has one of the best collections of this bit of Americana), and from the pages of more than half a dozen festschriften to which he was asked to contribute, to popular journals for the preacher, with pithy advice about current foibles in church life and the proper use of the Bible. In this volume we share with him in the sentiment he once voiced about Scripture at the close of *Christian Beginnings* (p. 510):

> To love it you must know it;
> To know it you must love it.

J. R.

30 April, 1971

List of Abbreviations

JPS	The Jewish Publication Society of America, Bible translation. 1917. *The Torah* (Philadelphia, 1962).
JQR	*Jewish Quarterly Review*
JR	*Journal of Religion*
JTS	*Journal of Theological Studies*
KJV	King James Version
LXX	Septuagint
NEB	New English Bible
NovTest	*Novum Testamentum*
NTA	*New Testament Abstracts*
NTS	*New Testament Studies*
par.	parallel
PG	Patrologia Graeci, Migne
PL	Patrologia Latina, Migne
PPTS	Palestine Pilgrims' Text Society (1885-1897, reprinted 1971)
PW	*Real-Enzyklopädie der classischen Alterumswissenschaft,* ed. A. Pauly and G. Wissowa
RevBib	*Revue Biblique*
RSV	Revised Standard Version
SBL	Society of Biblical Literature
SBT	Studies in Biblical Theology (First Series, unless noted)
SNTS	Society for New Testament Studies
TDNT	*Theological Dictionary of the New Testament,* tr. of *TWNT*
ThViat	*Theologia Viatorum.* Jahrbuch der Kirchliche Hochschule Berlin
TU	*Texte und Untersuchungen*
TWNT	*Theologisches Wörterbuch zum Neuen Testament,* ed. Kittel-Friedrich
VT	*Vetus Testamentum*
ZAW	*Zeitschrift für die alttestamentliche Wissenschaft*
ZNW	*Zeitschrift für die neutestamentliche Wissenschaft*
ZThK	*Zeitschrift für Theologie und Kirche*

The conventional abbreviations are employed for books of the Bible and other ancient sources, including the Dead Sea scrolls (e.g., 1 QS denotes the Manual of Discipline or *sérek* from cave 1)

Contents

THE GOSPELS AND CHRISTIAN ORIGINS

The Sum
of
Many Parts
by Theodore V. Enslin

A son may be prejudiced in favor of his father, and it is right that he should be, but there are other elements which go far beyond mere filial pride in the honor I feel in attempting to sketch briefly some of the elements which make up my father's unique qualities and contributions, together with the more obvious *vita*. Despite its mere chronological sequence, a *vita* reveals a continuity, with direct bearing on the achievement which can be seen in outline—a slow, whole growth, which continues at a time when many men think of retirement, in terms of winters in Florida and summers on a golf course.

The pace is still such that its exactness and steadiness would make many younger men quail, and to me it is a study in industry which I despair of equaling. I can hear his retort: "I would rather wear out than rust out," and it is true that what is used constantly keeps an edge and usefulness which is soon blunted when a tool is put away on a dark shelf, to be used occasionally. This is an obvious truism, but one which is too little heeded by those who, for one reason or another, bow to arbitrary age requirements for retirement when actually they are very probably of more value in their particular fields than they were in their so-called prime. I cannot conceive of a time when my father would be satisfied with this sort of "leisure."

To think of him is to think simultaneously of the many hours each day which he spends at his desk, and at the quantity of work, as well as the variety, which passes in front of him, from many sources, requiring his attention as scholar, teacher, and editor. It is typical of him that several years ago, while undergoing convalescence from a serious operation and still confined to a hospital, he pressed my mother into service as secretary, troubleshooter, and general legman, so that the forthcoming issue of the *Journal of Biblical Literature* might appear on time. It did. If a teaching or other engagement is to be met, it *is* met, and there are no excuses given. Many times, in the years which he spent at St. Lawrence University in upstate New York, I am sure that the attendance at class, church, or lecture platform was cut by the type of winter weather which is common there. The lecturer arrived invariably, and on time.

These are simply outward manifestations of the meticulous care with which all of his work is invested. I have no competence in the fields where he is eminently at home, but in reading his work, occasionally visiting his classes or a Sunday morning service, I am always struck by the whole-souled honesty of the work which has been done in preparation, the integrity of the scholarship, which I sense in a way that I cannot know (it is impossible to fake such integrity), and the highly interesting manner of presentation. These are not separate qualities, but are integral parts of a fully aware intelligence — one that is completely in command of each situation that confronts it. A pitiless examination of himself, and of each step as he takes it, is one of the most evident qualities of all of his work.

One of my earliest recollections in this respect has to do with his definition of scholarship as a following of truth wherever it may lead, regardless of consequences. And there are no details too small for his attention. As an editor and proofreader, of his own and others' work, he has often taught printers things which they should have known, but didn't. No matter how heavy the load of commitments, no prospective contributor to the several journals which he has edited has ever had to hang by his thumbs awaiting a decision. Usually the answer goes out by the next mail. These are not run-of-the-mill qualities, nor qualities to be taken lightly.

Emerson once made a list which he entitled "My Men," beginning with Thoreau and ending with John Muir. I have never, consciously, made such a list, but if I were to do it, my father, Morton Scott Enslin, would figure in a preeminent position.

The following list of important events, honors, and publications is subjoined, not as a mere directory, as I hinted above, but as a guide to an enviable achievement:

Born, Somerville, Massachusetts, March 8, 1897. Parents, Theodore V. Enslin — Ada E. Scott.

Graduated from Somerville High School, 1915.

Commissioned, Ensign, U.S. Naval Reserve, December, 1918.

A.B., Harvard (war degree) as of 1919.

B.D., Newton Theological Institution, 1922.

Ordained, Baptist ministry, 1922.

Married, Ruth May Tuttle, 1922.

Th.D., Harvard, 1924.

Children: Theodore V., II, 1925; Priscilla, 1929.

Professor of New Testament Literature and Exegesis, Crozer Theological Seminary, Chester, Pa., 1924–1954.

Lecturer, Textual Criticism, Philadelphia Divinity School, 1924–1925.

Lecturer, Patristics and the History of Religions, Graduate School, University of Pennsylvania, 1925–1954.

Craig Professor, Biblical Languages and Literature, Theological School, St. Lawrence University, Canton, N.Y., 1955–1965.

Visiting Professor, Chicago Theological Seminary, summer, 1929.

Visiting Professor, Drew Theological Seminary, 1953, 1954.

Visiting Professor, Iliff School of Theology, summer 1956.

Visiting Lecturer, Bryn Mawr College, 1965–1968.

Professor, Dropsie University for Hebrew and Cognate Learning, 1968–

President, Society of Biblical Literature and Exegesis, 1945.

President, American Theological Society, 1952.

Honorary D.D., Colby College, 1945.

Honorary L.H.D., Hebrew Union College, 1964.

Honorary Phi Beta Kappa, St. Lawrence University, 1962.

[for publications, see pp. 19-26.]

A Select Bibliography
of the Writings
of Morton Scott Enslin

BOOKS

The Ethics of Paul. New York: Harper & Row, Publishers, 1930. 2d ed., Nashville: Abingdon Press (Apex Books), 1962 (paperback), with a new introduction, pp. xxi-xxvi. Excerpts, pp. 63-78, were printed in *CQ*, 4 (1927), pp. 159-170, and in *Contemporary Thinking About Paul: An Anthology*, ed. Thomas S. Kepler, Nashville: Abingdon-Cokesbury Press, 1950, pp. 302-308, "The Central Place of Morality in the Life and Thought of Paul."

Christian Beginnings. New York: Harper & Row, Publishers, 1938. Paperback reprint, in 2 vols. (pp. 1-200, 201-512) : *Christian Beginnings, Parts I and II; The Literature of the Christian Movement, Part III of Christian Beginnings.* New York: Harper & Row, Publishers, Torchlight Books 5 and 6, 1956. Sections are reprinted in *Religion from Tolstoy to Camus*, selected, with an introduction and prefaces, by Walter Kaufmann. New York: Harper & Row, Publishers, 1961, pp. 298-317, cf. pp. 23-25.

The Prophet from Nazareth. New York: McGraw-Hill Book Company, 1961. 2d ed., New York: Schocken Books, 1968 (paperback), with a new Preface, pp. xi-xiv.

Letters to the Churches: 1 and 2 Timothy, Titus. Bible Guides, ed. William Barclay and F. F. Bruce, No. 18. London: Lutterworth Press, and Nashville: Abington Press, 1963 (paperback).

From Jesus to Christianity. Boston: Beacon Press, 1964. The Winter Lectures for 1964 at All Souls Unitarian Church, Tulsa, Oklahoma.

Judith, in the Dropsie College (Philadelphia) series, Jewish Apocryphal Literature (in press).

SECTIONS OF BOOKS

"Athos, Laura 184 [B¹64] (Greg. 1739; von Soden α 78), Acts, Catholic Epistles, Paul," in *Six Collations of New Testament Manuscripts*, ed. Kirsopp Lake and Silva New. Harvard Theological Studies, 17; Cambridge, Mass.: Harvard University Press, 1932, pp. 141-219 (with K. Lake and J. de Zwaan). Cf. Bruce M. Metzger, *The Text of the New Testament: Its Transmission, Corruption, and Restoration.* New York: Oxford, 1964, p. 65.

"The Credo of an Unregenerate Liberal," in *The Protestant Credo*, ed. Vergilius Ferm, pp. 73-98. New York: Philosophical Library, 1953.

"Biblical Criticism and Its Effect on Modern Civilization," in *Five Essays on the Bible*, by Erwin R. Goodenough, Roland H. Bainton, Morton S. Enslin, Howard Mumford Jones, and Nelson Glueck, pp. 30-44. New York: American Council of Learned Societies, 1960. Papers read at the 1960 Annual Meeting of ACLS.

FESTSCHRIFTEN ARTICLES

"The Date of Peter's Confession," in *Quantulacumque, Studies presented to Kirsopp Lake by Pupils, Colleagues and Friends*, ed. Robert P. Casey, Silva Lake, and Agnes K. Lake, pp. 117-122. London: Christophers, 1937.

"Preaching from the New Testament: An Open Letter to Preachers," in *The Joy of Study, Papers on New Testament and Related Subjects Presented to Honor Frederick Clifton Grant*, ed. Sherman E. Johnson, pp. 87-98. New York: Macmillan, 1951.

"Concerning Experience and Revelation," in *Studies and Essays in Honor of Abraham A. Neuman*, ed. M. Ben-Horin, B. D. Weinryb, and S. Zeitlin, pp. 154-169. Leiden: Brill, 1962.

"Paul—What Manner of Jew?" in *In the Time of Harvest: Essays in Honor of Abba Hillel Silver on the Occasion of his 70th Birthday*, ed. D. J. Silver, pp. 153-169. New York: Macmillan, 1963.

"Rome in the East," in *Religions in Antiquity (Essays in Memory of Erwin Ramsdell Goodenough)*, ed. Jacob Neusner, pp. 125-136. Leiden: Brill, 1968.

(Dr. Zeitlin's Contribution to) "New Testament Studies," in *Solomon Zeitlin: Scholar Laureate, An Annotated Bibliography, 1915–1970, With Appreciations Of His Writings*, ed. Sidney B. Hoenig, pp. 56-60. New York: Bitzaron, jointly with Dropsie University Alumni Association, Philadelphia, 1971—5731.

"Luke, the Literary Physician," in *Crucial Issues in Early Christian History: A Volume of Essays in Honor of Allen Wikgren*, ed. David E. Aune. Leiden: Brill, 1972.

"How the Story Grew—Judas in Fact and Fiction," in *Festschrift for F. W. Gingrich*, ed. Eugene H. Barth (in press).

TRANSLATIONS

Couchoud, Paul-Louis, "Was the Gospel of Mark Written in Latin?" *CQ*, 5 (1928), pp. 35-79. From the French, "L'Évangile de Marc a-t-il été écrit en Latin?" *Revue de l'Histoire des Religions* (1926), pp. 161-192, revised and expanded by the author.

Boegner, Marc, *God, the Eternal Torment of Man*. New York: Harper & Row, Publishers, 1931. From the French, *Dieu, l'éternal torment des hommes* (1929).

Bertram, Georg, "The Problem of Death in Popular Judaeo-Hellenistic Piety." *CQ*, 10 (1933), pp. 257-287.

Dibelius, Martin, "Gethsemane." *CQ*, 12 (1935), pp. 254-265. German in *Botschaft und Geschichte: Gesammelte Aufsätze von Martin Dibelius †*, ed. G. Bornkamm with H. Kraft. Tübingen: J. C. B. Mohr, 1953, vol. 1, pp. 258-271.

EDITOR

The Crozer Quarterly, vols. 18—29,2 (Jan., 1941—April, 1952). From January, 1943 (20, 1) on, the editor wrote a 2-3 page editorial, "Where Ignorance Is Bliss, 'Tis Folly," discussing biblical passages often misconstrued or garbled. *CQ* ceased publication in 1954.

The Journal of Biblical Literature, vols. 79-88 (March, 1960—Dec., 1969).

The Parables as Recorded in the Gospels, with drawings by Cyrus LeRoy Baldridge. New York: Harper & Row, Publishers, 1942.

The Apocrypha: A Facsimile of the Famous Nonesuch Edition of 1924, with an Introduction by Morton S. Enslin. New Hyde Park, N.Y.: University Books, 1962.

Studies in Pharisaism and the Gospels, First and Second Series (1917, 1924), by Israel Abrahams, reprinted with a Prolegomenon by Morton S. Enslin. Library of Biblical Studies, ed. Harry M. Orlinsky. New York: KTAV Publishing House, Inc., 1967. Prolegomenon, pp. v-xxvii.

The Interpreter's One-Volume Commentary on the Bible. Nashville: Abingdon Press, 1971. One of the New Testament editors, handling 22 articles.

ENCYCLOPEDIA ARTICLES

"Allegory," etc., many articles. *An Encyclopedia of Religion,* ed. Vergilius Ferm. New York: Philosophical Library, 1945. Contributor and contributing editor.

"New Testament Times: II. Palestine." *The Interpreter's Bible.* Nashville: Abingdon Press, vol. 7 (1951), pp. 100-113.

"Abdias, Apostolic History of," "Abgarus, Epistles of Christ and," "Acts, Apocryphal," etc., 150 articles on the New Testament Apocrypha. *The Interpreter's Dictionary of the Bible.* 4 vols. Nashville: Abingdon Press, 1962.

"Emperor Worship," "Herod." *Dictionary of the Bible,* ed. James Hastings, rev. ed. by Frederick C. Grant and H. H. Rowley. New York: Charles Scribners' Sons (1963), pp. 246-248, 378-381.

"Bethsaida," etc., 20 articles. *Biblisch-Historisches Handwörterbuch,* ed. Bo Reicke and Leonhard Rost. 3 vols. Göttingen: Vandenhoeck & Ruprecht, 1962–1966.

"Galatians, Epistle to the," *Encyclopaedia Britannica* (1952 ed., until 1964), vol. 9, pp. 969-971.

Ten articles (unsigned) —*Harper's Bible Dictionary,* ed. Madeleine S. and J. Lane Miller. New York: Harper & Row, Publishers, 1952.

"The Apocalyptic Literature," *The Interpreter's One-Volume Commentary on the Bible.* Nashville: Abingdon Press (1971), pp. 1106-1109.

"Old Testament, Christian Attitude towards." *Encyclopaedia Judaica* (in press).

ARTICLES

(In alphabetical order, excluding "a" and "the"; where a summary is available in *NTA,* the reference is also indicated.)

"An Additional Step Toward the Understanding of Jesus," *JR,* 9 (1929), pp. 419-435.

"Along Highways and Byways," *HTR,* 44 (1951), pp. 67-92.

"And That He Hath Been Raised," *JQR,* 43 (1952–1953), pp. 27-56.

"Another Gospel Come to Light," *Christian Register* (Boston), June 6, 1935, pp. 376-377.

"The Artistry of Mark," *JBL,* 66 (1947), pp. 385-399.

"The Ascension Story," *JBL*, 47 (1928), pp. 60-73.

"The Atoning Work of Christ in the New Testament," *HTR*, 38 (1945), pp. 39-61.

"The Bible—Asset or Liability." Lecture at Harvard, originally published in the Harvard Divinity School *Bulletin*, reprinted in *The Pulpit*, 28, 12 (Dec., 1957), pp. 6-8, 26-27.

"A Breeze in the Treetops," *Christian Leader* (Boston), 129 (May, 1947), pp. 197-200.

"But Is It 'Cruel and Unusual'?" *Religion in Life* (forthcoming).

"But What About the Pew?" *Iliff Review* (Denver), 4 (1947), pp. 108-113.

"Cain and Prometheus" (Critical Note), *JBL*, 86 (1967), pp. 88-90.

"Changing Horizons in the Gospels," *CQ*, 16 (1939), pp. 3-15.

"A Check List of Horatio Alger, Jr.," *Antiquarian Bookman*, July 6-13, 1959.

"Christianity's Debt to Torah," *CQ*, 2 (1925), pp. 60-67.

"The Christian Stories of the Nativity," *JBL*, 59 (1940), pp. 317-338.

"Concerning Disturbers of the Peace," *Pulpit Digest*, 37, 225 (January, 1956), pp. 9-13.

"Concerning Questionnaires," *Religion in Life*, 31 (1961-1962), pp. 131-132.

"The Constraint of Christ," *CQ*, 11 (1934), pp. 315-322 (sermon).

"Dr. Piper's Bible," *The Christian Century*, 63, 15 (April 10, 1946), pp. 460-462.

"The Essential Principles of Christian Morality as Gathered from the New Testament," *CQ*, 5 (1928), pp. 280-297.

"The Ethical Core of Our Religion," *Religion in Life*, 40 (1970-1971), pp. 331-342.

" ἐφοβοῦντο γάρ, Mark 16.8," *JBL*, 46 (1927), pp. 62-68.

" 'The Five Books of Matthew': Bacon on the Gospel of Matthew," *HTR*, 24 (1931), pp. 67-97.

"The Future of Biblical Studies" (Presidential Address to the Society of Biblical Literature and Exegesis, Dec. 27, 1945). *JBL*, 65 (1946), pp. 1-12.

"Gamaliel and the Fundamentalist," *CQ*, 25 (1948), pp. 332-336.

"A Gentleman Among the Fathers," *HTR*, 47 (1954), pp. 211-241.

"Hagiographic Mistletoe," *JR*, 25 (1945), pp. 10-24.

"Horatio Alger, Jr., After Seventy Years," *Dime Novel Roundup* (Lawrence, Kansas), 39, 4 & 5 (April, May, 1970), pp. 39-45, 49-55.

"The Idea of God as Affected by Modern Knowledge." The 28th annual Garvin Lecture at the Church of our Father (Unitarian), Lancaster, Pa., April 24, 1969. © 1969 by the Garvin Trust.

"In Darkness and the Shadow of Death," *Pulpit Digest*, 36, 218 (June, 1956), pp. 11-16.

"Interpreting the Bible and the Role of Myth," *Andover-Newton Quarterly* (Newton, Mass.), 8 (1968), pp. 163-179. Greene Lecture for 1967. *NTA*, 12 (1967—1968), no. 785.

"Irenaeus: Mostly Prolegomena," *HTR*, 40 (1947), pp. 137-165.

"Justin Martyr: An Appreciation," *JQR*, 34 (1943), pp. 179-205.

"Light from the Quest," *HTR*, 42 (1949), pp. 19-33.

"Like a Mighty River," *CQ*, 27 (1950), pp. 1-13.

"A List of Alger Titles," *Dime Novel Roundup*, 40, 8 & 9 (August, September, 1971), pp. 73-84, 89-106.

"Luke and Matthew," *JQR*, 75th Anniversary Volume, 1967, pp. 178-191.

" 'Luke' and Paul," *JAOS*, 58 (1938), pp. 81-91.

"Luke and the Samaritans," *HTR*, 36 (1943), pp. 277-297.

"The Meaning of the Historical Jesus for Faith," *JBR*, 30 (1962), pp. 219-223. *NTA*, 7 (1962-1963), no. 477.

"Musings by the Dead Seaside," *Universalist Leader*, 138 (June, 1956). Reprinted in *Torch*, 30, 2 (April, 1957).

"A New Deal in Ordinations," *The Christian Century*, 54, 30 (July 28, 1937), pp. 949-950.

"A Notable Contribution to Acts," *JBL*, 52 (1933), pp. 230-238 (review article, *The Beginnings of Christianity*, 1933).

"The Old and the New," *The Baptist*, 4 (March 31, 1923), p. 269.

"Once Again: John the Baptist," *Religion in Life*, 27 (1957–1958), pp. 557-566.

"Once Again, Luke and Paul," *ZNW*, 61 (1970), pp. 253-272. *NTA*, 15 (1970-1971), no. 907.

"Our Challenge: A Liberal View," *The Baptist*, 12 (Mar. 7, 1931), pp. 300-301.

"The Parting of the Ways," *JQR*, 51 (1960—1961), pp. 177-197. *NTA*, 6 (1961–1962), no. 61.

"Paul and Gamaliel," *JR*, 7 (1927), pp. 360-375.

"The Perfect Tense in the Fourth Gospel," *JBL*, 55 (1936), pp. 121-131.

"The Pontic Mouse," *ATR*, 27 (1945), pp. 1-16 (on Marcion).

"The Puritan of Carthage," *JR*, 27 (1947), pp. 197-212 (on Tertullian).

"The Relevance of the Bible in Preaching Today," *Unitarian-Universalist Christian*, 25, 3-4 (Autumn 1969—Winter 1970), pp. 10-15.

"The Relevance of Theology," address at the 18th Biennial Meeting of the American Association of Theological Schools, June 10-11, 1952, at Louisville, Kentucky, published in *AATS Bulletin*, 20 (June, 1952), pp. 118-127.

"Roger Williams Goes to Rome," *CQ*, 19 (1942), pp. 311-318.

"A Second Century Pastor," *CQ*, 6 (1929), pp. 278-298.

"Some Further Considerations Regarding the Origin of Christian Baptism," *CQ*, 8 (1931), pp. 47-67.

"Special Reading List: Lives of Jesus," *Bulletin* of General Theological Library, Boston, 22, 1 (Oct., 1929), pp. 10-21.

"The Temple and the Cross," *Judaism*, 20 (1971), pp. 24-31. *NTA*, 15 (1970-1971), no. 815.

"Twixt the Dusk and the Daylight," *JBL*, 75 (1956), pp. 19-26.

"Where Do They Get Them?" *The Pulpit*, 21, 7 (July, 1950), pp. 164-165. This article led to a regular column in *The Pulpit*, "Pulpit Patter," vols. 22-28 (January, 1951—January, 1957).

"Why Not Use a Prayer Wheel?" *The Christian Century*, 52, 11 (Mar. 13, 1935), pp. 332-334.

"Why Technical Scholarship?: A Theological Professor Looks at His Task," *CQ*, 7 (1930), pp. 328-340.

Book Reviews have not been included. They occur especially in *CQ* and *JBL*, the indexes in each volume of which should be consulted.

BIOGRAPHY

Kepler, Thomas S., ed., *Contemporary Thinking About Paul: An Anthology.* Nashville: Abingdon-Cokesbury Press, 1950, p. 427.

Twentieth Century Encyclopedia of Religious Knowledge (Schaff-Herzog Extension; Grand Rapids: Baker Book House, 1955), vol. 1, p. 385.

New Testament Abstracts, 5 (1960–1961). p. 103.

Henderson, R. Melvin, "Interpreting the New Testament: Morton Scott Enslin," *Bulletin* of Crozer Theological Seminary (Centennial Issue III), 60, 3 (July, 1968), pp. 14-18.

Directory of American Scholars: A Biographical Dictionary, vol. 4, *Philosophy, Religion and Law*. 5th ed., 1969. New York: Jaques Cattell Press and R. R. Bowker Co., p. 102.

Interview, "Is Christian Ethics Biblical?" *Salt* (ed. T. Y. Mullins, Adult Quarterly Discussion Material, Lutheran Church in America), 6, 3 (Autumn, 1969), pp. 32f.

Who's Who in America, vol. 36 (1970–1971). Chicago: Marquis-Who's Who, p. 669.

The Ancient
Mind
and Ours

by Samuel Sandmel

Phenomena in the Tanak, the Gospels, and rabbinic literature involving inconsistencies or direct contradictions increasingly intrigue me. Some of these I discussed in my essay, "The Haggada Within Scripture" (*JBL*, 80 [1961], pp. 105-122) as an aspect of my personal dissent from the usual source analysis of the Pentateuch. My purpose here is quite different, for it is not to prolong the dissent already public, but rather to wonder if I can satisfy a persistent desire, namely, to bring myself to the point of possibly beginning to understand the ancient mind. Perhaps our Western mentality impedes our full appreciation of the ancient mind. Let us take as our first example our commitment to logic and consistency. Out of the scholarly notice of the phenomena of inconsistency and contradiction there have arisen rational hypotheses to explain the origin of these phenomena. Are such modern explanations right because they are rational? Or does the modern mind work on premises so different from the ancient mind as to be beside the point? Or, if a rational hypothesis is apropos at one point, is it equally apropos at each and every point?

The normal rational hypothesis points to inconsistency or contradiction as evidence for diversity either in authorship or in the sources which an author has utilized. Certainly there are such cases, which we shall see. Yet even in those cases it seems to me that there remains a residual problem of accounting for the toleration in the ancient writings of a particular inconsistency or contradiction which is, logically, disruptive of a context.

To the extent that I have been pursuing this quest of understanding the ancient mind, which this essay can reflect only in aspects because of space, I find a new enlightment in the ancient documents. I am led to wonder whether this is only a subjective

29

aberration, or whether the pursuit might objectively open a new vista for scholarship. I wonder if there is not some virtue in setting aside the prevailing scholarly preoccupation with history in the sense of events and their dates, and in probing into the craft of writing on the part of the ancient authors. The Hebrews and early Christians have not left us any significant information on their literary methods; there is bequeathed to us, however, the observation in Ecclesiastes that too many books were being written and one could get tired of reading them! Our knowledge of the craft of writing comes from sparse and indistinct clues, such as Jeremiah 36, or from our own adventurous analysis of what has been written. I relish the datum about writing in Esther that Mordecai's informing on the would-be assassins of the king Ahasuerus was duly recorded in the royal Persian chronicles which were read to the king on a later occasion as a soporific when he suffered from insomnia (Esther 2:21-23; 6:1-3).

I

The habits of mind among peoples seem to reflect generations of accumulated dispositions. We and the British seem to differ, for example, in our after-dinner speeches. Among us there is the habit of beginning with a quite irrelevant joke, so as to warm up the audience, and if it falls flat, to try one more and still another. Thereafter comes the body of the speech, earnest and solemn, but seldom with an effort at wit. The British seem to skip the introductory joke, and then proceed to an exposition, enhanced by wit or marred by a desperation toward it by one who lacks it.

Such habits of mind are in a sense quite different from the basic passions of men, such as anger, lust, sorrow, or joy. Men, to turn to a truism, are basically the same, and I imagine they have been so at least for the past four thousand years. The habits of mind result from social situations or controls, and in a sense are accidental, rather than essential. The kind of language spoken or written exercises its own measure of influence. A language highly inflected, such as Greek or Latin, with verbs compounded with prepositional prefixes and an array of abstractions, leads to precision, to shades of meaning, even subtle ones. Hebrew, on the other hand, is not highly inflected, is poor in abstractions, disposed to the concrete, and forced to struggle to express desired shades of meaning. Philosophy could and did develop among the Greeks; it did not follow a similar course among the Hebrews.

This Hebrew bent for the concrete explains the frequency with which Hebrew prose expresses theological ideas by means of narration. When Abraham bargains with Yahweh (in Gen. 18:17-33), there is theology at stake; when Yahweh asks Cain where Abel is (Gen. 4:8-12), again there is theology at stake. The story of David and Bathsheba, with its remarkable ironic contrast between David's elaborate machinations and Uriah's simple piety, proceeds (2 Sam. 11:1-27a) as if it is the most secular of stories, until the pregnant words (2 Sam. 11:27b) "What David had done was evil in the eyes of Yahweh." That is to say, the Hebrews had no difficulty in expressing ideas, but they did so in didactic narratives.

The consequence of the bent for narration manifests itself in a variety of ways. Hosea makes his point about Israel's infidelity through the account of Gomer (Hosea 1:2-9); Isaiah (in 5:1-7) sings the Song of the Vineyard; Jeremiah (in 24:1-10) relates his vision of two baskets of figs. The divine displeasure of Yahweh with his people and his abortive intention to destroy them is expressed in the dialogue between Yahweh and Moses, both in Exodus 32:7-14, after the incident of the golden calf, and also in Numbers 14:11-20, after the return of the twelve spies.

The dialogue between Yahweh and Abraham in Genesis 18:17-33, though essentially theological, is not too different from that between Abraham and Ephron about the cave of Machpelah (Genesis 23:1-20), in that the Deity is presented in 18:17-23 in a markedly anthropomorphic way. In itself this would not be surprising; in context it is so. For example, the narrative of the theophany at Sinai presents an awesome Yahweh of whom the people are so frightened that they implore Moses to be their representative (Exodus 20:18-21). Yet neither Abraham in Genesis 18:17-23 nor Moses in Exodus 32:7-14 and 14:11-20 is portrayed as overawed; the Deity reacts to the words they address to him much as a man would, and, indeed, the omnipotent Deity becomes persuaded. The dialogue between the Deity and Satan in the prologue to Job is so written that the omniscient Deity asks Satan where he has been, as if not knowing. But we now advert to the literary tone of Genesis 1, wherein the Deity is portrayed so majestically; the disparities in writing about the Deity seem all the more vivid.

Does the fact of such disparity of itself necessitate the view of diverse stages? That is, does the treatment in Genesis 1 of itself alone necessitate the hypothesis that Genesis 18:17-33 comes from a different age? I suppose the answer one gives reflects the whole complex of the factors that make up his approach. Parenthetically, respecting value, I personally do not regard the folksy dialogues alluded to as religiously inferior to Genesis 1. Could not the same ancient writer have thought on two different levels?

But there seem to me to be additional matters to turn to. For example, the Western mind so thoroughly associates religion with solemnity that modern men have thoroughly exiled humor from religion and from Scripture. Perhaps there is an inconsistency in us, not in the ancient mind. First Samuel 24:1-15 relates that while David and his men were hidden in a cave at Engedi, Saul entered the cave to relieve himself. David cut off the skirt of Saul's robe. Caird, in his exegesis in *IB*, makes no comment on the humor in the incident, focusing on the end of the story to comment, "David with his usual unfailing generosity puts the blame for Saul's conduct toward him on his bad advisers." [1] The exposition by John C. Schroeder comments that "David even feels humiliated that in cutting off Saul's skirt he has been guilty of lese majesty. . . . The ruler . . . whatever his personal weaknesses or foibles . . . ought never to be held in contempt." [2] (What else is the funny incident about but contempt for Saul?) The narrative of Ehud ben Gera and the fat king of Moab (Judges 3:15-25) is comparably coarse, and funny. Myers, in the exegesis in *IB*, informs us, "The whole episode must be interpreted in the light of the times. Ehud, like Jacob (Gen. 30–31), was regarded as a clever fellow because he succeeded in deceiving Eglon and his servants." [3] Elliott, in the exposition, comments, "By even the most elementary standard of ethics [Ehud's] deception and murder of Eglon stand condemned." [4] Is this not a bit stuffy? To my mind, the story of Ehud is the kind of material which in our time leads to television or movie spy stories and is to be taken just as seriously. As to Samson, a comparable opaqueness in Myers's treatment continues as in the case of Ehud, for Myers himself seems to find no delight in the stories, though he manages to ascribe some to the narrator. How seriously Myers takes it all!

Again, in the matter of the Philistine foreskins, a hundred of which Saul demands as David's gift to him, the text (1 Sam. 18: 27) tells that David and his men killed two hundred Philistines and David brought the foreskins in full number to Saul. Caird comments: "The killing of two hundred Philistines is an unnecessary and unoriginal exaggeration. David paid the full number to Saul, viz., one hundred; and this is borne out by a later reference to this event (II Sam. 3:14)." [5]

To take these kinds of things as reliable history and to comment on them with utmost reverential piety is not my way of handling the materials. The veins of humor in Scripture are frequent and very rich, ranging from a commendable coarseness as above, through the delicate satire in Esther 1:13-22 where the seven royal counsellors, advising Ahasuerus what to do about the disobedient queen Vashti, pompously act as if they are confronting the most profound crisis to the state. Bernhard Anderson comments in the Introduction to the Book of Esther in *The Interpreter's Bible:* "There is humor in Esther, but it is the kind which is appreciated only by the victor." [6] In the body of the commentary, Anderson sees irony from time to time, but, as I read him, the ribald humor is seldom noted, whereas I see it as recurrent and frequent.

It is a bit puzzling to note this broad absence of the recognition of the intended humor in Scripture, despite the abundance of puns and the biting sarcasm found in many of the passages. These come to mind from a variety of contexts. The Sodomites say of Lot (Gen. 19:9), "This man came to dwell with us, and now he acts like a *šōpēṭ!*" The Hebrew slave rebukes Moses (Exod. 2:14): "Who made you a prince and *šōpēṭ* over us?" The opening words of some of the speeches in Job crackle with it, as in Job 8:2, 11:2, and 12:2, the latter especially: "With you wisdom perishes!"

It is not that the humor is in itself important, but that its ubiquitousness in the Tanak reflects for me a facet of the Hebrew mind, and a comprehension of that mind is inadequate if modern humorlessness in religion obstructs a genuine understanding. Because of this humorlessness, the supple and elastic minds behind the writings have become frozen into rigidity, and the written words come to be viewed as if they were composed not by wondrously vibrant human beings, but by robots.

II

As to the inconsistencies and contradictions, an easy example is the last five verses of Amos. Virtually all modern scholars regard these verses as an addition, chiefly on two premises. The first is general, that the hopeful, affirmative tone of these verses is totally out of keeping with the denunciation and gloom of the preceding substance of the book. The second is more specific. The text, 9:11, speaks of raising the "fallen tabernacle of David." The natural meaning would be that the dynasty of David has come to an end, as we know it did in the middle of the sixth pre-Christian century, about two hundred years after the time of Amos. We can rationally account for these verses added to the Book of Amos by supposing that there were circles in which the written prophecies were preserved and recurrently read; into these circles the affirmative hopes of perhaps an Ezekiel or a Second Isaiah penetrated. Someone was persuaded that the sacred words of Amos, valid as they had been for their own time, would be the more serviceable for the new age by appending the counter-balancing appendix of hope. We can wonder (fruitlessly, since evidence is lacking) whether the writer of this appendix, or else a copyist who discovered the floating verses and incorporated them into the book, had any qualms about his tampering with the text. It seems to me quite impossible that the person, whether the author or the copyist, was unaware that the appendix contradicted the rest of the book, for the appendix is there precisely because it contradicts. If, then, the determination existed to balance the gloom with this addition reflecting hope, then how can we grasp the bent of mind of a man who understood the gloom so well that he had no reluctance against diluting the one with the other?

There is, of course, another possibility — that someone added the appendix in a rather mindless way, as if he understood neither the substance of Amos nor the purport of the appendix.[7] This theory of mindlessness, moderate or extreme, or else a theory, that of sheer accident, is always an alternative to a theory of deliberate alteration. But any theory of deliberate alteration must raise for the student the inevitable questions about the ancient mind and inconsistencies and contradictions.

Three other phenomena from the Book of Amos merit some

attention. One is typified by Amos 9:8: "Behold, the eyes of
Yahweh are on the sinful kingdom, and I will destroy it from
the face of the earth, except that I will not utterly destroy the
house of Jacob. . . ." The underlined clause seems to most
scholars an addition. It modifies the threat of complete destruction found in the first half of the verse to the point of contradicting it. If the clause is indeed an addition, then its purpose
may not be that alone of relieving the portentous gloom of the
first part of the verse; it may be no more than attestation from
later times that, since Jacob survived when the destruction came,
the latter fell short of being total, and whoever added the clause
was, in a way, protecting Amos from palpable error. A somewhat
similar situation might be inferred respecting Jeremiah 1:10: "Behold I have appointed you this day against the nations and the
kingdoms to tear up, to break down, to destroy and tear down,
to build and to plant." Some scholars, though not as uniformly
as in the case of Amos 9:8, wish to strike the underlined words
as a comforting addition; if it is an addition, some later hand
might well have had Jeremiah 24 or even 29 in mind, and therefore added the words. It is just as likely, though, that these
words are by Jeremiah, reading back from the end of his career
the total mandate to him at the beginning of it. In any case,
the conclusion would seem to be that the clause in Amos or the
words in Jeremiah do not conform to a theory of mindlessness
or of accident.

Respecting Amos 5:18-24, a "Day of Yahweh" passage, the
words "it is darkness not light" at the end of 5:18 and "Is not the
Day of Yahweh darkness and not light" in 5:20 constitute a
repetition. In between, 5:19 is in prose and devoid of the meter
found in the remainder of the passage: "As when a man flees
from a lion and a bear meets him, and he comes home and leans
his hand against a wall and a serpent bites him." Harper, in *ICC*
denied Löhr's denial of the authenticity of this verse; [8] Löhr regarded it as "a proverb which has crept into the text from the
margin"; [9] Fosbroke in *IB* speaks not of the certainty but of the
possibility that the verse is a proverb;[10] Morgenstern is sure it is
an interpolation.[11] These who would strike 5:19 also wish to
eliminate the repetition of "darkness, not light," usually by striking the clause in 5:18, but retaining the clause in 5:20. If all this
is correct, then we may well have here the result of what has

been called the "Yom Yahweh" editor, someone who colorfully embroidered the Day of Yahweh passages.[12] Indeed, somewhat similarly, passages in Hosea and Amos against Israel are made to apply to Judah, by the addition of the appropriate words (cf. Amos 2:4-5; Hosea 1:6; 4:15; 8:14) ; this also implies some perceptive response to the text. To me, these phenomena, viewed cumulatively, suggest most strongly that in the time prior to the rigid fixing of the text by the Masoretes, the additions were a natural result of a quasi-existentialist response to the comprehension of the text by those who copied it. The text, in these early days, was sacred enough to warrant copying, but not so sacred as to be copied merely mechanically.

In Amos 4:13, 5:8-9, and 9:5-6 there are passages, denied to Amos by scholars, which King, in the *Jerome Biblical Commentary*, terms as "doxologies"; [13] others view the three passages as portions of a single poem, separated and scattered. Harper seems to view only 9:5-6 as an interpolation, apparently accepting the authenticity of the other two passages.[14] Within the diversity there is this common thread, that the verses are all deemed to be at least contextually difficult, with the weight of interpretation seemingly holding the verses to be secondary. If this latter is the case, then we are confronted here not by contradiction or marked inconsistency, but rather by an embroidering piety, which celebrates abstractly the universal power of the Deity. The person who interpolated these verses into the text was embellishing the sacred words by psalm-like sentences, simply because he felt that the text would be enhanced by them; these interpolations are his tribute to the majesty which he found in the Book of Amos.

Two Hebrew words, "This is Sinai," in Judges 5:5 interrupt the rhythm and present a grammatical and syntactical problem. A frequent explanation is that the words were once a marginal gloss which crept into the text. (Marginal glosses seem never to move except by creeping!) The origin of the gloss is conceivably a combination of piety and a bent toward identification; at any rate, the implication of a theophany in the text ("Yahweh, on your leaving the field of Edom, the earth trembled, even the heavens dripped, indeed, the clouds dripped water; mountains melted before Yahweh, before Yahweh, Israel's God") called to mind the narrative of the theophany as in Exodus 19:16-20. That a glossator noted that the verses in Judges 5 called to mind the Sinai episode points again to inescapable conclusion that the glossator read Judges with comprehension and, indeed, with a mind keen enough to make a ready association.

The words "glossator" and "glosses" are conveniently vague. A gloss is ordinarily a thing to put into a footnote, as C. F. Kent does in his *Student's Old Testament* or the *ICC* does usually in the fine print. Usually, though of course not always, one disposes of a gloss simply by denominating it for what it is. This procedure of dismissal seems to be especially the case in Ezekiel where the unusual words or unclear passages seem to have bred marginal explanations which later were incorporated into the text (cf. Ezek. 1:4, 11, 16, 20, 24).[15] But must one not note that a gloss, even a pedestrian, explanatory gloss, is a response to the content? And must one not wonder whether the incorporation of a gloss, with resultant syntactical confusion or metrical anomalies, troubled the incorporator? Is it right simply to pass over glosses?

A quite different type of gloss recurs in Ecclesiastes (Eccles. 2:26a; 3:17; 4:4; possibly 5:7; 7:18, 24; 8:5-6, 11-13; 11:9; 12:13b-14). What is common in the glosses in Ecclesiastes is that they deny, and seem pointed to refute, the argument in the text itself.[16] These glosses are normally termed either "pious" or "orthodox," and these descriptions seem quite in order. Surely we can glimpse in these glosses a resistance to the unorthodox views of Ecclesiastes. But did the glossator have no concern with the illogic, or even the disruptive nature of his comments, and was the copyist who brought the glosses into the text unaware of the anomalies he was creating, or, if aware, unconcerned? And why did the glossator seek to counter the trend of Ecclesiastes by mere addition? Why preserve a disagreeable or disconcerting text? Why not simply suppress it? Or, why not use a blue pencil on the most glaring of the offensive passages?

How shall we account for what went on in the mind of what we may here call the redactor of the "second edition" of Samuel-Kings? Let us assume that those scholars are right who hold that the Deuteronomic writings glorified proper kingship in general, as evidenced by the repetition of the phrase "there was then no king in Israel; each man did what was right in his own eyes," a phrase which occurs in Judges 17:6 and 25:6 and seems adumbrated in Deuteronomy 12:8, and in some other passages where *yāšār* occurs. The Deuteronomist glorified Josiah in particular (2 Kings 22:2; see 1 Kings 13:2). But Josiah died in battle, and after his time kingship culminated in defeat, exile, and in the liquidation of monarchy itself. The "second edition" carries the account beyond Josiah into the days of Jeconiah. Into 1 Samuel there were inserted anti-monarchy passages, put into the mouth of Samuel himself, wherein Samuel regards the wish for a human king as the equivalent of apostasy from Yahweh, as in 1 Samuel 8:1-22, 10:17-19, and 12:1-25. Hence, there are to be found in close juxtaposition pro-monarchy and anti-monarchy sentiments, in grossest contradiction of each other. Was the man who recast the "first edition" and produced the "second," totally oblivious of such contradiction? Surely not; he adds the contradicting factor deliberately to counter the earlier sentiments. But then where was his blue pencil?

Or, again, let us consider another matter. The succession of Deuteronomic writings seems to reveal a mind (or succession of related minds, perhaps a school) of high intelligence and creativity. This mind fashioned, in brilliant style, a religious history of Israel from the time of Moses until the Babylonian exile, no mean ambition and no mean accomplishment. His skill is best evidenced by the book of Deuteronomy itself, where he imagined himself Moses with such success that the denial of the Mosaic authorship of Deuteronomy came quite late in modern biblical scholarship.

So much literary skill abounds in Deuteronomy that I regard it as a supreme creation. But I am left to wonder. How did the author have the temerity to write as if it were Moses writing? Did he have any sense at all of perpetrating a fraud? To me this seems unlikely. The explanation I give to myself is double. First the author so thoroughly identified himself with the material that he had neither a sense of fraud nor any sense of artificiality in what he was doing. Second, the distinction between history and non-history is Western, not Hebraic; the Hebrew mind did not create some line of demarcation between the two. Precision was neither a goal nor a preoccupation. (Hence, the enslavement in Egypt could endure for three generations [Gen. 15:16], or for four hundred [Gen. 15:13] or four hundred and thirty years [Exod. 12:41] and in the interim the seventy souls of Jacob's

old age could proliferate into 600,000 males in Moses' time.) The
Hebrew historian, so it seems to me, was intuitive, not pedantic.
The step from intuition to the composition of the book of Deuteronomy seems to me characteristic of the kind of historical
mind the Hebrew possessed.

The Deuteronomist usually seems to be in good, even full,
control of his material. Surely no ordinary mind envisaged and
carried out the chore of writing the Deuteronomic sequence. But
what shall we make of two tiny items, the anointing of Saul and
of David? Each was, as it were, private. In the case of Saul, Samuel sent Saul's servant (1 Sam. 9:27) away so as to be alone with
Saul; in the case of David, the anointing was limited to the
presence of David's family (1 Sam. 14:11-13). In neither case is
there a direct sequel, and each man rose to *de facto* monarchy
through achievement and popular acclaim without reference at
all to the antecedent anointing. The inescapable impression is
that the Deuteronomist simply grafted these stories of anointing
onto his material in a manner that needs to be termed inept.
Yet his was a great and capacious mind. Then how could he have
done this? Did his *tendenz* outweigh his prudence and skill? Even
if we cannot answer such questions, can we avoid asking them?

III

Among the phenomena in the Pentateuch is the recurrent
interpolation of the name, and the role, of Aaron into narratives
which appear originally to have been only about Moses; that is,
in the traditional terms of the Higher Criticism, P utilized J and
E material by interpolation and minor recasting, though also by
adding the narrative (Exod. 4:10-16) that Moses' stated limita-
tion in fluency impelled the Deity to designate Aaron as Moses'
spokesman — something not carried out in fullest consistency in
the Pentateuch. The P author both created his basic framework
as an original composition and also cited and adapted older materials for his purpose. Within the created P framework, there
appears a remarkable consistency of conception and execution,
and I should think that we need to attribute a luminous mind
to P. Indeed, the remarkable literary conception which resulted
in Genesis through Numbers, plus the closing verses of Deuteronomy replaced from the end of Numbers, reinforces one's admiration for P as a thinker. As an author, we may well deem him

first-rate. As a compiler, though, we are led to wonder. How was it that the writer who added the narrative about Aaron as a spokesman for Moses, and who interpolated Aaron's name here and there, worked in what we might describe as a slovenly way? Again, why does he reproduce a genealogy from Adam to Noah in Genesis 5 which is inconsistent with the genealogy he has written in Genesis 4? Why does he allow us to be confused in the Sinai episode by the profusion of traditions about who ascended Sinai, Moses alone; Moses and Joshua; Moses, Aaron, Nadab, and Abihu; the seventy elders? Why does he leave the account of Korah's rebellion in Numbers 16 something of a shambles, as if he has coalesced two strands, a Levite rebellion and a lay, Reubenite, one? Why does he leave the diversity of endings? All these, and the countless other "discrepancies," and the instances of dissimilar materials in intimate juxtaposition, must puzzle us. Was P unaware of the differences in the two accounts of creation which the ancient rabbis and Philo were aware of (and ingeniously harmonized)?

The Chronicler might have chosen P's way of retaining older accounts and recasting. That is, the Chronicler might have reshaped the Deuteronomic writings by additions and interpolations and alterations. Why did he choose, instead, to embark on a completely new narration? Was it his purpose to have his account supplant and replace the Deuteronomic? Or was his effort merely to supplement? (The former, not the latter, seems to me to be right.) Perhaps the materials in the Tetrateuch were too well known for a P to embark on a totally supplanting version; perhaps P had to resist the penchant of the Chronicler for significant omissions.

In the Tetrateuch P chose merely to append his own composition and to engage in relatively minor alterations. Like all authors, he occasionally slipped. His recasting of Exodus 3:6-18 in Exodus 6:2-8 shows that he was fully aware of the supposition that the name Yahweh was unknown until the time of Moses, and for the most part Genesis conforms to this supposition. Yet the slips are present. Genesis 4:26, whatever it may mean that with Enosh there began "the calling on the name of Yahweh," [17] could well have been expunged, but was not. Again, P retains Yahweh in the long narration, and he almost always abstains from letting the name appear in words spoken of or to him by the patriarchs. Yet Genesis 32:11 and even more significantly Genesis 28:11-22 portray Jacob as knowing Yahweh's name and even as addressing him by it, despite Exodus 3 and 6. Such slips, if that is what they are, do not greatly disturb me. I have seen them in first-drafts of manuscripts by friends, and I am acutely aware of them in my own writing. Modern copy editors, even gifted ones, do not catch all the slips; anyone who writes something extended is guilty of them. But slips are quite different from a considered intention on the part of a mind of good capacity. The questions we could ask about P are interminable. Here are a few: Why did he, in Genesis 2—11, retain the folk-narratives (thank goodness he did!), so out of accord with his lofty theology? How could he let stand together the dual motives for Jacob's flight, one his fear of Esau, and the other his parents' disinclination for him to marry a local girl? If Abraham ordinarily did not offer sacrifices, why did he build so many altars? Or, in Exodus, why does he portray the Deity as simultaneously sending Moses to Pharaoh to obtain the release of the Hebrews, and yet hardening Pharaoh's heart, as if to delay or frustrate Moses' divine mission? [18] Why did he retain Aaron as the chief figure in the golden calf incident, in the light of the Chronicler's omissions of the trespasses of David? (How wondrously the ancient rabbis managed to exculpate Aaron and to blame the "mixed multitude" of Exodus 12:38!)

IV

Now, none of these many questions would arise on an assumption that biblical writers were either primarily feebleminded (which seems to me implicit in much of the recorded scholarship on source analysis of the Pentateuch) or if they were only copyists devoid of reaction to what they were copying. I am willing, as indicated above, to attribute usual auctorial slips to them, great as they were. But they read to me like vibrant human beings, men with perception and sensitivity, and hence I grapple to understand the workings of their minds. I tell myself, for example, that when they rewrote extant documents, they did not expunge, but they "neutralized" by addition; possibly they abstained from expunging because the material with which they dealt was firmly fixed in the public domain. They did omit (a procedure kindred to expunging) only when embarking on a brand-new manuscript, as in Chronicles or in Jubilees. Inconsistencies or contradictions demonstrably did not bother them to the same high degree that they bother the Western mind. I doubt that the gifted author who wrote the surviving prologue of Job, inconsistent as it is at many points with the poem itself, was unaware or at all concerned about the inconsistencies; for him it was sufficient that Satan, not Yahweh, needed to be the source of Job's disaster, and he needed to imply that the experience of Job was exceptional, and not the recurrent example of divine injustice which the poem sets forth. May I not conclude that he did not care about the anomalies he was fashioning? The toleration of diversity by the ancient mind suggests an elasticity which we moderns do not possess.

V

But we must guard ourselves against a wrong view that the ancient mind was devoid of any concept of consistency. It is true that in a tractate, *Pirke Aboth*, we can encounter diverse and contradictory sentiments,[19] and the Jewish tradition was not disturbed by such haggadic differences. But in halakic matters, wherein vagueness, a by-product of inconsistency, seemed inadmissable, the rabbis arrayed the frequent scriptural contradictions as contained in two separate verses against each other, and then called on a third verse as a means of judicious harmonization. The ancient rabbis, as their formulation of precise hermeneutical norms shows, were well disciplined in logic and dialectic. But they did not elevate consistency as the highest achievement of mankind.

VI

Why did Matthew write a new composition in his Gospel? Why did he not do with Mark what P seems to have done with J and E? And why did not Luke simply make interpolations into Mark? The obvious answer is that neither Matthew nor Luke found interpolation into Mark an adequate literary outlet. Like the Chronicler, they (and John) preferred each to prepare his own presentation. Like all authors, the evangelists have their own slips. Mark slips when he relates the incident of the Syro-Phoenician woman (7:24-30) in that the woman speaks the universal message and Jesus the narrow one. In his genealogy

(1:1-16) Matthew slips, tracing the Davidic ancestry of Joseph who is not Jesus' father; he misunderstands Zechariah so that in the best texts Jesus enters Jerusalem (21:7) on two animals. Luke slips when he speaks of having the sun eclipsed at Passover time (23:44f.), a situation which yielded the variant reading that the sun was darkened. The assertion of messianic claims through descent from David and the denial of Davidic descent (because the Christ preexisted, Matt. 22:41-46 par.) are found in the same Gospel. The different bases for justifying Christian claims, such as "Son of man," the virgin birth, eyewitness attestation, scriptural proof texts, point again to elasticity. One recalls that what is today called *Gospel Parallels* used to be called a "Harmony." And one remembers that Tatian wrote his *Diatessaron*.

A consequence is that all too often, so it seems to me, modern scholarship has so addressed itself in noting divergencies and discrepancies as to forget that there were elastic and intuitive minds behind the writings. Especially does this seem to me the case in "form criticism" wherein individuality and the individual mind tend to fade from all concern as if a "community" did the rewriting. The abundance of pseudepigraphs, whether Deuteronomy, Enoch, the Pastoral Epistles, or Second Peter, should alert us much more than they do to the imaginative factor in the ancient mind. The desperation of modern scholars to find secure, reliable history in the imaginative works of ancient authors rests as much on the failure of the modern mind to meet the ancient mind on the same plane as it does in the antecedent viewpoints, conservative or radical, of modern scholars.

My own interest becomes progressively less and less historical. I become more and more unconcerned with whether or not Ruth or Esther are historical persons (and I have absolutely no interest in theories which make Ezekiel or Ezra, like the magician's assistant, vanish from the scene) ; I am fascinated by the skill of the authors of Ruth and Esther, but even more curious about the creative minds behind the books, mostly because they are so different from my own.

But granted, as I firmly believe, that the biblical writers were individualistic, and defy reckless forcing into a single mold, there is nevertheless a community of characteristics which suit a description of the ancient mind in general and which do not suit the Western mind in general.

The ancient mind was elastic, ours is rigid. Theirs was essentially intuitive, creative; ours is self-consciously disciplined and restrained, prone to eclecticism; theirs was passionate, ours dispassionate; theirs was adventurous, ours is safe; they were artisans or artists; we, perhaps, are craftsmen; they were religious, and even superstitious; we are theological, and maybe even devoid of religion.

NOTES

[1] George B. Caird, "The First and Second Books of Samuel," *IB*, vol. 2 (Nashville: Abingdon Press, 1953), p. 1009.

[2] John C. Schroeder, *ibid.*, p. 1009.

[3] Jacob M. Myers, "The Book of Judges," *IB*, vol. 2, p. 710.

[4] Phillips P. Elliott, *ibid.*, p. 708.

[5] George B. Caird, *op. cit.*, p. 984.

[6] Bernhard W. Anderson, "The Book of Esther," *IB*, vol. 3 (1954), p. 831.

[7] Once an item, announcing in the press a lecture I was to give, dutifully reproduced certain facts about me and ended with these words: "The photograph is to be returned to the Temple Bethel office." This last sentence represents mindless copying at its extreme.

[8] W. R. Harper, *Amos and Hosea, ICC* (New York: Charles Scribner's Sons, 1905), p. 129.

[9] Max Löhr, *Untersuchungen zum Buch Amos*, Beihefte *ZAW*, 4 (Giessen: J. Ricker'sche Verlagsbuchhandlung [Alfred Töpelmann], 1901), p. 19.

[10] Hughell E. W. Fosbroke, "The Book of Amos," *IB*, vol. 6 (1965), p. 818.

[11] J. Morgenstern, "Amos Studies," *HUCA*, 11 (1936), p. 109.

[12] I accept this judgment. Moreover, it is my opinion that in Amos the Day of Yahweh is not eschatological, but the name of a festival, the precursor to what was later called the *Rosh-Ha-Shanah*, the New Year. The eschatological turn seems to me to come in Zephaniah.

[13] P. J. King, "Amos," *JBC*, p. 249.

[14] W. R. Harper, *Amos, ICC* (cited above, note 8), p. 190.

[15] Similarly Amos 7:1b seems to be a gloss explaining the import of *leqesh*.

[16] In the Hebrew Union College oral tradition, one of its past presidents is reputed to have used the benediction at the close of the service to refute the thesis offered by a visiting preacher in his sermon earlier in the service.

[17] In my "Genesis 4:26b," *HUCA*, 32 (1961), I traced the millennial history of the ingenious interpretations of this half-verse.

[18] In my *The Hebrew Scriptures: An Introduction to Their Literature and Religious Ideas* (New York: Knopf, 1963), p. 375, I offer an explanation, and suggest the obvious dependency on Isaiah 6. That explanation is that Yahweh controlled every historical event, including Pharaoh's adamancy.

[19] For example, Antigonos of Socho said, "Do not be like servants who serve their masters in the hope of receiving reward," whereas Rabbi Elazar said, "Know in whose service you toil, and who is your employer who will give you the reward of your labor." Again, *Genesis Rabbah* gives a variety of inconsistent suggestions about Abraham's age—one, three, ten, or forty-eight—when he came to the knowledge of the existence of God.

Midrash
and the
Old Testament
by Brevard S. Childs

A characteristic approach of recent biblical scholarship is the frequent application of the term "midrash" or "midrashic interpretation" to describe certain features within the biblical text. The practice of identifying elements as midrashic is hardly new in respect to New Testament studies, but the rash of recent publications on the subject would at least point to fresh interest in the subject.[1] However, until quite recently the attempt to find midrash within the Old Testament has not been widespread, especially in non-Jewish circles. When the term did appear, it was frequently employed in a negative sense and restricted to a development of the late post-biblical age.[2]

In the period since World War II a different attitude toward midrash in respect to the Old Testament has emerged. Several factors seem to have played a role in effecting the change of attitude. First of all, the discoveries at Qumran demonstrated the widespread importance of midrash, even if in a form which differed markedly from the traditional rabbinical form. Secondly, the impetus from the side of New Testament studies evoked interest in tracing the development of the method back into the Old Testament period. Then again, particularly French scholars sensed a new significance for theology in the hermeneutics of midrashic interpretation and directed much energy to exploring its early development within the Bible.[3] Finally, Jewish biblical scholars, fully conversant with the later rabbinic development, began to demonstrate with great illumination some of the possibilities for biblical interpretation contained in midrash which had been hitherto overlooked.[4]

In spite of the renewed interest in the subject, there remains a considerable lack of clarity in respect to a precise definition of midrash and its relation to the Old Testament. No consensus has

47

emerged as to what should be included under the term, and scholars continue to employ widely divergent concepts. The nature of the problem can best be illustrated by reference to several important articles which relate midrash to the Old Testament.

I

Samuel Sandmel's programmatic article is, above all, an attempt to offer another alternative to the source theory of the literary-critical school in respect to the Pentateuch.[5] Sandmel argues that the usual recourse to sources has robbed the biblical authors of all imagination and creativity and has transformed them into illogical and pedestrian copyists who did a poor job in patching together contradictory narratives. His own suggestion is rather to see the Pentateuch as a crystallization of tradition which provided the basis for later writers, often in different situations, to embellish the text. Sandmel uses the term "haggada" to describe this embellishment. Thus the three accounts in Genesis of the betrayal of the wife (chaps. 12, 20, 26) can be understood as creative and intelligent adaptations of the one story in order to soften Abraham's misconduct and to harmonize some of the difficulties present in the original account with later concerns.

Although Sandmel does not go into great detail in defining the term "haggada," he does make it clear that he intends to use the term as it is commonly employed in the study of Jewish midrash. He accepts the common distinction within midrash between "halakah," which is reserved for legal matters, and "haggada," which he summarizes as "the fanciful retelling of tales." [6] However, it is obvious that Sandmel does not intend to offer a complete definition of haggada, but assumes its general characteristics to be well known. His concern is rather with the application of a method familiar to Judaism of the hellenistic period to the much earlier stories of the Bible.

There are several strengths to Sandmel's proposal which come immediately to mind. Sandmel is able to attribute an integrity to the various adaptations of the original story which had often been lost by the exclusive concentration on unraveling different sources. In a real sense, many of Sandmel's concerns are similar to those expressed by Gunkel against literary criticism's all too narrow focus. Again, Sandmel's concern to exploit all the insights of folklore [7] in tracing the development of a story, while at the same time doing justice to the imagination and spontaneous capacity of the biblical authors, parallels Gunkel's. In fact, Sandmel's suggestions for interpreting various Genesis stories, although often differing in specific details, have many conclusions in common with Gunkel, although Sandmel seems to have reached them independently.

Nevertheless, in my opinion, there are some major problems involved with Sandmel's use of the category haggada in reference to the Old Testament. First of all, it seems to me that Sandmel's method assumes an understanding of the relationship between parallel stories which has not been established. In fact, the establishing of the relationship between the parallel stories remains the chief exegetical problem. Sandmel assumes that one story represents an embellishment of an earlier story. Thus the more elaborate story of Genesis 20 is a haggadic expansion of the bare account in Genesis 12. But by moving in this manner, a host of problems is bypassed. Is Genesis 20 actually dependent on the story as presented in Genesis 12 or upon some common oral tradition? What was the function of the different stories which account for the strikingly different forms? Wellhausen and his school of literary critics have rightly been criticized for employing a concept of unilinear development to connect the various sources. There is a real question whether Sandmel's midrashic method is guilty of a similar error in assuming a relation between stories in the Pentateuch which is analogous to *Genesis Rabbah's* relation to Genesis.

Secondly, Sandmel's proposal can also be faulted in not really doing justice to the basic character of midrashic interpretation. Although it is correct that midrash often entails a considerable amount of embellishment, this characteristic is shared by other non-midrashic methods. Rather, midrash is, above all, an interpretation of a canonical *text* within the context and for the religious purposes of a community, and is not just embellishment of tradition. Midrash can be related in different degrees of closeness to the literal meaning of the text, but what is constitutive of midrash is that the interpretation does attach itself to a text. Unless this characteristic is fully appreciated, the lines are blurred which distinguish the forces at work in shaping the Genesis stories and those which shaped the Chronicler's use of

Kings. Only in the latter case is it a question of one writer attempting to interpret a normative text. Again, midrashic interpretation occurs within the context of a specific religious community. To apply the term midrash to the Genesis stories is to assume more about the exegetical activities of early Israelite communities than is actually known.

In sum, Sandmel's use of the concept midrash suffers from being too broad a definition which therefore does neither justice to the Bible nor to the midrashic method.

II

Addison G. Wright's two lengthy articles [8] clearly qualify as being the most exhaustive study of the problem of midrash and the Bible yet to appear in English. Wright's primary concern is to bring some rigorous order into the confusing application of the term "midrash." The great strength of his articles lies in the precise terminological distinctions which are then tested on a wide range of scholarly hypotheses relating to midrash.

Wright is concerned to make a sharp distinction between midrash as an exegetical method and midrash as a literary genre. As a literary genre the term "midrash" denotes a "specific corpus of literature within Jewish oral tradition." [9] In order properly to understand the classification, he seeks to analyze the rabbinic midrashic literature and to describe its characteristics. He argues that it is essential to distinguish between characteristics which are constitutive of the form (primary) and those which are incidental (secondary). According to Wright the essential feature of midrash as a genre is that it is a literature about a literature, which has primarily a religious and edifying aim. "It seeks to make yesterday's text . . . meaningful and nourishing for today." [10] Naturally there are certain exegetical techniques which appear in rabbinic midrash, but Wright classes them as part of the exegetical activity which participated in the development and not a constitutive characteristic of the genre.

On the basis of his definition of the genre midrash as a literature about a literature, Wright turns to examine critically the numerous examples within the Bible which have been classified as midrashic by scholars. Chronicles cannot be correctly called a midrash on Kings because the author has used Kings as a source and not as an object of interpretation. Then Wright makes a further refinement of his definition of the midrashic genre. The citing of a text of Scripture is only midrashic if the new composition contributes something by way of understanding to the Scripture text. A citation does not form a midrash if it is simply used by the author as part of a new composition. With this clear distinction Wright then examines examples of the "anthological style" first suggested by Robert and Bloch, "redaction and glosses," and apocalyptic literature. None of these examples are judged to have been written for the sake of the biblical text and are therefore not to be classed as midrash. Finally, Wright includes several examples from the New Testament, particularly the infancy narratives, and again fails to find any evidence that the stories were intended to actualize biblical texts.

At first sight it would appear that Wright's use of the term "midrash" represents the other extreme from that of Sandmel. Whereas Sandmel's broad definition included far too much within the term to be useful, Wright has excluded midrash, by and large, from the Bible. Yet the issue is more complex than this. Wright cannot be faulted for applying too narrow a definition of midrash. The problem lies elsewhere, in my opinion. The basic issue at stake is whether Wright's sharp distinction between midrash as a genre of literature and midrash as an exegetical activity can be sustained. Wright feels constrained to eliminate midrash from the Bible because the characteristics which are described as midrashic are those analogous to the exegetical activity and not the literary genre. Can this distinction be justified?

One of the fundamental postulates of the form-critical method is the insistence that the form and function of a genre must be held together.[11] The attempt of the form-critical method to analyze the stereotyped form of a literary genre has the purpose of determining the sociological setting within the life of the community which by its recurrent pattern shaped the genre. The interest in combining the form and function distinguishes the method from a simple literary analysis of a composition. In my opinion, Wright's approach suffers from its failure to retain the combination of form and function. By concentrating only on the form, he arrives at distinctions which tend to be artificial and unhelpful when applied rigorously to the material. So, for example, the distinction whether the citation of a text contributes something to a new composition or is directed only to understanding the biblical text itself, is not only extremely difficult to apply, but does not touch the heart of the problem. The distinction is a wooden one, lacking the needed flexibility to register the interplay of form and function in the reapplication of biblical texts.

Moreover, the sharp separation cannot be maintained between understanding midrash as an exegetical activity and as a literary genre. Naturally to make such a distinction is in order, but by failing to relate the two, the essential form-critical problem is overlooked. The heart of the midrashic method is that the interpretation moves from the biblical text to seek a connection with a new situation. But then again, the reverse direction is equally important; namely, the interpretation comes from the situation and moves back to the text. In the first instance, the text interprets the new situation; in the second, the new situation illuminates the text. At times the connection between text and situation is more explicit than at others. But the persistent attempt to actualize the ancient text, while at the same time evaluating the present in the light of the past, provides the distinctive features of both the literary genre and the exegetical activity of midrash. So, for example, when the Mekilta expands on Moses' recovering the coffin of Joseph,[12] the haggadic interpretation arises initially from the midrash's sensing a problem in the text, one which incidentally was of no concern to the original biblical author. How did Moses know where Joseph was buried? However, the midrash addresses at the same time the larger issue, particularly acute in the hellenistic period, respecting Israel's relation to the burial practices of its neighbors. It does so by means of an interpretation of Moses' act of piety. The haggadic story both arises from the text and returns to it; it speaks both from a new situation and to a new situation.[13]

If one now turns to the biblical material with a form-critical understanding of midrash, quite a different evaluation from that proposed by either Sandmel or Wright emerges. Obviously one will not discover exact parallels to the fully developed midrashic forms of the Tannaite period, but the concern would be to trace analogous movements in the biblical period to the form and function of midrash as it is represented in the later hellenistic and Roman periods. Lying at the center of the enterprise is the endeavor to trace the forces which were exerted on the interpretation of the Bible by what has aptly been described as "the consciousness of canon." [14] Whereas Gunkel and his school felt that such institutions as cult in early Israel were the dominant sources for the tradition-building process, it is becoming increasingly clear that the formation of a sense of authoritative Scripture unleashed another set of forces which then tended to operate according to laws quite distinct from those at work in the development of oral tradition. The study of the development of midrash should be significant in attempting to describe the nature and impact of these new factors on the composition of the Bible.

III

The basic question at stake is how the biblical text was reinterpreted by later authors. It is obvious that a great variety of methods was used, none of which can be identified straight away with midrash. However, the similarities both in the form and function of these different approaches to the text raise the question whether these techniques are early responses to forces which ultimately developed into midrash.

1. Scriptural Citation

The effect of an earlier text on the later tradition has long been recognized. In an important article H. W. Hertzberg spoke of this phenomenon as the "Nachgeschichte alttestamentlicher Texte." [15] Still there is a great variety in the way in which texts have been reapplied. Certainly there is an enormous difference between Second Isaiah's use of First Isaiah and "Third" Isaiah's use of Second. In the latter instance far more is involved than the influence of earlier prophetic preaching. The author of Third Isaiah is clearly working with written texts which are quoted, adjusted, and adapted.[16] The same history of development can be seen in comparing Deuteronomy's use of the early laws of Exodus in comparison to Chronicles' use of Kings. In the latter instance the Chronicler actually quotes from earlier texts as part of his parenesis.[17] Again, in the Psalter there are many clear examples of historical texts being reinterpreted in a poetic form in order to be used for a later age and in a different situation.[18]

Wright would surely object to this line of argument and argue that such a use of earlier texts by the Chronicler cannot be related to midrash because the older text forms part of a new composition. But such a move fails to appreciate those features in the Chronicler's work which are akin to later midrash and which prepared the ground for its growth. First of all, it is clear that the words of the biblical text have assumed an integrity of their own quite apart from the way in which they functioned in their original setting. The Chronicler does not attempt to draw analogies between like *situations* in Israel's history, but uses the *text* as such for his new purpose. Again, the Chronicler feels free to choose texts from different parts of the Bible and to weave the parts into a whole (cf. 2 Chron. 15:2-7, etc.). Moreover, he even uses the same text in two completely different contexts which becomes a standard technique in Qumran and the New Testament (cf. Jer. 29:13f. in 1 Chron. 28:9 and 2 Chron. 15:2).

Now it is true that the major function of these earlier texts is to assist in creating a new composition. An ancient text illuminates a new situation. Yet the reverse influence can also be felt; namely, the new context in which the older texts were placed effected a fresh interpretation of the text itself. Second Chronicles 15:2ff. can apply a text from Jeremiah (29:14) to a situation which historically preceded Jeremiah's ministry by several hundred years so that it serves to universalize a prophetic word far beyond the borders of the original word addressed to despondent exiles. One can also argue that the Chronicler's altering an original unconditional promise into one conditioned on obedience reflects exegetical activity to meet a problem in the text.

The problems connected with the so-called "anthological style," popularized by Robert and his school, are similar to the Chronicler although not identical. Once again it is a case of reapplication of older texts, particularly the liturgical material of the Psalter [19] and the didactic wisdom literature,[20] in which implicit and explicit use is made of earlier texts. At times there appears to be but a slight echo of an earlier text, while at other times the reuse borders on actual citation. Again a basic characteristic of the anthological method is the forming of an actual catena of older psalms into a new composition. Wright is certainly correct in insisting that such psalms are far removed from rabbinic midrash. Still there are analogies in both form and function which should not be overlooked. When one compares the Hodayoth of Qumran with the biblical Psalter, one is struck with the high degree of dependency of the former upon the latter. Yet it would be a mistake to draw from this fact the conclusion that the Qumran psalms are lacking in all creativity. Rather, the biblical psalms have assumed such a normative role as to provide the framework and idiom in which even a highly sectarian Jewish community expressed its peculiar worship. The anthological use of texts provides another example of interaction between an old text and a new situation in which the growing effect of a concept of canon can be felt.

Finally, the explicit reinterpretation of a former prophecy by a later prophecy shares many of these same features. The classic passage which illustrates this phenomenon is Daniel's reinterpretation of Jeremiah's prophecy of the seventy years (Dan. 9:2ff.). Daniel is informed by Gabriel that the seventy years are in fact seventy weeks of years=490 years. Now this reinterpretation does not function to cast doubt on the validity of Jeremiah's original word. His prophecy was not rejected by its reinterpretation by Daniel, but simply clarified. The number 70 is not just corrected to 490, but supplemented by a computation with 7. This is to say, the old prophetic text is adjusted to the new situation, but the new is still understood by means of the old text. The fact that an ancient text is used to address the new situation of the writer is not directly akin to the *pesher* interpretation of Qumran, but at least one can see some lines of continuity.

2. Harmonization Between Texts

A principle of harmonization between conflicting biblical texts receives an explicit formulation in the thirteenth rule of R. Ishmael ("When two passages are in contradiction to each other, the explanation can be determined only when a third text is found, capable of harmonizing the two"). Irrespective of what exactly the original principle entailed—the question is in some debate — certain elements in the rule are clear. A concept of contradiction has emerged which is based on an idea of truth as logical consistency. Lest this development be taken for granted, one should be reminded of the manner in which truth was tested in the ordeal of Numbers 5. Again, the hermeneutical rule assumes basically a closed canon which by definition reflects an inner consistency. The harmonization of texts is not for a moment conceived of as a tortuous making true that which was actually in conflict. Rather, working from the assumption that the testimony of every part of Scripture is true, the harmonizing of passages by means of a variety of techniques is simply making explicit what was believed about the canonical Scripture as one harmonious deposit of truth.

Attempts at early harmonization have long been detected by scholars within the biblical tradition and have exercised an important influence in the compilation of the Old Testament. In the early levels of tradition concerning the Egyptian plagues, there seemed to be little concern over the inconsistencies of a later plague once again annihilating what had earlier been reported as destroyed. However, at some point in the transmission of the text the addition of harmonizing notices, such as Exodus 9:31-32, would indicate that inner consistency had become a problem for the biblical redactor.

Particularly in the work of the Chronicler one can notice an exegetical activity which, among other things, directed its attention to problems of harmonization. So, for example, in 2 Chronicles 32 the author harmonizes the different accounts in Kings. The Chronicler weaves together a portrayal of Hezekiah in which he is reticent to pray directly without the assistance of Isaiah with another portrayal in which he confidently offers a long prayer on his own.[21]

Wright is critical of describing as midrash such attempts at harmonization whether in the work of the literary redaction of the Pentateuch or in the composition of the Chronicler. His concern that the sharp differences not be blurred between the later midrashic techniques and those present within the Bible is well taken; however, the emergence of exegetical methods, well within the biblical period, which in time developed into midrash cannot be eliminated simply by definition.

3. *Establishment of a New Context*

One way to reinterpret a text is to reshape it within a new composition. Another equally effective way is to change the context from that in which the text originally functioned. The text itself is not altered, but a new framework is provided which assigns to it a new role. The classic illustration of this second approach is to be found in the superscriptions of certain psalms. To at least thirteen psalms there has been appended in the Masoretic Text a superscription which refers to some incident in the life of David, to which the particular psalm is a response. For example, the writing of Psalm 34 is connected with the incident reported in 1 Samuel 21:10ff. in which David fled from Saul to the Philistines and there feigned madness in order to gain sanctuary.

A close study of these historical titles reveals that the superscriptions are not derived from independent historical tradition, but are the result of inner biblical exegesis. Working on the assumption that these psalms were written by David, the redactor of the psalms reasoned from the content of the psalm which incident recorded in Scripture afforded the most apt setting. Now it is also clear that there is a wide variation in the exegetical techniques employed by this biblical redactor and the author of *Midrash Tehillim*. In the case of the biblical writer, little weight has been placed on word plays. The major factor at work in the formation of the titles appears to be general parallels in content. Certainly there is no indication that a set of hermeneutical rules has been developed as yet.

Nevertheless, there are again some strikingly similar features, both in form and function, between the formation of secondary superscriptions and midrashic interpretation. Psalms which originally functioned within a cultic role for the community have been secondarily given a specific historical setting in the life of an individual. Lying at the base of this process of "historization" is the conviction that Scripture can best be interpreted by Scripture *(Scriptura sui ipsius interpres)*, which is a corollary derived from a consciousness of canon. At the same time there is a reverse process of interpretation set in motion by the establishing of a new context. If the superscription provided the historical occasion for a psalm's composition, the psalm in turn now provides insight into the emotional life of the psalmist. A new access into the subjective side of David's life has been unlocked. A striking parallel to this process is found in the use of Psalm 40 by Hebrews 10 in order to reveal the inner life of Christ. Once again there is an analogy between a process initiated in the biblical period and a later midrashic form.

To summarize: The relation between midrash as a genre, which is known primarily in rabbinic Jewish literature, and the Old Testament can best be determined by clarifying the form and function of various exegetical activities within the Bible which are analogous to later midrash. Although the early biblical parallels to full-blown rabbinic midrash are often only remotely connected, there is enough similarity between the two to speak of proto-midrashic forms within the Old Testament.

NOTES

[1] Cf. such representative works as Birger Gerhardsson, *Memory and Manuscript: Oral Tradition and Written Transmission in Rabbinic Judaism and Early Christianity*, trans. E. J. Sharpe, ASNU, 22 (Uppsala: Gleerup, 1961) ; Barnabas Lindars, *New Testament Apologetic* (Philadelphia: The Westminster Press, 1961) ; Wayne A. Meeks, *The Prophet-King: Moses Traditions and the Johannine Christology*, Suppl. to *NovTest*, 14 (Leiden: Brill, 1967) .

[2] J. Wellhausen, *Prolegomena to the History of Israel* (Edinburgh: A. & C. Black, 1885) , p. 227.

[3] The basic works are listed by Reneé Bloch in her article "Midrash," *DBS*, 5, p. 1281. Add to this, Geza Vermes, *Scripture and Tradition in Judaism: Haggadic Studies*, Studia Post-Biblica, 4 (Leiden: Brill, 1961) .

[4] The most important article was certainly I. L. Seeligmann's "Voraussetzungen der Midrashexegese," Suppl. to *VT* 1 (1953) , pp. 150ff. Mention should also be made of the articles by D. Daube, J. Weingreen, and others. F. Maass's article "Von den Ursprüngen der rabbinischen Schriftauslegung," *ZThK*, 52 (1955) , pp. 129ff., is significant in his reference to the major works of the previous generation of scholars on the subject.

[5] Samuel Sandmel, "The Haggada Within Scripture," *JBL*, 80 (1961) , pp. 105-122; reprinted in *Old Testament Issues*, ed. Samuel Sandmel (New York: Harper & Row, Publishers, 1968) , pp. 94-118.

[6] *Ibid.*, p. 110.

[7] H. Rosenfeld, *Legende* (Stuttgart: J. Metzler, 1961). The relation of midrash to folklore is also explored in an excellent introductory essay by S. Spiegel in *Legends of the Bible*, by Louis Ginzberg (New York: Simon & Schuster, Inc., 1956) , pp. xi-xxxix. Finally much basic material is still to be found in I. Heinemann, *Darke Haggadah* (reprinted Jerusalem: Magnes, 1949) .

[8] Addison G. Wright, "The Literary Genre Midrash," *CBQ*, 28 (1966) , pp. 105-138, 417-457. Reprinted as *Midrash—The Literary Genre* (Staten Island, N.Y.: Alba House, 1968).

[9] *Ibid.*, p. 120.

[10] *Ibid.*, p. 120.

[11] H. Gunkel, "Ziele und Methoden der Erklärung des A. T.,"*Reden und Aufsätze* (Göttingen: Vandenhoeck & Ruprecht, 1913) , pp. 11ff.

[12] *Mekilta de Rabbi Ishmael*, ed. J. Z. Lauterbach, (Philadelphia: The Jewish Publication Society, 1933-1935), vol. 1, pp. 177ff.

[13] Cf. the many examples of this midrashic dialectic in S. Spiegel, *The Last Trial*, trans. J. Goldin (New York: Schocken Books, Inc., 1969), pp. 28ff., 54ff., 73ff.

[14] Seeligmann, *op. cit.*, p. 152, used the term "Kanonbewusstsein."

[15] "Die Nachgeschichte alttestamentlicher Texte innerhalb des Alten Testaments," in *Werden und Wesen des Alten Testaments*, ed. P. Volz *et al.*, Beihefte ZAW, 66 (Berlin: Töpelmann, 1936), pp. 110-121.

[16] Cf. W. Zimmerli, "Zur Sprache Tritojesajas," *Gottes Offenbarung* (Munich: Christian Kaiser Verlag, 1963), pp. 217ff.; Diethelm Michel, "Zur Eigenart Tritojesajas," *ThViat*, 10 (1966), pp. 213-230.

[17] G. von Rad, "The Levitical Sermon in *I* and *II Chronicles*," in *The Problem of the Hexateuch and other Essays*, trans. E. W. Trueman Dicken (New York: McGraw-Hill Book Company, 1966), pp. 267-280.

[18] Cf. the impressive essay of Nahum M. Sarna, "Psalm 89: A Study in Inner Biblical Exegesis," *Biblical and Other Studies*, ed. A. Altmann, P. W. Lown Institute, Brandeis University, Studies and Texts, 1 (Cambridge: Harvard University Press, 1963), pp. 29-46.

[19] Cf. A. Deissler, *Psalm 119 (118) und seine Theologie, Ein Beitrag zur Erfassung der anthologischen Stilgattung im Alten Testament* (Munich: Zink Verlag, 1955).

[20] A. Robert, "Les attaches littéraires bibliques de Prov. I-IX," *RevBib*, 43 (1934), pp. 42-68, 172-204, 374-384; 44 (1935), pp. 344-365, 502-525; A. Robert and R. Tournay, *Le Cantique des Cantiques* (Paris: Gabalda, 1963).

[21] Cf. the fuller discussion in B. S. Childs, *Isaiah and the Assyrian Crisis*, SBT Second Series, 3 (Naperville, Ill.; Allenson, 1967), pp. 104ff.

Nationalism—
Universalism in
the Book of Jeremiah

by Harry M. Orlinsky

In an essay on "Nationalism-Universalism and Internationalism in Ancient Israel"[1] I tried to demonstrate the proposition that the biblical writers regarded YHWH at one and the same time as their national God and as the only Deity in the universe; they did not consider him the God of any other nation. The only God in existence had a mutually exclusive contract with Israel. As I expressed it there:

> To the biblical writers, from first to last, God is not only Israel's God alone, but he is at the same time, and naturally so, also the God of the universe, the only God in existence in the whole wide world, the only God who ever existed and who will ever exist. As God of the universe, he is the sole Creator and Master of all heavenly bodies (sun, moon, stars), of all natural phenomena (lightning, thunder, rain, drought, earthquakes), and of sky, earth, waters, and all living beings therein, human and animal. All natural phenomena, all heavenly bodies, all living creatures, all people, nations and individuals alike, are subject to his direct supervision and will. He is their Master in the fullest sense of the term.
>
> And so the God of Israel is at the same time the sole God and Master of the universe without being the God of any nation but Israel: the *national* [so for erroneous *natural*] God of biblical Israel is a *universal* God, but not an *international* God. With no people other than Israel did God ever enter into a legally binding relationship. To the biblical writers God was never the God of Moab, or of Egypt, or Canaan or Assyria or Aram or Ethiopia or Philistia, *et al.* He was the God of Israel alone. . . .[2]

In that connection I dealt with such notable passages as Malachi 2:10 ("Have we not all one father? Has not one God created us?"); Leviticus 19:18 ("Love your fellow as yourself"); Amos 9:7 (" 'You are to me the same as the Ethiopians, O children of Israel,' declares the Lord. 'I brought up Israel from the land of Egypt, and the Philistines from Caphtor, and the Arameans from Kir' "); Isaiah 2:2-4 par. Micah 4:1-4 ("In the days to come, the mount of the Lord's house shall be established as the highest mountain. . . . And all the nations shall stream to it . . . and say: 'Come, let us go up

to the mount of the Lord . . . that he may instruct us in his
ways. . . .' For instruction [tôrāh] shall come forth from Zion . . .");
and Isaiah 56:7 (". . . For my house shall be called a house of
prayer for all peoples"); as well as such passages as Isaiah 19:18-25,
Isaiah 14:1-2, Zechariah 2:14-16, Malachi 1:11, and the books of
Ruth and Jonah. Elsewhere[3] I have discussed in some detail Jeremiah 1:5 ("I appointed [or: designated] you a prophet concerning
[or: "for"; hardly "to"; see below] the nations"); Isaiah 42:6 ("I
have created you and appointed you a covenant-[or: of]people, a
light of nations"); and 49:6 ("I will make you a light of nations").
The present essay is a study of the subject as it pertains to the Book
of Jeremiah.

The passages in Jeremiah that are clear-cut in their attitude
toward God in relation to Israel and to the rest of the world are
those that should be dealt with first; after a clear picture has been
achieved, the passages that are less than clear may be dealt with.
Unfortunately, too often the principle of obscurus per obscurius has
been applied to the study of biblical problems such as ours.

A second point: Everyone recognizes the fact that Jeremiah is
not the author of every verse of all fifty-two chapters of the received
Hebrew text that bears his name, so that different — even conflicting — points of view might well be the result of multiple authorship. For our problem it is methodologically preferable to treat the
book as a unit, as though Jeremiah were its sole author, in order to
obtain a picture of the Book of Jeremiah as a whole. If the picture
obtained does justice to every part of the book, then the matter of
authorship — be it Jeremiah's or that of one or more additional
writers — is of no concern for our problem. Only if problems arise
that require close analysis of authorship need further study be made.

No part of the Book of Jeremiah is without a reference to YHWH
as the God of Israel. Thus the prophet, and whoever else contributed
to the making of the book, employed no less than about seventy
times such expressions as "the Lord your/our God," "the God of
Israel," and "their/its [viz., Israel's] God" when addressing or
referring to his fellow Judeans.[4] Even Nebuzaradan, King Nebuchadrezzar's representative, recognized this when he is said to have
told Jeremiah (40:2 f.), ". . . The Lord your God Himself pronounced this calamity upon this place. . . ."

In conjunction with this concept, the Book of Jeremiah frequently puts in the mouth of God the term "My people" (*ʿammî*) in reference to Israel;[5] twice the term is "Your people" (31:7[6]; 32:21). In this connection, mention might be made also of the phrases "this people" (*hā-ʿām haz-zeh*)[6] and simply "the people" (*hā-ʿām*),[7] both of which denote God's people.

As elsewhere in the Bible, no nation other than Israel is referred to as the "servant" (*ʿébed*) of God; this is understandable if no people but Israel has a special relationship with God. The expression employed is *ʿabdi yaʿaqōb*, "Jacob, my servant" (30:10; 46:27, 28).[8]

There are several passages in which the idea of Israel as God's people and of YHWH as Israel's God — to the exclusion of all other peoples and gods — finds expression: 7:23 (". . . this is what I commanded them [viz., your ancestors in Egypt]: 'Obey me, and I will be your God and you shall be my people . . .' "); 11:4 (". . . you shall be my people, and I will be your God [*wih-yîtem lî lᵉʿām wᵉ-ʾānōkî ʾehyeh lākem lēʾlōhîm*]"); 13:11 (". . . I brought close to me the whole house of Israel and the whole house of Judah — declares the Lord — to be my people . . ."); 24:7 (". . . and they [viz., the Judean exiles] shall be my people, and I will be their God . . ."); 30:22 ("And you [viz., the restored Judean community] shall be my people, and I will be your God"); 31:1 [30:25] (". . . I will be the God of all the [restored] families [or: clans, *mišpᵉhôt*] of Israel, and they shall be my people"); 31:31-33 ("Days are coming — declares the Lord — when I will make a new covenant [*bᵉrît hᵃdāšāh*] with the house of Israel and with the house of Judah . . . and I will be their God, and they shall be my people"); 32:38 (". . . they [viz., the restored Judean exiles] shall be my people, and I will be their God").

These bare references and quotations, however, receive their full import only when their respective contexts are fully comprehended, when it is realized that from the bondage in Egypt through the distant future, with no exceptions, it was always and it will always continue to be the exclusive God-Israel relationship that prevails: *tertium non datur*! (See further below.)

If God and Israel have a relationship that is not shared by any people or deity, it should follow that expressions deriving from that exclusive relationship are not applied to others. This is borne out completely in Jeremiah. Thus God is referred to on three different occasions as the "hope" of Israel: 14:8 and 17:13, "the hope of

Israel" (*miqwēh yiśrā°ēl*); and 50:7, ". . . because they sinned against the Lord . . . and the hope [*miqwēh*] of their fathers. . . ." Consequently, it is natural for Jeremiah, speaking for his fellow Judeans, to petition the Lord (14:22): ". . . no one but you, O Lord our God, and we hope in you [*û-n°qawweh-lāk*]. . . ." In line with this, the prophet can extend to his people the hope that God will restore the Babylonian captivity: 29:11, "For I am mindful of the plans that I have for you — declares the Lord . . . to give you a hopeful future [lit., a future and a hope, *tiqwāh*]." The same assurance is given in 31:17 (16), "There is hope [*tiqwāh*] for your future, declares the Lord, and [your] children shall return to their territory."

Or take the root *qdš*. Only "Israel was holy [*qōdeš*] to the Lord" (2:3). And by the same token God is the "Holy One" of Israel, never of anyone else: 50:29, ". . . for she [Babylon] has acted presumptuously against the Lord, against the Holy One of Israel" (*°el-q°dôš yiśrā°ēl*); 51:15, "For Israel and Judah are not left widowed by their God, by the Lord of Hosts . . . by the Holy One of Israel." Since God, Israel, and the land of Israel constitute an inseparable unit in biblical thought, it is only the last named that will be graced by the term "holy": 25:30, ". . . The Lord makes his voice heard from his holy dwelling [*mim-m°°ôn qodšô*]"; and of course Jerusalem-Zion, and no other site, will be called "Holy Mount" (31:23 [22]).

Terms of devotion, endearment, and kindness characterize God's attitude toward Israel, in contrast to that shown to the Gentile nations. Thus in 31:9(8), in dealing with restored Israel, God is described as asserting: ". . . for I will be [or: have become] a father to Israel, and Ephraim is my first-born [*ki-hāyîtî l°yiśrā°ēl l°°āb w°°eprayim b°kōrî hû°*]." The same term *°āb* "father" is employed also in 3:4 (". . . you have called me 'Father' [*qārā°t lî °ābî*] . . .") and 19 (". . . and I thought: you would call me 'Father' . . ."). In contrast, note the bitter irony in 2:27 f., where God is said to taunt his people: "They said to wood, 'You are my father' [*°ābî °attāh*]. . . . And where are those gods you made for yourself? . . ." In one Jewish tradition, 3:4 follows on 2:27-28 in the *haftarah* for the *sidrāh Mas°ê* (Num. 33–36).

Very moving is the description of God and Israel in 2:2 f.:

Go proclaim to Jerusalem: Thus said the Lord:
I remember[ed] fondly [or: in your favor; lit., for you] the devotion [*hesed*]
of your youth,
Your love [*°ah°bat*] as a bride:

How you followed me in the wilderness,
In a land not sown.
³Israel was holy [qōḏeš] to the Lord,
First fruits of his harvest:
All who partook of it were held guilty;
Disaster befell them. . . .

And the same terms for "love" and "devotion" will be employed by the prophet to describe, in the opposite direction, God's feelings for Israel (31:3[2]):

I conceived for you [lit., I loved you] an eternal love [ʾahᵃḇaṯ ꜥ ôlām ᵃhaḇṯiḵ]; Therefore I extend [my] devotion [ḥesed] to you.

And in 33:11 God's ḥesed is bound up with the return of Judah's exiles: " 'Praise the Lord of Hosts . . . for his devotion [ḥasdô] endures forever, . . . for I will restore the fortunes of the land as of old,' said the Lord." These terms, ḥesed and ʾāhaḇ, will not be found in passages involving God and a non-Israelite people.

The same holds true, for example, for rāḥam, "have compassion." In 12:15 God is quoted as asserting that "After I have torn them out [viz., the people of Judah], I will take them back into favor [wᵉ-riḥamtîm, have compassion on them]." In 30:18, "Thus said the Lord: 'I will restore the fortunes of Jacob's tents and have compassion [ʾᵃraḥēm] upon his dwellings' "; or compare 33:26, ". . . for I will restore their fortunes [viz., of the descendants of the patriarchs and David] and have compassion upon them [wᵉ-riḥamtîm]"; 42:12, "I will have compassion upon you [viz., the Judeans under the Babylonian ruler] and he will treat you with compassion [wᵉ-ʾettēn lāḵem raḥᵃmîm wᵉ-riḥam eṯᵉḵem]." God's relationship with the non-Israelite nations does not require the use of the term raḥam.

In a couple of instances God is said to be so angry with his people for their transgression of the covenant that his decision to punish them is irrevocable; he will not change his mind (niḥam); compare 4:28, "(²⁷For thus said the Lord: 'The whole land shall be desolate . . .) ²⁸. . . For I have spoken, I have planned, and I will not relent [wᵉ-lōʾ niḥámtî] or turn back from it' "; 15:6, " 'You cast me off' — declares the Lord — 'ever going backward. So I stretch out my hand to destroy you; I cannot relent [nilʾêṯî hinnāḥēm].' " However, the reverse is asserted in several other passages. In 26:1-3 the Lord commands Jeremiah to stand at the entrance of the temple in Jerusalem and tell the incoming worshipers to amend their evil ways: ³"Perhaps they will give heed and turn back, each from his evil way, that I may renounce [wᵉ-niḥamtî] the punishment . . .";

and similarly in v. 13, where Jeremiah pleads with his fellow Judeans: "Therefore mend your ways and acts, and heed the Lord your God, that the Lord may renounce [w^e-yinnāḥēm] the punishment he has decreed for you." Or compare 31:13 (12), referring to the Judeans in exile whom he will restore to their homeland, ". . . I will turn their mourning to joy, and I will have compassion on them [w^e-niḥamtîm]. . . ." In the case of niḥam, 18:8-10 apparently employs this term in connection with non-Israelites (see further below).

Terms that indicate "joy" are part of the vocabulary that derives from God's covenant with Israel. On several occasions mention is made of the fact that "the sound of mirth and the sound of gladness [qôl śāśôn w^e-qōl śimḥāh], the voice of the bridegroom and the voice of the bride" will either be banished from Judah because of her faithlessness to God (7:34; 16:9; 35:10) or "shall be heard again in this place" (33:10-11). Or compare the following passages: 31:7(6), "For thus said the Lord: 'Cry out in joy [rānnû . . . śimḥāh] for Jacob . . .' "; vv. 10-13 (9-12):

> Hear the word of the Lord, O nations,
> And tell it in the isles afar,
> And say . . .
> 11. . . the Lord will deliver Jacob . . .
> 12They shall come and shout in joy [w^e-rinn^{e}nû]
> On the heights of Zion;
> They shall be radiant over the bounty of the Lord . . . .
> 13Then shall the maidens dance gaily [tiśmaḥ . . . b^{e}māḥôl] . . . .
> I will turn their mourning to joy [l^{e}śāśôn],
> I will comfort them and cheer them [w^e-śimmaḥtim] in their grief.

In 32:41, the Lord assures the Judean exiles: "I will rejoice over them [w^e-śaśtî] . . ."; in 33:9, again addressed to the captivity and Jerusalem restored, the Lord asserts that "It shall become for me a symbol [lit., name] of joy [l^{e}śēm śāśon], a praise and a glory, before all the nations of the earth. . . ." Contrast 50:11 ff., where Babylon, rejoicing in her victory over God's people, is assured by God of utter, irrevocable destruction — this as against the glorious future of his people as expressed in vv. 4-5, 19-20:

> 11Though you rejoice, though you exult [ki tiśm^{e}ḥi ki ta^{ca}lzi],
> O plunderers of my heritage, . . .
> 12Your mother shall be utterly shamed. . . .
> 13Because of the wrath of the Lord
> She shall not be inhabited,
> She shall be an utter desolation;
> All who pass by Babylon
> Shall be appalled. . . .

(^{19}But I will restore Israel to his pasture,
And he shall graze on Carmel and Bashan;
In the hills of Ephraim and in Gilead
He shall satisfy his desire.)

Such terms as *ḥēleq* "portion" and *naḥ^{a}lāh* "allotment, inheritance, heritage, share," arising from the idea that God as the creator and master of the world had granted his favorite land to Israel and had apportioned it among her tribes, will occur for God vis-à-vis Israel and no other people: 10:16 par. 51:19,

But the portion [*ḥēleq*] of Israel is not like these [gods],
For He is the creator of everything
And Israel is his own allotted tribe [*šēbeṭ naḥ^{a}lāṭô*]. . . .

One cannot refrain from noting the direct association of the foregoing with several passages in Deuteronomy; e.g., 32:8-9,

When the Most High gave nations their homes [*b^{e}hanḥēl*]
And set the divisions of man,
He fixed the boundaries of peoples
In relation to Israel's numbers.
^{9}For the Lord's portion [*ḥēleq*] is his people,
Jacob his own allotment [*ḥebel naḥ^{a}lāṭô*].

It is precisely the non-Israelite peoples and their gods who were denied this *ḥēleq* and *naḥ^{a}lāh*: Deuteronomy 4:19-20, ". . . These [viz., everything in the world that is worshiped as a deity] the Lord your God allotted (*ḥālaq*) to the other peoples everywhere under heaven; ^{20}but you the Lord took and brought out of Egypt, that iron blast furnace, to be his own allotted people [*lihyôṭ lô l^{e}cam naḥ^{a}lāh*], as is now the case." And compare Deuteronomy 29:25 (26), "They [viz., violators of the covenant in time to come] turned to the service of other gods . . . whom he had not allotted [*w^{e}lō^ɔ ḥālaq*] to them."

To get back to these terms in the Book of Jeremiah. According to 3:18-19, ". . . they [Judah and Israel] shall come together from the land of the north to the land that I allotted [*hinḥálṭî*] to their fathers.^{19} . . . and I gave you a desirable land, the fairest allotment [*naḥ^{a}laṭ ṣ^{e}bî*] . . ."; and 12:14 has it that "Thus said the Lord: Concerning all . . . who encroach on the heritage which I allotted [*han-naḥ^{a}lāh ^ɔašer-hinḥálṭî*] to my people Israel. . . ." To these may be added the use of *naḥ^{a}lāṭî*, "My [God's] portion," for the people Israel in such passages as 2:7; 12:7, 8, 9; 50:11, and for the land of Israel in 16:18 and 17:4. (On ^{ɔ}îš l^{e}naḥ^{a}laṭô in 12:15, see below.)

All three standard terms denoting restoration of God's exiled people — *qābaṣ* "gather in," *gāʾal* "redeem," and *pādāh* "ransom" — are found in 31:10-11 (9-10),

Hear the word of the Lord, O nations . . .
And say:
He who scattered Israel will gather them in [*yᵉqabbᵉṣénnû*] . . .
¹¹For the Lord will ransom [*pādāh*] Jacob,
Redeem him [*û-gᵉʾālô*] from one stronger than he.

In 50:33-34 the Babylonian captors are warned that Judah's God, "their Redeemer [*gōʾᵃlām*], is strong . . . He will plead their case. . . ." Jeremiah's usual term for "deliver, rescue" is *yāšaᶜ*, and as with the terms just mentioned, this word also refers to Israel as against the Gentile peoples, never the reverse. Thus 30:10 (par. 46:27)-11 (cf. 42:11) read:

Have no fear, my servant Jacob —
Declares the Lord —
Be not dismayed, O Israel!
For I will deliver you [*môšiᶜᵃḵā*] from afar. . . .
¹¹For I am with you . . .
To deliver you [*lᵉhôšiᶜᵉḵā*]. . . .

Or compare 14:8, "O Hope of Israel, / its deliverer [*môšiᶜô*] in time of trouble . . ."; 31:7(6), "For thus said the Lord . . . 'Cry out in joy . . . and say: "Save [*hôšaᶜ*], O Lord, your people . . ." ' "; and 23:6 par 33:16, "In his [par. those] days [viz., of the restored dynasty of David], Judah shall be delivered [*tiwwāšaᶜ yᵉhûḏāh*]. . . ."

In keeping with the agricultural character of Israel's social structure, God will be referred to as a "shepherd" (*rōᶜeh*) in relation to his people: 31:10(9), "Hear the word of the Lord, O nations, . . . He will guard [Israel] as a shepherd his flock"; and God will see to it that in restored Judah "there shall again be habitations of shepherds [*nᵉwēh rōᶜîm*] resting their flocks" (33:12), that "[Israel] shall graze [*wᵉ-rāᶜāh*] on Carmel and Bashan" (50:19), and that reliable "shepherds" lead his people (3:15; 23:4). On the other hand, God is never the shepherd of a Gentile nation, nor will he provide them with reliable shepherds or enable them to graze in peace and prosperity. (On chaps. 48–49, see below toward the end.)

There are additional terms that shed light on our problem. Thus the phrase *šāb šᵉbût* "restore the fortunes" (traditional "captivity") is used frequently for Israel: 29:14; 30:3 (*wᵉ-šabtî ʾet-šᵉbût ᶜammî . . .*, "and I will restore the fortunes of my people . . ."), 30:18; 31:23 (22); 32:44; 33:7, 11, 26. (On the use of this phrase for Moab

[48:47], Ammon [49:6], and Elam [49:39], see below toward the end.) However, it is to the larger segments of the Book of Jeremiah that we may now turn our attention.

In receiving the call from God as his spokesman, Jeremiah is described as having heard this word of God (1:5),

> Before I created you in the womb, I selected you;
> Before you were born, I consecrated you;
> I appointed you a prophet to [or: for] the nations [nābīʾ lāg-gôyim neṯattīḵā].

Strange as it may seem, it has been essentially the last line — "I appointed you a prophet to/for the nations" — that has been made to serve as the major evidence for the universally held belief that Jeremiah was an internationalist, that his message from God was directed not to his people alone but to all nations everywhere, to all mankind. As in the case, e.g., of Amos 9:7, Isaiah 56:7, and Malachi 2:10, not to mention Isaiah 42:6 and 49:6 (see the beginning of this essay), this phrase has been taken at its face value without being investigated further in the light of the rest of the Book of Jeremiah. No one asked himself the natural, and crucial, question: precisely where in the book does Jeremiah bring God's message to the Gentile peoples?

Indeed, immediately after receiving the call, Jeremiah replied (v. 6),

> Ah, Lord God!
> I don't know how to speak,
> For I am still a boy.

To which the Lord responded (vv. 7-8),

> Do not say, "I am still a boy,"
> But go wherever I send you. . . .
> 8Have no fear of them,
> For I am with you to deliver you. . . .

But whom did Jeremiah have to fear? From whose hands would God have to deliver him? Did Jeremiah have to go to Babylonia or Egypt to report to the government or to the populace the word of God, and thereby incur their wrath? Or from Jerusalem did he have to attack these foreign powers and depend on God to protect him from vengeance at the hands of their emissaries? But of course the answers to these questions are well known, if one bothers to look for them in this connection, because they are present in the text of Jeremiah's book. After preparing Jeremiah for his career (1:9, "The Lord put out his hand and touched my mouth, and . . . said to me: 'Herewith I put my words into your mouth' "),[9] and advising him (v. 10),

> See, I have set you (or: given you authority) [*hipqadtikā*] this day over the nations and kingdoms,
> To uproot and to pull down,
> To destroy and to overthrow,
> To build and to plant,

God tells him that he would soon bring in foreign nations with which to punish Judah for her sins (vv. 11-19),

> . . . [15]For I am summoning all the peoples of the kingdoms of the north. . . . They shall come and shall each set up a throne before the gates of Jerusalem and against its walls round about and against all the towns of Judah. [16]And I will argue my case against them for all their wickedness. . . . [17]But you, gird up your loins and go speak to them all that I command you. Do not be dismayed by them [or: break down before them], or I will dismay [or: break] you before them. [18]And I, I make you this day a fortified city, and an iron pillar, and bronze walls against the whole land — against the kings of Judah, its officials, its priests, and its citizens [lit., the people of the land]. [19] They will attack you, but they will not overcome you, for I am with you — declares the Lord — to deliver you.

It is clear, then, that it is not the foreign nations, even those on Judean soil as victors, that Jeremiah is told by God not to fear in his divine mission, but his fellow Judeans, and it is from their hands that God assures him deliverance. Note also, in this connection, the phraseology:

> ⁷ וַיֹּאמֶר יהוה אֵלַי . . . וְאֵת כָּל־אֲשֶׁר אֲצַוְּךָ תְּדַבֵּר:
>
> ⁸ אַל־תִּירָא מִפְּנֵיהֶם כִּי־אִתְּךָ אֲנִי לְהַצִּלֶךָ נְאֻם־יהוה:
>
> ¹⁷ . . . וְדִבַּרְתָּ אֲלֵיהֶם אֵת כָּל־אֲשֶׁר אָנֹכִי אֲצַוֶּךָּ אַל־תֵּחַת מִפְּנֵיהֶם פֶּן־אֲחִתְּךָ לִפְנֵיהֶם:
>
> ¹⁹ . . . כִּי־אִתְּךָ אֲנִי נְאֻם־יהוה לְהַצִּילֶךָ:

Cf. also 15:20-21, immediately below.

This conclusion is borne out fully by everything in the book that bears on Jeremiah's relationship with his own Judean countrymen, as well as on his experiences with the foreign nations; indeed, if Jeremiah appears from his book as something of a "bellyacher," it is precisely because of this relationship with his fellow Judeans. One recalls readily such passages as 11:18-23; 15:10,

Woe is me, my mother, that you ever bore me —
A man of conflict and strife with all the land!
I never lent to them
And they never lent to me,
Yet everyone curses me;

and verses 15-21 (where the last two verses read, "Against this people [viz., the Judeans] I will make you / as a fortified wall of bronze . . . For I am with you to save you and deliver you — declares the Lord [*ki* *ʾittᵉḵā* *ʾᵃnî* *lᵉhôšîʿᵃḵā* *û-lᵉhaṣṣîleḵā* *nᵉʾum YHWH*]. ²¹I will deliver you [*wᵉ-hiṣṣaltîḵā*] from the hands of the wicked . . ."); and 17:14-18 ([note the use of the root *ḥtt*, as in 1:17] ¹⁸"let them [viz., Jeremiah's opponents] be dismayed, and let not me be dismayed" [וְיֵחַתּוּ הֵמָּה וְאַל־אֵחַתָּה אָנִי]). Also 18:18-23; 20:1 ff. (cf. v. 2: "And Passhur had Jeremiah flogged and put in a cell . . ."), 7 ff. (cf. vv.7-8: ". . . I have become a constant laughingstock, / everyone jeers at me. ⁸. . . For the word of the Lord brings upon me / constant disgrace and contempt"), 14 ff.; 26:7 ff. (cf. v. 11: "The priests and the prophets said . . ., 'This man [viz., Jeremiah] deserves the death penalty, for he has prophesied against this city [viz., Jerusalem] . . .' "). Indeed, were it not for the intervention of Ahikam, son of Shaphan, Jeremiah would have been killed just as his fellow ("true") prophet Uriah was (26:20-24); 26:14 ff.; 37:12 ff. (Jeremiah beaten and jailed, and almost starved); 38:1 ff. (Jeremiah rescued from death by starvation); etc.

What is more: it is not the Egyptians whom Uriah feared when he fled to Egypt from his Judean opponents; and it is not to the Egyptians that Jeremiah prophesied when he was carried off by a group of his fellow Judean opponents, but to his fellow Judeans with him in Egypt or back home in Judah. Neither does Jeremiah prophesy to the Babylonian victors on Judean soil (chaps. 40–44). And when Jeremiah sends a message from Jerusalem to Babylonia (chap. 29), it is not to the Babylonians at all but "to the rest of the elders of the exile community — to the priests, prophets, and all the people whom Nebuchadnezzar had exiled from Jerusalem to Babylonia . . ." (v. 1).

One need merely render the prepositions *lᵉ-*, *ʿal*, and *ʾel* naturally in context, that is, by "concerning, about" (sometimes "against" for *ʿal* or *ʾel*), to do justice to the text of Jeremiah. When Jeremiah's rejoinder to the "false" prophet Hananiah in 28:8 is rendered "The prophets who lived before you and me in ancient times prophesied against [or: concerning; *ʾel*] many lands and great kingdoms of war and calamity and pestilence," the passage makes sense; and the standard English versions do so. If, however, 'el were rendered here "to," then the truly — as well as unnecessarily — embarrassing question would be asked: which prophets, to which lands and kingdoms? The same is true, e.g., of 27:19 ff., where the standard English versions read, "For thus said the Lord of Hosts concerning [ʾel] the columns, the [wᵉ-ᶜal] tank, the [wᵉ-ᶜal] the stands, and the [wᵉ-ᶜal] rest of the vessels . . .," where "to" (or hardly even "against") would make no sense. Of especial pertinence are the statements about the nations in chapters 46–50, where ᶜal, lᵉ-, and ʾel are all employed and where only "concerning, about" (or perhaps "against") — but never "to" — fits the context: "concerning [ᶜal] the nations" (46:1); "About/Concerning [lᵉ-] Egypt" (46:2); "about/concerning [lᵉ-] the coming of Nebuchadrezzar" (46:13); "c./a. [ʾel] the Philistines" (47:2); "C./A. [lᵉ-] Moab" (48:1); "Concerning [lᵉ-] the Ammonites" (49:1); "Concerning [lᵉ-] Edom" (49:7); "Concerning [lᵉ-] Damascus" (49:23); "Concerning [lᵉ-] Kedar" (49:28); "The word of the Lord that came to the prophet Jeremiah concerning [ʾel] Elam" (49:34); and "The word which the Lord uttered concerning [ʾaŝer dibber YHWH ʾel] Babylon, concerning [ʾel] the land of the Chaldeans" (50:1).[10]

Yet with all these clear and ample data before them, scholars and translators have mechanically — and unnecessarily misleadingly — rendered (nābîʾ) la(g-gôyim nᵉtattikā) in 1:5 by "(I appointed you a prophet) to (the nations)." No one would have rendered lᵉ- here by anything but "concerning," were it not for the universally assumed notion that the prophets, including Jeremiah, were internationalistic, and hence the failure to ask oneself the obvious question: to what nations?

Parenthetically, this additional point might be made here. A "diehard," insisting on rendering lᵉ- in 1:5 by "to" and disregarding the rest of the Book of Jeremiah, might point to the Book of Jonah as an instance where God sent a prophet to a Gentile nation — as though this one fact were decisive and justified ignoring all the other evidence to the contrary. However, apart from the several serious problems with which the Book of Jonah confronts the scholar (cf. pp. 228-231 of my essay in the May volume mentioned in note 1 above; and see now Millar Burrows's essay in the same volume, "The Literary Category of the Book of Jonah," pp. 80-107), it should at least be recognized that — in contrast to the careers of the main heroes of the other prophetic books — the career of Jonah is postexilic fiction, created when there was no Nineveh to which to deliver God's message. As long as Nineveh was in existence — and it reached its zenith precisely during the *floruit* of Israel's prophets — there is no record of a prophet, even Nahum, who devoted his entire prophecy to Nineveh, going there or being sent there for any purpose. It might also be mentioned in passing that such exilic prophets as Ezekiel and Second Isaiah had nothing to say *to*, but quite a bit *concerning*, even their Gentile "host" nation.

Not only is Jeremiah a prophet to his fellow Judeans and never to the Gentile nations, but also the nations themselves have no independent existence for him. That is to say: whatever happens to the nations is of no concern to Jeremiah — in other words, is of no concern in the covenant between God and his people Israel — unless they are involved in some action between God and Israel. Thus, e.g., when warning the Judeans that God is omnipotent and that Judah is, in his hands, what clay is in the hands of the potter (18:1-6), Jeremiah says that just as God, master of the universe, can change his mind about any nation in the world if that nation deserves it, so will he act toward his people (vv. 7-11):

> At one moment I may decree that a nation or a kingdom shall be uprooted and pulled down and destroyed; [8]but if that nation . . . turns back from its wickedness, I will change my mind concerning the punishment. . . . [9]At another moment I may decree that a nation or a kingdom shall be built and planted; [10]but if it does evil in my sight . . ., then I will change my mind concerning the good that I planned to bestow upon it. [11]And now, say to the men of Judah and the inhabitants of Jerusalem: "Thus said the Lord: 'I am shaping punishment for you . . . Turn back, each of you from your wicked ways, and mend your ways and your actions!' "

It is, again, but rhetoric when Jeremiah proceeds two verses farther on to argue and to rebuke (vv. 13 ff.):

> . . . thus said the Lord:
> "Inquire among the nations:
> Who has heard anything like this?
> Fair Israel has done
> A most horrible thing:
> [14]Does one forsake Lebanon snow
> From the mountainous rocks?
> Does one abandon cold waters
> Flowing from afar?
> [15]Yet my people have forgotten me . . .,"

just as it is but rhetoric in 2:10-13,

> Just cross over to the isles of the Kittim and look,
> Send to Kedar and observe carefully;
> See if aught like this has ever happened:
> [11]Has any nation changed its gods —
> Even though they are no gods?
> But my people has exchanged its glory
> For what can do no good.
> Be appalled, O heavens, at this;
> Be horrified, utterly dazed!
> — declares the Lord.
> [13]For my people have done a twofold wrong:
> They have forsaken me, the fount of living waters,
> And hewed them out cisterns, broken cisterns,
> Which cannot even hold water,

and in 16:19-21 (the whole world will come to realize that Israel's God alone is real). So that, when Jeremiah warns of the destruction of the royal palace in Jerusalem (22:1-7) and says (vv. 8-9),

> And when many nations pass by this city and one man asks another,
> "Why did the Lord do thus to that great city?" [9]the reply will be,
> "Because they forsook the covenant with the Lord their God and bowed down
> to other gods and served them,"

he is using "nations" in the same manner as "heavens" in 2:12 quoted above ("Be appalled, O heavens, at this;/Be horrified . . .!"); surely no one need argue that the "many nations" will hardly explain the defeat as due to God's punishment for transgression of the covenant, when the superiority of their weapons, men, god(s), and the like, was so self-evident. Similarly, when Nebuzaradan, captain of the Babylonian guard, is described as having said to Jeremiah (40:2-3), "The Lord your God pronounced this calamity upon this place [3]. . . because you sinned against the Lord and did not obey him . . .," this is only a literary-psychological device to influence the Judean people to believe that Jeremiah was the true spokesman of Israel's omnipotent God.

In their secondary and incidental role, this role is one of the two main functions that the nations, Babylonia among them, serve in the Book of Jeremiah, viz., as a figure of speech, as a literary-psychological device; the other main function is that of agents of God in his actions involving Israel. Sometimes, indeed, it is difficult to distinguish between the two functions; in either case, however, the nations, whether only rhetorically or actually, are but helpless pawns in God's plans.

Thus in chapter 27, Jeremiah relates that God said to him (vv. 2 ff.),

... Make for yourself thongs and bars of a yoke, and put them on your neck. [3]And send them [better, with emendation, send a message] to the king of Edom, the king of Moab, the king of the Ammonites, the king of Tyre, and the king of Sidon, by envoys who have come to Jerusalem to King Zedekiah of Judah; [4]and give them this charge to their masters: "Thus said the Lord of Hosts, the God of Israel: ... [5]It is I who made the earth and, the men and beasts who are on the earth ..., and I give it to whomever I deem proper. [6]I herewith deliver all these lands to my servant, King Nebuchadnezzar of Babylon; I even give him the wild beasts to serve him. [7]All nations shall serve him, and his son and his son's son, until the turn [lit., time] of his own land comes, when many nations and great kings shall subjugate him. [8]The nation or kingdom that does not serve him ... and does not put its neck under the yoke of the king of Babylon, that nation I will visit ... with sword and famine and pestilence, until I have destroyed it by his hands. [10]So do not listen to your prophets, augurs, dream[er]s, diviners, and sorcerers, who say to you, 'Do not serve the king of Babylon.' [11]For they prophesy falsely to you, with the result that ... you shall perish. ..."

Whether it was Jeremiah himself or a later writer who composed the above, and whether the statement is to be taken literally or symbolically[11] — that is, whether the yokes or the messages alone were or were not actually sent to the kings east and north of Judah who were involved in Nebuchadnezzar's western campaigns — the fact is that the nations were arbitrarily and summarily being handed over to Babylonia, along with Judah; but whereas Judah had broken the covenant with God and was being punished for it by Babylonia, the other nations had done no wrong. They merely suited God's interests in the process of punishing Israel by means of Babylonia.[12]

The same may be said of Jeremiah's statement in 25:15-31:

For thus said the Lord, the God of Israel, to me, "Take from my hand this cup of wine — of wrath — and make all the nations to whom I send you drink of it. [16]Let them drink and stagger about and go mad, because of the sword which I am sending among them." [17]So I took the cup from the hand of the Lord and gave all the nations drink to whom the Lord had sent me: [18]Jerusalem and the towns of Judah, and its kings and officials ...; [19]Pharaoh king of Egypt, his courtiers, his officials, and all his people; [20]all the mixed [or foreign] peoples; all the kings of the land of Uz; all the kings of the land of the Philistines ... [21]Edom, Moab, and Ammon; [22]all the kings of Tyre and all the kings of Sidon, and all the kings of the coastland across the Sea; [23]Dedan, Tema, and Buz ... [24]all the kings of Arabia ... [25] ... and all the kings of Elam and all the kings of Media; [26]... all the kingdoms of the world which are on the face of the earth. And at the end, the king of Sheshach [traditionally regarded as a cipher for *bābel* =Babylon] shall drink. ... [28]And if they refuse to take the cup from your hand and drink, say to them, "Thus said the Lord of Hosts: You must drink! [29]If I am bringing the punishment first on the city that bears my name, do you expect to go unpunished? You will not go unpunished . . ." [31]. . . For the Lord has a case against the nations, He contends with all flesh. He delivers the wicked to the sword. . . . [32]. . . Disaster goes forth From nation to nation; A great storm is unleashed From the remotest parts of the earth. [33]In that day, the earth shall be strewn with the slain of the Lord . . . [38]because of his fierce anger.

Two things are readily apparent: (1) whatever symbolism or sympathetic magic the "cup of wine, of wrath" was meant to represent, it is hardly likely that any of the wine was ever sent out to the nations; and (2) the nations, Babylonia included, are to experience calamity not because of any wrong that they have committed but because Judah has to be punished. Here is what the text of vv. 8-10 of the same chapter (25) says, "Assuredly thus said the Lord of Hosts: 'Because you [viz., Judah] would not listen to my words, [9]I am going to send for all the peoples of the North, and for my servant, King Nebuchadnezzar of Babylon, and bring them against this land and its inhabitants, and against all those nations round about. I will exterminate them and make them a desolation, an object of hissing — ruins for all time. . . .' " And as for Nebuchadnezzar and his Babylonia (vv. 11-14), ". . . Those nations shall serve the king of Babylon seventy years. [12]When the seventy years are over, I will punish the king of Babylon and that nation for their sins . . . and I will make it a desolation for all time. . . . [14]For they too shall be enslaved by many nations and great kings; and I will requite them according to their acts and according to the deeds of their hands." One will look in vain for a serious description of the "sins" that merited such an end. Or compare 43:8-13, where Jeremiah is told by God to tell the Judean refugees in Egypt that God will bring Nebuchadnezzar to Egypt and destroy it; what the guilt of Egypt is, is not revealed.

Chapter 33 is another of the numerous typical statements in Jeremiah concerning the status of Babylonia and the other nations (vv. 4-9):

For thus said the Lord . . . concerning the houses of this city [viz., Jerusalem] and those of the kings of Judah which were torn down . . . [5]whom I struck down in my fierce anger . . . because of all their wickedness. [6]I will bring healing to them . . . [7]I will restore the fortunes of Judah and Israel . . . [8]I will purge them of all their guilt . . . [9]And it [viz., Jerusalem] shall become to me a name of joy, a praise and a glory before[13] all the nations of the earth who, when they hear of the good that I do for them, shall fear and tremble because of all the good and all the prosperity that I provide for them.

Another of the clear-cut passages which assert the uniqueness and universality of Israel's God and his exclusive national covenant with Israel — and where Babylonia is only a temporary tool, to be discarded when no longer needed — is provided by 32:26-41,

> The word of the Lord came to Jeremiah: [27]"I am the Lord, the God of all flesh [ʾelōhê kol-bāśār]. Is anything too wondrous for me? [28]Assuredly ... I am delivering this city [viz., Jerusalem] into the hands of the Chaldeans ... [30]because the people of Israel and Judah have done nothing but wickedness in my sight...," [36]Now therefore thus said the Lord ... [37]"I will gather them from all the countries to which I banished them in my fierce anger ... [39]I will give them one heart and one way to fear me forever.... [40]And I will make with them an everlasting covenant [berit ʿōlām] ... [41]I will rejoice in them and do them good...."

Babylonia as a mere tool is well described, e.g., in 51:7-8,

> "A golden cup was Babylon,
> In the Lord's hand,
> Making all the earth drunk.
> Of its wine the nations drank,
> And so the nations went mad.
> [8]Suddenly Babylon fell and was broken;
> Wail over her!..."

Poor Babylon, destined in the view of the authors of the Book of Jeremiah to constitute only a passing incident in the long and eternal relationship between God and Israel! The author of 50:6-10 asserts,

> My people have been lost sheep, led astray by their shepherds ... [7]All who have come upon them have devoured them, and their enemies have said "We shall not incur guilt, for they have sinned against the Lord..." [8]Flee from Babylon ... [10]For Chaldea shall be plundered....

Or as put by the author(s) of 51:15-24, speaking of God as the master of the universe, the covenanted partner of Israel and nemesis of Babylonia:

> He who made the earth by his might.... [17]All mankind is stupid and witless, ... for their images are false....
> [19]But not like these is the portion [i.e., God] of Jacob,
> for he is the one who formed all things,
> and Israel is his very own tribe....
> [24]And I will repay Babylon and all the inhabitants of Chaldea for all the calamity that they wrought in Zion....

More, much more, can readily be cited from Jeremiah in this vein; virtually every chapter provides several pertinent passages. But enough has been adduced for our purpose directly from the text of the book, and the limitations of space in this volume must be respected. Every passage in the Book of Jeremiah, whether cited or not in this essay, derives from a specific historical circumstance and serves the interests of whatever group(s) may be involved. Further, the exclusive covenant between God and Israel, the only basis on which argument between God's prophets and his people is possible, must always be justified and explained. So that if Nebuchadnezzar attacks Judah and her neighboring countries, it is because God is utilizing his Babylonian army; if Egypt will be destroyed, it is because this serves God's purpose in relation to his covenanted people; if, when the final editor of the statement about Moab in chapter 48 lived, Moab seemed destined to survive whatever calamity it was experiencing or had experienced, then v. 46, which is the culmination of the long prophecy against Moab and which reads, "Woe to you, O Moab! / The people of Chemosh are undone. / For your sons have been taken captive, / your daughters into captivity," is supplemented by v. 47, "Yet I will restore the fortunes of Moab in the days to come — declares the Lord. Thus far the judgment on Moab." (As to why Moab should merit restoration — that is not explained. If Moab will be restored, it is because Israel's God wanted it so.) The same prospect of restoration is promised to the Ammonites (49:6), after the prophecy proper (vv. 1-5) had promised nothing but destruction — again without explanation. And similarly Elam (49:34-39). But no restoration of fortunes is promised to Edom (49:7-22), Damascus (vv. 23-27), and Kedar (vv. 28-33) — again without explanation. It is hardly possible to date with any confidence these several utterances, and their component parts, concerning the nations, since the precise historical circumstances are not known to us.[14] And the same is true of such passages as 12:14-17:

> Thus said the Lord concerning my wicked neighbors who encroach on the heritage which I allotted to my people Israel, "I am going to tear them up from their soil, and I will tear up the house of Judah out of the midst of them. [15]Then, after I have torn them out, I will take them back into favor, and restore them each to his own inheritance and his own land. [16]And if they learn the ways of my people, to swear by my name — 'As the Lord lives' — just as they once taught my people to swear by Baal, then they shall be built up [or: incorporated] in the midst of my people. [17]But if they do not listen, I will tear out that nation, tear it out and destroy it," declares the Lord.

Most scholars now seem to agree that the date and authorship of such passages can no longer be determined; not only was this utterance not delivered to the nations round about Judah, but it holds out for these nations only the certainty of destruction unless they adopt Israel's God and way of life and become absorbed within the Judean community. In any case, Jeremiah is no prophet of theirs, and their role in the unfolding events involving God and Israel is not one of their choosing or one that they can in any way determine. This role is exclusively Judah's, and Jeremiah's function is to tell his fellow countrymen how God wants them to comprehend and play that role.[15]

As a matter of fact, so dependent are the actions and experiences of the nations upon the covenant between Israel and God that the essence of the whole Book of Jeremiah could be summed up fairly in the one single statement uttered by God to Jeremiah (36:2-3), "Take a scroll and write on it all the words that I have spoken to you concerning [or: against] Israel and Judah and all the nations. . . . ³Perhaps the house of Judah, hearing of the harm that I plan to do to them, will turn from their wicked ways, and I will pardon their sinful wrongdoing." Whether the phrase "all the nations" in v. 2 is original or secondary, the fact is that it is exclusively Judah's decision, by continuing in its conduct or by repenting, that will determine the fate of the nations, i.e., whether Babylonia will come and conquer and punish and, in the end, itself be destroyed, and whether the other nations will remain independent or be conquered by Babylonia.

NOTES

[1] In *Translating and Understanding the Old Testament: Essays in Honor of Herbert Gordon May*, ed. Harry T. Frank and William L. Reed (Nashville: Abingdon Press, 1970), pp. 206-236.

[2] *Ibid.*, pp. 213 f.

[3] H. M. Orlinsky, *The So-Called "Servant of the Lord" and "Suffering Servant" in Second Isaiah* (Suppl. to *VT*, 14, 1967), Appendix: "A Light of Nations" (*ʾôr gôyim*) — "A Covenant of People" (*bᵉrit ᶜam*), pp. 97-117.

[4] I have noted 2:17, 19; 3:13, 21, 25; 5:4, 5; 7:3, 21, 28; 9:14; 11:3; 13:12, 16; 16:9; 19:3, 15; 21:4; 22:9; 23:2; 24:5; 25:15, 27; 26:13; 27:4, 21; 28:2, 14; 29:4, 25; 30:2, 9; 31:23; 32:14, 15, 36; 33:4; 34:2, 13; 35:13, 17, 18, 19; 37:7; 38:17; 39:16; 42:4, 6, 9, 13, 15, 18, 20, 21; 43:1, 10; 44:2, 7, 11, 25; 45:2; 46:25; 48:1; 50:4, 18; 51:5, 10, 33.

[5] See 2:11, 13, 31, 32; 4:11, 22; 5:26, 31; 6:14, 26, 27; 7:12; 8:7, 11, 19, 21, 22, 23; 9:1, 6; 12:14, 16 [*bis*]; 14:17; 15:7; 18:15; 23:2, 13, 22, 27, 32; 29:32; 30:3; 31:14 [13]; 33:24; 50:6; 51:45.

[6] See 4:10, 11; 5:14, 23; 6:19, 21; 7:16, 33; 8:5; 9:14; 11:14; 13:10; 14:10,

11; 15:1, 20; 16:5, 10; 19:1, 11; 21:8; 23:32, 33; 27:16; 28:15; 29:32; 32:42; 33:24; 35:16; 36:7; 37:18; 38:4.

⁷ Cf. 14:16; 19:1, 14; 21:7; 23:34; 26:7, 8 [bis], 9, 11, 12, 16, 17, 24; 28:1, 5, 7, 11; 29:1, 16, 25; 34:8, 10; 36:6, 9 [bis], 10, 13, 14; 37:12; 38:1, 4 [bis] 9 [bis], 10, 14; 40:5, 6; 41:10 [bis], 13, 14, 16; 42:1, 8; 43:1, 4; 44:15 [where wᵉ-ḳol-hā-ᶜām hay-yōšᵉbim bᵉ-ᵓéreṣ-miṣrayim, "all the people who dwelt in the land of Egypt," denotes Judeans], 20, 24; 52:15, 28.

⁸ It is unnecessary for our purposes to analyze the precise character of this relationship, i.e., what the term ᶜébeḏ denotes specifically in connection with the God-Israel relationship: is it an economic-social term that derives from the lord-servant element in the Israelite economic-social (agricultural) structure — and so essentially an inner-Israelite development — or is it a political-diplomatic (=military) term that derives from treaty relationship, specifically vassal treaties? The past decade has witnessed the rise of "pan-vassal-treatyism," to the point where even data that are hardly comparable are used uncritically; I have drawn attention to this current obsession in my presidential address for the Society of Biblical Literature, "Whither Biblical Research?" *JBL*, 90 (1971), pp. 1-14. Since the troublesome phrase "My servant, King Nebuchadnezzar of Babylon" (*N. meleḳ-bāḇel ᶜaḇdî*) in 25:9; 27:6; and 43:10 does not involve a people, it need not be discussed here.

⁹ It has not been sufficiently noted that the resistance to becoming God's spokesman (*nāḇiᵓ*) to his people need not always and automatically be taken literally. This "resistance" constitutes a stereotype throughout the Bible; cf., e.g., Elijah, Amos, Isaiah, Ezekiel, Jonah, and (retroactively) Moses. See my study, *The So-Called "Servant of the Lord"* (cited above, note 3), pp. 56 f. and 57, note 1.

¹⁰ It may be repeated here that the question of authorship of these chapters (46–50), as of any other passages in the Book of Jeremiah, does not concern us here; scholars differ as to when who wrote what, and in many systematic studies and commentaries on Jeremiah it is often next to impossible to locate many passages without the use of an index. For our problem, the picture that emerges from the book as a whole is clear and consistent.

¹¹ The precise character and function of these actions are not our concern here. So whether Jeremiah did or did not purchase a linen loincloth, wear it, and then go to *pᵉrāṯ* and cover it up in a cleft of the rock (13:1 ff.) — and whether Perath is the Euphrates or an otherwise unknown place in or near Judah — our concern here is merely to note that only God's covenanted Judeans are involved in the symbolism. It need, further, scarcely be noted that if v. 23 reads,

> "Can the Ethiopian change his skin,
> Or the leopard his spots?
> Just as much can you do good,
> Who are practiced in doing evil!"

nothing international is involved in the use of the term "Ethiopian" (*kuši*) any more than in the parallel term "leopard."

¹² Behind the statement in this chapter (18), as throughout the Book of Jeremiah and the Bible, lay the belief that, as the only Deity in the world, it was naturally Israel's God who was responsible for everything that happened to and among the nations, animals, heavenly bodies, etc., of the universe. This is the point, e.g., in Amos 9:7 (cf. above at the beginning of this essay, with reference to pp. 211 ff. of my article cited in note 1).

¹³ The first part of v. 9 is clearly corrupt, and it is generally — and probably correctly — rendered so as to accord with the clear text and reasonable

statement of the second half of the verse. Our rendering "before" for *l^e*(*kōl gôyê hā-ʾāreṣ*) follows such standard English versions as JPS (1917), RSV, JB, and NEB.

[14] A passage such as 3:17 ("At that time Jerusalem shall be called 'The Throne of the Lord,' and all the nations shall assemble there, in the name of the Lord at Jerusalem; they shall no longer follow the willfulness of their evil hearts") might be adduced here, except that the term *ḵōl-hag-gôyim*, generally rendered "all the nations," may actually — as I believe — refer only "to the house of Judah together with the house of Israel" in the verse immediately following (18), especially since the whole chapter otherwise (vv. 1-16 and 18-25) deals only with these two parts of God's covenanted people. The term *goy*(*im*) not infrequently refers to Judah-Israel in Jeremiah. And this, too, should be noted, that the phrase *š^erirûṯ lēb*, "willfulness of heart," occurs in seven additional passages in Jeremiah (only in Deut. 29:18 and Ps. 81:13 elsewhere in the Bible) and always with reference to Judah.

[15] What Jeremiah and the group(s) whose views he shared really desired is a problem that only a trained historian can determine; neither the textual or the literary critic nor the theologian can comprehend this problem. Thus when God commands Jeremiah (7:2-3),

"Stand at the gate of the house of the Lord, and proclaim this word there: 'Hear the word of the Lord, all you of Judah who enter these gates to worship the Lord!' ³Thus said the Lord of Hosts, the God of Israel: 'Mend your ways and your actions, and I will let you dwell (or, with change of vocalization: I will dwell with you) in this place,' "

with which, compare 26:2-3,

"Thus said the Lord [to Jeremiah]: 'Stand in the court of the house of the Lord, and speak to all the towns(men) of Judah, who are coming to worship in the house of the Lord, all the words which I command you to speak to them. Do not omit anything. ³Perhaps they will listen and turn back, each from his evil way, that I may renounce the punishment that I am planning to bring upon them for their wicked acts' " (cf. also 36:6-7),

it is noteworthy that precisely those "who enter these gates to worship the Lord" are being denounced as evildoers. If then the "wicked acts" did not really involve sacrifices and prayers to other gods — i.e., did not really involve idolatry — they must have been political and economic and social acts which Jeremiah and his supporters opposed. So that while the terminology is religious (cf. 7:4 ff.), the significance of these terms is basically far more than religious. That is why, as put at the end of the address cited in note 8 above, "in his analysis of the momentous events that befell Judah at the turn of the sixth century B.C., the historian will go seeking behind such terms as 'sin' and 'covenant' for the fundamental economic, political, and social forces that determined the use and content — and, so frequently, the utter disregard — of these terms. There is a great future for biblical research and the trained historian who devotes himself to it."

Some Remarks on the New English Bible

by William F. Stinespring

This token is presented to Morton Enslin in gratitude for his friendship and in admiration of his careful scholarship and his painstaking devotion to the highest ideals of our profession.

To another festschrift of recent date, I contributed an article calling attention to a certain idiom in the Old Testament that seems to be understood by the grammarians, but has been mishandled by some of the translators, even self-styled modern ones. Reference was also made to two previous articles dealing with two other idioms sometimes similarly mishandled. Finally, a few words were added concerning "the 'Red Sea' blunder."[1] When this previous article was written, the New English Bible Old Testament had not been published and therefore could not be included for comparison with the other translations. This was unfortunate, owing to the influence which NEB will exert throughout the English-speaking world for some time to come.

The purpose of this article is to subject NEB to the same scrutiny already applied to other modern translations, and to add any general conclusions that may follow from the examination. To be sure, the points to be examined are few and perhaps not tremendously important, though they may be typical enough to afford an indication of the care with which this new translation was made.

In biblical Aramaic, the third-person plural active voice of verbs with meaning equivalent to a passive is very common. There are about twenty-seven examples in Daniel and eight in Ezra.[2] NEB shows good awareness of this idiom, so that in only about four instances in Daniel and two in Ezra does the idiom fail to come through clearly as a passive. NEB paraphrases in Daniel 2:13, "men were sent to fetch Daniel and his companions for execution," whereas the Aramaic simply says, "Daniel and his companions were sought for execution." The meaning, however, is perfectly clear.

מהודעין in Ezra 7:24 is controversial because it is a participle and cannot be inflected for person. NEB follows the King James Version (KJV) and the Revised Standard Version (RSV) in keeping it active ("we make known") by supplying the first-person plural pronoun as a subject instead of the more natural third person, whereas Moffatt and *An American Translation* (AT) take the latter course, which yields passive meaning.[3] The NEB translators of course were not obligated to follow KJV, but they had read it and were sometimes influenced by it.[4]

In biblical Aramaic this idiom is also used with the infinitive, which cannot be inflected for number, gender, or person. Nevertheless, when an active infinitive clearly demands a passive translation, a "hidden third-person plural indefinite" must be recognized. There are about thirteen examples of this in Daniel and three in Ezra (Dan. 2:12, 46; 3:2, 13, 19; 4:3 [Eng. 6]; 5:2, 7; 6:9 [Eng. 8], 16 [Eng. 15], 24 [Eng. 23]; 7:26 [*bis*]; Ezra 4:21; 5:13; 6:8). Of these sixteen examples, only one in Ezra (4:21, "must desist" instead of "must be stopped") and one in Daniel (5:2, "to fetch" instead of "to be brought in") seem to have been overlooked in NEB, as against three in RSV. (In some cases the idiom is obscured in English by a paraphrase, but that is legitimate for reasons of style or clarification.) Thus it can be safely concluded that the NEB translators were well aware of the use of the third-person plural active of the finite verb as a substitute for the passive voice, including the extension of this usage to the infinitive.

The next idiom to be considered is the much overlooked appositional genitive, best exemplified by the expression בת־ציון, often mistranslated as "the daughter of Zion," as though the genitive were possessive. Zion, or Jerusalem, of course did not have a daughter; she *was* the daughter or maiden (the real meaning in this case).[5] The appositional genitive exists in English, but it is of limited application. We can say "the city of Jerusalem" or "the tribe of Judah," but we cannot use the "of" in "the river Euphrates" or "my daughter Mary." The translator must be on his guard to translate Hebrew idiom into English idiom to avoid spoiling the sense. An attempt to stay too close to the original words of the text sometimes produces mistranslation.

Unfortunately, the performance of the translators of NEB in this instance was not as good as might be expected. One notes that ubiquitous yet nonexistent "daughter of Zion" in about twenty instances. There are also several instances of the parallel expression "daughter of Jerusalem" (Isa. 10:32; 16:1; 37:22 [=2 Kings 19:21]; 52:2; 62:11; Lam. 1:6, 2:1, 4, 8, 10, 13, 15, 18; 4:22; Mic. 1:13; 4:8, 10, 13; Zeph. 3:14; Zech. 2:10; 9:9; cf. Jer. 4:31; 6:2, 23).

Another such mishandled phrase is בת־עמי, conventionally translated as "the daughter of my people." This phrase occurs about fifteen times, all but one in Jeremiah and Lamentations (Isa. 22:4; Jer. 4:11; 6:26; 8:11, 19, 21, 22; 9:1, 7; 14:17; Lam. 2:11; 3:48, 4:3, 6, 10). The translator of Jeremiah, whoever he was, seems to have been somewhat aware of the appositional genitive and the pitfalls in translating it. He rendered the three occurrences of בת־ציון in Jeremiah (4:31; 6:2, 23) simply as "Zion," which makes sense but destroys the connotation of tender pity achieved in the Hebrew by prefixing the word *baṭ*.[6] Likewise, among the nine occurrences of בת־עמי in Jeremiah, he rendered six of them simply by "my people"; in two instances he relapsed into the conventional and misleading "daughter of my people" (6:26; 14:17), whereas in the ninth instance (8:22) he evaded the problem by a paraphrase. In every case, of course, the translation should have been something equivalent to "my beloved people." In no case did the translator show real understanding of the Hebrew.[7]

It remains to look at the six instances of בת־עמי not in Jeremiah. In Isaiah (22:4), the rendering is "my own people," which shows a faint reflection of the pathos inherent in the idiom. Of the five occurrences in Lamentations, four of them have simply "my people," the more common rendering also in Jeremiah. The fifth instance (4:3) is rendered "the daughters [sic] of my people," without any textual support for the plural number or any note of explanation for the emendation, though such notes are fairly common in the translation as a whole. The effect is a strained interpretation that destroys the imagery of the line. In the light of what has been seen above, it is all the more surprising to find three instances of בתולת־ישראל in Jeremiah (18:13; 31:4, 21) and one in Amos (5:2) translated correctly as "virgin Israel" or "the virgin Israel," contrary to KJV but in agreement with RSV, which also mostly retains "the daughter of Zion." It is indeed strange that translators who can see Israel personified as a virgin cannot see Zion or Jerusalem personified as a maiden even though the grammatical construction is similar in all three cases.

In Isaiah 40:9 the NEB text reads "You who bring Zion good

news" and "you who bring good news to Jerusalem" מבשרת־ציון
מבשרת־ירושלם). Notes *g* and *h* read "*or* O Zion, bringer of good news"
and "O Jerusalem, bringer of good news." The reading in the notes
is according to the Hebrew, while the reading in the text would require about nine emendations (changing verbs, nouns, and pronouns from feminine to masculine) in this one verse. This is another
example of the often overlooked appositional genitive. Clearly, here,
the "bringer of good news" is Zion (Jerusalem), feminine gender.
When some other messenger brings good news to Zion (Jerusalem),
as in 41:27 and 52:7, then the gender of that messenger is masculine,
with verbs and pronouns in agreement, and Zion (Jerusalem)
standing alone in the feminine. Incidentally, RSV has the reading
according to the Hebrew in the text, and the conjectural reading in
a footnote. Thus it would seem that in this case NEB is more beholden to KJV than is RSV.

We come now to the matter of the participle of the immediate
future.[8] This usage sometimes occurs when the participle is func-
tioning as a pure verb, either in a main clause or in a subordinate
clause. The usage is well recognized by the grammarians[9] but the
translators are just now beginning to sense it. It occurs in both
Hebrew and Aramaic and is so common that exhaustive consideration is impossible; Bergsträsser, e.g., lists about thirty-five examples,
Gesenius-Kautzsch-Cowley about twenty-five. Proper translations
are "about to" or "going to" (preceded by the present tense of the
verb "to be"), often with a threatening connotation, as in "I am
about to punish you" or "I am going to punish you" (soon).

Let us take first a few examples from Genesis, all from threatening
situations:

6:17 (מביא)

KJV: I <u>do bring</u> a flood of waters . . . .
RSV: I <u>will bring</u> a flood of waters . . . .
NEB: I <u>intend to bring</u> the waters of the flood . . . .
Probably "I am about to bring . . ." would be the best translation,
though NEB's "I intend to bring . . ." is a fair substitute.

7:4 (ממטיר)

KJV: For yet seven days, and I <u>will cause it to rain</u> . . . .

RSV: For in seven days I <u>will send rain</u> . . . .
NEB: In seven days' time I <u>will send rain</u> . . . .
"I am about to cause it to rain . . ." would be literally correct, but
"I will send rain . . ." seems to get the sense very well.

19:13 (משחיתים)

KJV: For we <u>will destroy</u> this place . . . .
RSV: . . . for we are <u>about to destroy</u> this place . . . .
NEB: . . . because we <u>are going to destroy</u> it . . . .
Both RSV and NEB are entirely correct.

20:3 (מת)

KJV: . . . thou <u>art but a dead man</u> . . . .
RSV: . . . you <u>are a dead man</u> . . . .
NEB: You <u>shall die</u> . . . .
"You are about to die . . ." would be best, though "you shall die . . ."
recognizes that מת is here a verb, not a noun.

The early and late chapters of Deuteronomy also furnish good
examples. Moses is about to repeat the Law, he is about to die, the
people are about to cross the river, etc.:

1:20 (נֹתֵן)

KJV: . . . which the Lord our God <u>doth give</u> to us.
RSV: . . . which the Lord our God <u>gives</u> us.
NEB: . . . which the Lord our God <u>is giving</u> us.
NEB attempts to render the Hebrew participle more correctly by
using an English participle; the correct translation is, however,
"which the Lord our God is about to give us."

5:1 (דִּבֶּר)

KJV: . . . which I <u>speak</u> in your ears this day.
RSV: . . . which I <u>speak</u> in your hearing this day.
NEB: . . . which I <u>proclaim</u> in your hearing today.
The present tense is not adequate here; the meaning is, "which I
am about to proclaim . . ." (the Ten Commandments, which follow
immediately).

32:47 (עברים)

KJV: . . . the land, whither ye <u>go over</u> Jordan to possess it.

RSV: . . . the land which you <u>are going over</u> the Jordan to possess.

NEB: . . . the land which you are to occupy <u>after crossing</u> the Jordan.

The literally correct translation would be, ". . . the land which you are about to cross the Jordan to possess." NEB's paraphrase gets the meaning effectively.

A passage in Jonah is very characteristic:

1:3 (באה)

KJV: . . . he found a ship <u>going to</u> Tarshish.

RSV: . . . and found a ship <u>going to</u> Tarshish.

NEB: . . . where he found a ship <u>bound for</u> Tarshish.

All of these renderings get the idea very well, though "a ship about to go to Tarshish" would make it clear that the ship was to sail soon.[10]

An interesting example occurs in the Aramaic of Daniel:

2:13a (מתקטלין)

KJV: And the decree went forth that the wise men <u>should be slain</u>.

RSV: So the decree went forth that the wise men <u>should be slain</u>.

NEB: A decree was issued that the wise men <u>were to be executed</u>.

All three versions make the second clause subordinate; this makes excellent sense and avoids saying, "and the wise men were being slain," which was not the case. Yet the second clause is probably coordinate, meaning "and the wise men were about to be slain"; the participle expresses not the present progressive, but the immediate future, with threatening connotation.

To summarize what has been observed so far, it can be said that the NEB translators had good understanding of the active infinitive used as a passive (in Aramaic), rather poor understanding of the appositional genitive, and only limited understanding of the participle of the immediate future. Of previous translations, Moffatt shows the best understanding of the appositional genitive, the American Translation of the participle of the immediate future.

We come now to "the 'Red Sea' blunder." As was pointed out in the previous article,[11] "the Red Sea" occurs at least twenty-four times in conventional translations of the Old Testament as a rendering of the Hebrew term *yam sûp*, following the Greek versions, which have ἡ ἐρυθρὰ θάλασσα in these places (Exod. 10:19; 13:18; 15:4, 22; 23:31; Num. 14:25; 21:4; 33:10, 11; Deut. 1:40; 2:1; 11:4; Josh. 2:10; 4:23; 24:6; Judg. 11:16; 1 Kings 9:26; Nch. 9:9; Pss. 106:7, 9, 22; 136:13, 15; Jer. 49:21. Cf. Exod., chaps. 14 and 15, where the word *yām* is used several times alone in the same sense). But *yam sûp* (literally "Sea of Reeds" or "Lake of Reeds") never means the Red Sea proper as shown on modern maps of the area. It seems to be a rather inexact term with at least four possible meanings: (1) any one of a series of small lakes or marshes along the route of the present-day Suez Canal; (2) the Gulf of Aqaba; (3) the Gulf of Suez; (4) a mythical place symbolic of difficulties to be overcome or easement to be achieved in the realm of the spirit.[12] Suggestions (2) and (3) are of course arms of the Red Sea, but are not included in that sea in modern geographical terminology.

One can only speculate why the LXX and other Greek translators of the Old Testament used ἡ ἐρυθρὰ θάλασσα. As far back as Herodotus the ancient term included the Indian Ocean and the Persian Gulf, which would make the idea of crossing the Red Sea even more ridiculous. But perhaps to the LXX "the Red Sea" simply meant any water east of the Nile. Their decision, followed by many English versions, has had an unfortunate effect on interpretation, beginning with the New Testament (Acts 7:36; Heb. 11:29; cf. Wisd. of Sol. 10:18; 1 Macc. 4:9).

Both terms, Red Sea (*yammā šimmôqā*) and Sea of Reeds (*yam sûp*), occur in the *Genesis Apocryphon* (col. 21, ll. 17–18), where they are distinguished from one another in meaning. The Red Sea includes the Persian Gulf and Indian Ocean, whereas the Sea of Reeds is called "the tongue [i.e., "gulf"] . . . which leads out from the Red Sea," presumably meaning the Gulf of Suez, or even the Gulf of Aqaba.[13]

Since the modern term "the Red Sea," in contrast to ancient usage, has a definite, restricted, and well-known meaning which excludes it as a sensible translation of *yam sûp*, the question remains what to do. In 1924 James Moffatt simply substituted "Reed Sea" everywhere for "Red Sea."[14] This was a sensible solution, being a reasonably exact translation of the Hebrew, which at the same time avoided the various geographical, exegetical, and theological difficulties inherent in the traditional translation. In 1927 the AT paid no attention and kept the traditional "Red Sea"; subsequent editions and printings brought no change. In 1952 RSV likewise opted for "the Red Sea," a great misfortune because of the continuing influence of this version. In 1962 the Pentateuch volume of the new Jewish Publication Society's version gave "the Sea of Reeds" as the translation of *yam sûp*, with an added footnote, "Traditionally, but incorrectly, 'Red Sea.' "[15] This is an excellent example of taking the right stand and taking it strongly. In 1966 the Jerusalem Bible appeared with "the Sea of Reeds" offered in all relevant passages without comment, following the usage of the French version from which JB is derived.[16] The NEB translators were apparently vaguely aware of some of this, but they were too steeped in tradition to make a clean break. They used "the Red Sea" in the text, with a note at the first occurrence in each biblical book, saying: "*Or* the Sea of Reeds." This reminds one of the RSV translators, who were a bit too timid to remove the erroneous but very traditional "valley of the shadow of death" from the text of Psalm 23:4 and relegated the correct translation, "valley of deep darkness," to a footnote. Incidentally, at this particular spot, the NEB translator, by rendering "a valley dark as death," has managed to retain the "death" and thus throw a sop to tradition by using a slight overtranslation rather than an actual mistranslation.

There are some additional problems in the translation of the NEB. The word נחשת is rendered in the older English versions everywhere as "brass." Modern research has shown that this word means "copper," in its original state as taken from the mine (as in Deuteronomy 8:9), or "bronze" when denoting a worked metal (as in 1 Samuel 17:5–6). NEB seems to have this right every time. In the case of Ezekiel 1:4, 27; 8:2, where the word חשמל has traditionally been translated "amber," which is obviously wrong, NEB translates "brass," but very properly adds a note, thus: "Meaning of Hebrew word uncertain." One wonders why such objectivity and freedom from erroneous tradition could not have been exercised in some other instances already noted.

In Hosea 11:9, the translation reads "I will not turn round and destroy Ephraim." KJV has "I will not return to destroy Ephraim." RSV and some other recent versions have "I will not again destroy Ephraim." The last seems to be the only grammatically legitimate translation.[17] There is a serious problem of interpretation here, and it seems fair to say that one should start with exactly what the Hebrew says, as nearly as that can be determined, and then go on from there to the interpretation.[18] Once again NEB seems more beholden to KJV than is RSV.

The New Testament portion of NEB has been available for some years, receiving wide acclaim from clergy, laity, and scholars alike. It now appears in a second edition (1970) with little change. No further comment need be made at this point. The effect of rather rapid reading of large portions of the Old Testament and Apocrypha is very pleasing. It is fairly obvious that the consultants on English style have done their work well and thus have contributed substantially to the production of an English Bible that will be easier to read than any heretofore offered to the public, with the possible exception of Moffatt's remarkable one-man production in his own inimitable, personal style, free from the restrictions of a committee.

This aspect of readability shows itself particularly in the Apocrypha. Most of the current translations of these books have been made as a sort of afterthought, without proper care to make them readable. But in NEB the translations of the Apocrypha are an integral part of the entire work, and they read extremely well. Particularly good is the rendering of Ecclesiasticus; one can now read this book in English with real pleasure. Commendable also is the title "Bel and the Snake," instead of "Bel and the Dragon," in the Additions to Daniel. Surely the creature was more like a snake than a dragon, though one might compromise by using the word "serpent."

Returning to the Old Testament and reading the Psalms and Job, one gets an impression similar to that created by Ecclesiasticus. The Psalms and Job are notoriously difficult to translate, and we may well have here the best attempt made so far. Particularly noteworthy are the revised rendering of Psalm 23:4 (mentioned above), 23:6 ("my whole life long"), and 121:1 ("If I lift up my eyes to the hills, where shall I find help?"). The same could be said of Job 13:15 ("If he would slay me, I should not hesitate; I should still argue my cause to his face"). The incredibly difficult passage, Job 19:25-29, is treated fairly and sensibly, even though drastic emendation is required to make any sense at all.

Apart from the unfortunate "daughter of Zion" blunder, and a few other slips, the books of prophecy are rendered in a refreshingly new fashion. An excellent example, among many, is Isaiah 1:18, where the note of uncertainty is so properly preserved by the word "may," to achieve consistency with the verses that follow (which RSV utterly fails to do with its unconditional "shall"):

> Though your sins are scarlet,
> they _may_ become white as snow;
> though they are dyed crimson,
> they _may_ yet be like wool.

Like the books of prophecy, the narrative books read smoothly and with a feeling of freshness. Nevertheless, in a few instances, there is evidence of haste, carelessness, or domination by tradition. One example is 2 Kings 15:38. This involves the ubiquitous conjunction _waw_, traditionally translated "and," but having many other meanings, and often serving in lieu of punctuation, which was mostly lacking in ancient writing. In the latter case the best translation is omission. NEB renders the verse as follows: "And Jotham rested with his forefathers and was buried with them in the city of David his forefather; and he was succeeded by his son Ahaz." This could have been improved thus, without any change in style: "Then Jotham rested with his forefathers and was buried with them in the city of David his forefather; he was succeeded by his son Ahaz."

All in all, NEB is a worthy and worthwhile project. It will enable many people to read the Scriptures with new understanding. To be sure, it is not perfect, but no translation can ever be so. New translations must appear from time to time to maintain the layman's understanding of his Bible, as language changes and new knowledge is made available by scholarly research. In this series of necessary efforts, NEB will stand high.[19]

NOTES

[1] "The Participle of the Immediate Future and Other Matters Pertaining to Correct Translation of the Old Testament," in _Translating and Understanding the Old Testament: Essays in Honor of Herbert Gordon May_, ed. Harry T. Frank and William L. Reed (Nashville: Abingdon Press, 1970), pp. 64–70.

[2] W. F. Stinespring, "The Active Infinitive with Passive Meaning in Biblical Aramaic," _JBL_, 81 (1962), pp. 391–394.

[3] J. Moffatt, _The Old Testament: A New Translation_ (New York: G. H. Doran Co., 1924–1925); J. M. P. Smith, ed., _The Old Testament: An American Translation_ (Chicago: University of Chicago Press, 1927).

[4] As M. Burrows points out in his review, _JBL_, 89 (1970), p. 221.

[5] W. F. Stinespring, "No Daughter of Zion: A Study of the Appositional Genitive in Hebrew Grammar," _Encounter_, vol. 26, no. 2 (1965, Biblical Studies in Honor of Toyozo W. Nakarai), pp. 133–141.

⁶ The same thing was done in Isa. 1:8 and Zeph. 3:14; compare "Zion's city" in Ps. 9:14.

⁷ Note, by contrast, the perceptive remark of J. Bright, in his Anchor Bible volume, *Jeremiah* (New York: Doubleday & Co., Inc., 1965), p. 32: "The term is a poetic, and endearing, personification of the people, and is a favorite one with Jeremiah. EVV 'the daughter of my people' is misleading: 'daughter' and 'people' are in apposition."

⁸ See note 1 above.

⁹ E. Kautzsch, *Gesenius' Hebrew Grammar*, 28th ed., rev. and trans. A. E. Cowley (Oxford: Clarendon Press, 1910), § 116 *p*, pp. 359–360; G. Bergsträsser, *Hebraische Grammatik*, II. Teil: Verbum (Leipzig: J. C. Hinrichs, 1929; reprinted Hildesheim, 1962), § 13 *h*, p. 72; P. Joüon, *Grammaire de l'Hebreu Biblique*, 2d ed. (Rome, 1947), § 121 *e*, p. 339; R. J. Williams, *Hebrew Syntax: An Outline* (Toronto: University of Toronto Press, 1967), p. 42.

¹⁰ Another good example is in Isa. 7:14. The young woman is already pregnant; thus it is better to say "and is about to bear a son" (AT) than simply "will bear" (NEB). The whole context is, of course, threatening.

¹¹ See note 1 above.

¹² This fourth meaning is suggested by J. R. Towers, *JNES*, 18 (1959), p. 151, on the basis of a similar meaning of "Sea of Reeds" or "Lake of Reeds" in Egyptian mythology. M. Copisarow, *VT*, 12 (1962), pp. 1–13, and N. H. Snaith, *VT*, 15 (1965), pp. 395–398, wish to read *yam-sôp*, literally "sea of the end," "distant sea," "remote sea" to contrast with the Mediterranean, which was the "nearby sea." It is noteworthy that the LXX read ἐσχάτη θάλασσα ("remote sea") in 1 Kings 9:26, where the meaning obviously is the Gulf of Aqaba.

¹³ See J. A. Fitzmyer, *The Genesis Apocryphon of Qumran Cave I*, Biblica et Orientalia, no. 18 (Rome, 1966), pp. 136–137, for a clear discussion. Another appositional genitive is involved here (col. 21, l. 18), and Fitzmyer does not miss it.

¹⁴ While Moffatt probably has the priority on "Reed Sea" in English, it should not be forgotten that Luther's German translation (about 1532) used *Schilfmeer*, of which "Reed Sea" is a fairly exact counterpart.

¹⁵ *A New Translation of the Holy Scriptures: First Section, The Torah* (Philadelphia: The Jewish Publication Society of America, 1962). Compare the statement of the translator in M. Noth, *Exodus* (Philadelphia: The Westminster Press, 1962), p. 11: "The traditional 'Red Sea' . . . is not an accurate translation of the Hebrew text and has a confusing effect on any discussion of the route of the Exodus."

¹⁶ *The Jerusalem Bible* (Garden City: Doubleday & Company, Inc., 1966), based on *La Sainte Bible traduite en français sous la direction de l'École Biblique de Jérusalem* (Paris: Les Éditions du Cerf, 1956), which uses throughout "*la mer des Roseaux*." E. Dhorme's French translation (Paris, 1956) uses "*la mer de Jonc*," with similar meaning.

¹⁷ E. Kautzsch, *op. cit.*, § 114 *n*, p. 350, n. 2; F. Buhl, *Wilhelm Gesenius' Hebraisches und Aramaisches Handwörterbuch über das Alte Testament*, 17th ed. (Leipzig: F. C. W. Vogel, 1921), art. שוב, 1.(0), p. 811, col. 1; L. Koehler and W. Baumgartner, *Lexicon in Veteris Testamenti Libros* (Leiden: E. J. Brill, 1953), p. 952, col. 2, ll. 11–12.

¹⁸ For an unpopular attempt to resolve the problem, see W. F. Stinespring, "Hosea, Prophet of Doom," *CQ*, 27 (1950), pp. 200–207.

¹⁹ On the very day when the first draft of this article was completed (August 25, 1970), a local newspaper ran this headline: "Catholics in U.S. to Get

New Bible." The brief story went on to say that a committee of U.S. Catholic scholars had been working for twenty-five years on a new Bible translation, that the product of their labors was soon to be published, that the language would be "up to date," and that the name would be "The New American Bible." The writer welcomes this latest addition to the family of modern translations and looks forward to the privilege of comparing NAB with NEB and other members of the family. NAB should be a worthy American companion to JB, which was effectively produced by French and British Catholics.

Sarepta
in History
and Tradition

by James B. Pritchard

That Sarepta was an important city on the Phoenician coast between Tyre and Sidon, with a history that spans more than three
millennia, is known from numerous ancient written sources as
well as from the archeological soundings made at the site, now
called Sarafand, in 1969 and 1970.[1] The city was prominent
enough in the thirteenth century b.c. to have been listed in an
Egyptian papyrus along with the more important of the Phoenician cities, Byblos, Beirut, Sidon, and Tyre. The Assyrian kings
Sennacherib and Esarhaddon boasted of their conquests of
Sarepta. It is known to have had its own tutelary, referred to as
"the holy god of Sarepta"; and its fame as a source for purple
dye and for wine is well attested in classical sources. Thus from
writings in Egyptian, Assyrian, Greek, and Latin and from the
artifacts discovered in two campaigns of archeological excavations, the history of the city of Sarepta may be said to be well
documented.

Yet what is known about the city's history from these sources
is considerably augmented by a single circumstance: Sarepta was
the setting for two miracles wrought by a Hebrew prophet. The
story of Elijah's visit with a widow of the Phoenician city was
cherished by folk audiences until it eventually became a part of
Hebrew writings and was later incorporated into a canon sacred
first to the Jew and then to the Christian. Certainly it had wide
currency in first-century Palestine since it was used effectively
as an analogy to drive home a point in Luke 4:25-26. This prom-
inence given to Sarepta in the Gospel further enhanced the fame
of the place, especially among Christians, which was already
associated with two of the more dramatic episodes of the Elijah
cycle of stories. Located, as the site was, on a much traveled
coastal road, it attracted pilgrims, crusaders, and ecclesiastics,

who visited it and subsequently recorded, sometimes inadvertently, important details about the city or its ruins through more than fifteen centuries. The tradition of Elijah's miracles has been an effective agent in the recording of important details about the history of this city on the coast of Phoenicia which was important in its own right.

One may well pose the question as to whether one of the principal Phoenician cities of the Iron Age might not have lost its identity completely had it not been for the tradition that attracted so many pilgrims to the ancient site. Would the former name of Sarepta have survived in the modern name of Sarafand without the aid of the dramatic story about Elijah's visit? Be this as it may, it is certain that the itineraries, diaries, and memoirs of the many visitors to the shrine to Elijah have provided the historian with observations that serve to chart the course of the city's life through what otherwise would have been its dark ages.

In the following sketch of the history of Sarepta we shall deal first with those sources that are independent of the Elijah tradition. In the second section we shall present those references to Sarepta that reflect the influence of the dominant tradition about Elijah's visit and shall seek to cull from them what can be learned about the history of the site.

I

The earliest known reference to Sarepta occurs in a letter written by an Egyptian scribe who sought to discredit his correspondent by satirizing his lack of firsthand knowledge about Asiatic geography.[2] The argument implied in the section of the letter from which the following paragraph is taken is that the correspondent does not even know the most elementary facts about the geography of the Phoenician coast:

> Let me tell thee of another strange city, named Byblos. What is it like? And its goddess? Once again—[thou] has not trodden it. Pray, instruct me about Beirut, about Sidon and Sarepta. Where is the stream of the Litani? What is Uzu [Tyre on the mainland] like? They say another town is in the sea, named Tyre-the-Port. Water is taken (to) it by the boats, and it is richer in fish than the sands.[3]

The listing in this late thirteenth-century B.C. papyrus of Sarepta along with Sidon and Tyre, which in the Iron Age sources far outstrip Sarepta in importance, suggests that in the earlier period the latter was more of a political equal to her neighbors.

Some five centuries later Sennacherib recounts his march down the Phoenician coast in the famous campaign of 701 B.C. Sarepta belonged to Luli, king of Sidon, who fled to Cyprus, leaving his cities with no choice but to capitulate and to accept the terms of an annual tribute to the Assyrian king. The listing of cities in which Sarepta appears is as follows:

> Great Sidon, Little Sidon, Bit-Zitti, Sarepta [URU Za-ri-ib-tu],
> Mahalliba, Ushu, Akzib (and) Akko, (all) his fortress cities, walled (and
> well) provided with feed and water for his garrisons. . . .[4]

Yet the submission of Sarepta, which Sennacherib claimed to have received, did not outlast the next generation. Esarhaddon, Sennacherib's son, mentioned the city and remarked that he turned it over to Ba'li, king of Tyre, from whom he required a yearly gift in addition to the earlier tribute.[5]

Except for a mention of the city in Pseudo-Scylax and an obscure mythological reference of the third century B.C. in Lycophron to the Cretans carrying off captive "in a bull-formed vessel the Sareptian heifer to the Dictaean palace to be the bride of Asteros, the lord of Crete," [6] there are no classical references to Sarepta until the first century A.D. Pliny mentions, in his *Natural History*, Sarepta, Birdtown, and Sidon, "where glass is made." [7] More important, however, are two fragments of a Greek inscription, found at Puteoli in 1901, which deals with "the holy god of Sarepta." C. C. Torrey, aided by a similar inscription on a bronze plaque from Syria, now in the Babylonian collection at Yale, succeeded in reading the text on the Puteoli pieces. It tells that in A.D. 79, ". . . there sailed from Tyre to Puteoli the holy god of Sarepta, conducted by a man of the Elim, in accordance with the [divine] command." [8] A third reference to "the holy god of Sarepta," would seem to appear in a Greek inscription (as yet unpublished) on a building stone found by a villager at Sarafand in 1969 and now in the National Museum in Beirut. Although the precise name of the deity is unknown, Sarepta was at least important enough in the first century A.D. to have had its own tutelary deity and to have been in this respect independent of its neighbors Tyre and Sidon.

Evidence for the existence of a fishing village at the site at the end of the third century is to be seen in some local color which

Achilles Tatius injects into his novel *Clitophon and Leucippe*. The author described Callisthenes' plans to abduct Calligone, with whom he was enamored, from Tyre:

> When he had arrived at Sarepta, a Tyrian village on the sea-board, he acquired a small boat and intrusted it to Zeno. . . . Zeno picked up with all speed some fishermen from that village who were really pirates as well, and with them sailed away for Tyre.[9]

Occasional references in classical sources name the products and commodities for which Sarepta was noted. Purple dye, the grape, the olive, and wheat are specifically mentioned in the fourth-century *Expositio totius mundi et gentium;* [10] the item of "four handkerchiefs from Sarepta" is found in a list of heterogeneous commodities found in a letter of Gallienus in *Divus Claudius*.[11] The Latin poets of the fifth and sixth centuries made mention of the wine of Sarepta, along with other well-known brands, although there was a difference of opinion as to its strength. Sidonius Apollinaris wrote a couplet that was often repeated:

> I have no wine of Gaza or Chios or Falernian field
> And what the Sareptan vine sent forth is yours to drink.[12]

Fulgentius, who wrote at the end of the fifth century, must have exaggerated the strength of Sareptan wine when he wrote: "So great is the strength of this wine that a man can hardly drink a pint in a whole month even if he were a toper." [13] For Alexander Trallianus, however, the contrary was true: "And there is a wine of weak strength and indeed quite watery such as the wines of Cnidus, Samos, and Sarepta." [14] The appearance rather than the strength was the concern of Fortunatus when he described the wines of Falerna, Gaza, Crete, Samos, Cyprus, Colophon, and Sarepta as "wines sparkling and vying with tiny precious stones." [15]

Arab geographers and historians of the twelfth and thirteenth centuries knew Sarafand, as Sarepta came to be called, and mention some topographical details of interest. Idrîsî places the city ten miles from Sidon and notes that it had a beautiful citadel, possibly the same building described as a fortress on the "very beach of the sea" by Joannes Phocas when he visited the site in 1177, some twenty-five years after Idrîsî wrote.[16] Yet apparently the fortification was not effective against Saladin, to whom Sarafand surrendered without resistance on July 29, 1187, the same day that Sidon was taken.[17] Yâkût merely mentions that the village belonged to Tyre,[18] but the author of *Livre des deux jardins* speaks of the beautiful town, with abundance of cisterns, surrounded by gardens, trees, and wild flowers.[19]

None of the sources cited above (with the exception of Phocas) — and all of them, except the thirteenth-century B.C. Egyptian papyrus, are later than the stories about the ninth-century prophet Elijah — mentions or alludes to the story which is dominant among the references to Sarepta. We shall now turn to the Elijah story and the influence of that tradition on the literature about the site.

II

The account of Elijah's visit to Sarepta (Zarephath), "which belongeth to Sidon," is known exclusively from the seventeen verses in 1 Kings 17:8-24.[20] The theme of the story is basically that of hospitality rewarded by two miracles, one which provided food in time of famine and the other, the resuscitation of the lifeless child of a widow,[21] but there are some significant overtones. The geographical location outside the borders of Israel is a detail which serves to heighten the wonder: the "man of God" had the power to work miracles beyond the land of Yahweh, in fact in the very domain of Baal. There is very little specific detail of a topographical nature, apart from the mention that the meeting of Elijah with the widow took place at "the gate of the city." It would be rash to take this as trustworthy evidence that the city was walled at the time, particularly since the gate of the city was the common meeting place in ancient Israel. Yet this specific detail about the meeting place was to determine, as we shall see, the location of the memorial to the event, at least from the twelfth century onward.

It is not surprising that this story, dealing as it does with two such popular themes as the need for food in time of drought and the resurrection of a widow's only son, should have been remembered and even enlarged upon. Josephus repeats the biblical story essentially in paraphrase,[22] but the Jerusalem Talmud adds the detail that the widow's son, so miraculously restored to life, became in fact the prophet Jonah.[23] A further indication of popularity of the Sarepta miracles is to be seen in the wall paintings of the third-century synagogue at Dura-Europos. Here both miracles are depicted in a manner remarkably faithful to the details of the biblical stories.[24]

It was, however, the Christian, and not the Jew, who commemorated the site made famous by the deeds of the Old Testament prophet. From the time that the Bordeaux Pilgrim's visit took place early in the fourth century, there is a long list of pilgrims who paid visits to Sarepta and recorded a variety of observations. The pilgrims were finally succeeded by the explorers, like Pococke and Robinson, who noted some details of the ruins which have now disappeared completely. Finally with Ernest Renan, who made observations there in 1861, the period of archeological investigation may be said to have begun.

The contents of the passages written by pilgrims, travelers, and explorers who visited Sarepta vary. However, except for two, all twenty-four of this list of visitors from the fourth to the nineteenth centuries mention the biblical story of Elijah's visit. Some take the pains to record the distances in miles, leagues, or versts, from Sarepta to Sidon and to Tyre and mention specific features, such as a church, a chapel, the city gate, or tombs that had been cut in the rocks.

The Bordeaux Pilgrim in A.D. 333 has the distinction of being the first to record his visit to Sarepta, where "Helias went up to the widow and begged food for himself." [25] Half a century later the Roman matron Paula, the disciple of Jerome, paid a visit which was described by her mentor:

> Leaving Berytus, a Roman colony, and the ancient city of Sidon; on the shore of Sarepta, she entered the tower (turricula) of Helias, in which she adored the Lord and Saviour; she then passed over the sands of Tyre, in which Paul impressed his knees.[26]

About 530 Theodosius gives some topographical data and mentions for the first time the church of St. Elijah. He recalls that in the Bible "it was called Sarepta of Sidonia, because at that time Sidon was a metropolis to Sarepta, but now Sarepta is the metropolis." [27] This is interesting evidence for the relative importance or size of the two cities, Sarepta and Sidon, in the sixth century.

The author of the *Antoninus Placentinus Itinerarium,* writing about 560–570, goes into more detail than did previous pilgrims in describing the shrine and its contents:

From Sidon we came to Sarepta, which is a small *(modica)* and very Christian city. In it is the chamber which was built for Helias, and the bed on which he lay, and a marble trough in which the widow (in Scripture) made her bread. In this place many offerings are made, and many miracles wrought.[28]

It is from about this time that we have mention of the Monophysite see at Sarepta in the *Notitia Antiochena (ca.* 570).[29]

Toward the end of the twelfth century, William of Tyre described the march of crusaders in the previous centuries from Sidon to Tyre and noted that the see of Sidon held Sarepta at that time. More important for the topographical information that it gives about the location of the city in the eleventh century is his description of the route from Sidon to Tyre: "The first part of the route on the succeeding day was through a country generally hilly. At last, however, they came into more level land. They passed on the right of the ancient city Sarepta of the Sidonians, the nurse of Elijah, the man of God." [30] Obviously the new site in the hills had not yet been established, since that would have been on the left.

By the twelfth century pilgrims, such as the Pseudo Beda, were aware of the earlier Jewish tradition about the name of the widow's son being Jonah.[31] Another visitor who wrote of his trip about 1130, Fetellus by name, enlarged upon this tradition and gave some additional, although erroneous, topographical detail: "In the mountains of Sydon and Sarepta is Gethagofer, the town from which came the above-named Jonah." [32] Two other pilgrims of the twelfth century, Theoderich *(ca.* 1172) [33] and John of Würzburg (1160–1170),[34] are explicit in equating the widow's son who was raised to life with the prophet Jonah.

Two visitors toward the end of the twelfth century have left some observations on the location of the church dedicated to Elijah. Jacques de Vitry, Bishop of Acre, who preached at Sarepta and complained that the Christians were a little lost among the Muslim majority,[35] wrote in his *History of Jerusalem* that the "Christians have built a small chapel at this place, near the gate of the city." [36] A similar, but not quite identical, testimony is that of Joannes Phocas, a pilgrim of *ca.* 1185, who also mentions the church dedicated to the prophet:

After Sidon stands the fortress of Saraphtha, built upon the very beach of the sea, and in the midst of the city a church dedicated to the prophet

Elias is built upon the site of the house of the widow who showed him hospitality.[37]

A century later there seems to have been a radical change in the appearance of the city. Burchard of Mt. Zion (*ca.* 1280) approached Sarepta from the south and recorded his observations thus:

> . . . before whose southern gate men show a chapel in the place where Elijah the prophet came to the woman of Sarepta, where he abode and raised her son from the dead. The chamber wherein he took his rest is shown there. Sarepta has scarce eight houses standing, albeit its ruins show that it was once a noble city.[38]

There is no hint that the ruined state into which the city had fallen by the end of the thirteenth century was ever remedied subsequently. Marino Sanuto (1321) makes mention in the notes to his map of the chapel before the southern gate and of the little chamber wherein the prophet lodged, but there is no intimation that the ruinous state of the city described by Burchard of Mt. Zion had been changed.[39] When John Poloner came to Sarepta just a century after Marino Sanuto, it was the ruins of the former great city that impressed him, along with, of course, the traditional holy places, "the place where Elijah went to the widow of Sarepta." He added that "not far from thence is the chapel where he raised her son from the dead." [40]

When Georges Sandys visited Sarepta in April, 1611, he reported that there was "a small solitary mosque, not far from the sea, erected, as they say, over the widow's house that entertained Elias. Close by it are the foundations of Sarepta commended for her wines." [41] After quoting the famous couplet of Sidonius Apollinaris, he notes the establishment of what is the present-day village of Sarafand high above the ruined Sarepta and mentions the presence of the rock tombs with a quaint interpretation as to their date. The passage reads:

> It was the seat of a bishop, and subject unto Tyre. Right against it, and high mounted on a mountain, there is the handsome new town, now called Sarapanta. Beyond, on the left hand of the way, are a number of caves cut out of the rock; the habitations, as I suppose, of men in the Golden Age, and before the foundation of cities.[42]

Almost a half century later, in 1659, Chevalier d'Arvieux described the newly established village on a hill with a fine view and with olive and fruit trees.[43] By this time the Elijah tradition had attached itself to the mosque of the new village and the Christians paid their devotion to St. Elijah at caves a short distance from the village. As for the mosque beside the sea, the Christians believed it to have been the place where "*Notre-Seigneur s'arrêta pour parler à la Cananée.*" At the time of d'Arvieux's visit, a dervish lived in the mosque and received alms for the fresh water he offered to the travelers.

Little had changed on the occasion of Richard Pococke's visit on May 29, 1738.[44] He noted the modern town in the hills, the mosque by the seaside, the sepulchres, and various ruins and foundations of ancient buildings. Just a century and a month later, Edward Robinson approached the site from the south, passed the Wely el-Khŭdr and judged it to have been built upon the site of the earlier chapel.[45] Five minutes beyond the Wely he noted ruins on the left and the modern vilfage on the hills to the right, as well as the rock-cut tombs at the foot of the hills.

Second only to the concern of the visitors for the tradition about Elijah was that for recording distances in Roman miles or leagues. The following list gives figures for distances from Sarepta to Tyre and to Sidon.

	Miles to Tyre	Miles to Sidon
Bordeaux Pilgrim [46]	16	9
Theodosius [47]	—	12
Antoninus Placentinus [48]	7	—
Pseudo Beda [49]	8	6
Fetellus [50]	8	6
Idrîsî [51]	—	10
John of Würzburg [52]	8	6
Theoderich [53]	8	6
Willebrand [54]	8	6
Burchard of Mt. Zion [55]	5 (leagues)	2 (leagues)
Marino Sanuto [56]	5 (leagues)	2 (leagues)
Maundeville [57]	8	5
Guide-Book to Palestine [58]	8	6
Poloner [59]	4 (leagues)	2 (leagues)
Reconstruction from Roman milestones and itineraries [60]	16	10
Modern road distances (in English miles) [61]	17	9

It is apparent from this tabulation that the distances given by the Bordeaux Pilgrim match almost exactly those that have been worked out by R. G. Goodchild on the basis of the Roman milestone system and the itineraries. The uniformity in measurements given by five of the twelfth- to thirteenth-century travelers, Pseudo Beda, Fetellus, John of Würzburg, Theoderich, and Willebrand, may indicate that one copied from another when writing his account. Nevertheless, if one assumes that the coastal road in medieval times followed the same course as did the Roman road, at least the ratio of 8 to 5 for the two distances measured has been maintained. One must conclude, however, from these figures that the concern for measuring accurately the distances traveled was not as great as the identification of sacred traditions that were attached to the places visited.

Some hints can be gleaned from the references about the size and the duration of the city. At the end of the fourth century Jerome writes of Sarepta as a small town *(oppidulum)* of Sidon.[62] By the early sixth century, however, it would seem that it was no longer dependent upon one of its neighbors, for according to Theodosius, Sarepta, once a dependent of Sidon, had by that time become the metropolis.[63] This hint of the increased size and importance may have some confirmation in a reading of a fragment of the sixth-century Medaba map that glossed Sarepta with "Longville" (ΣΑΡΕΦΘΑ [η] ΜΑΚΡΑ ΚΩ[ΜΗ]).[64] The same designation for the city appears in a passage of St. Sophronius of the seventh century, where a certain Philemon is said to have been a Macrocomite, that is one from Sarepta.[65] It was during the period of growth in the sixth century that Sarepta was first made a bishopric under the Patriarchate of Antioch.[66]

This extensive settlement of the sixth to seventh centuries dwindled away in the following half dozen centuries until, as Burchard of Mt. Zion noted in 1280, scarce eight houses were standing of the once noble city. The city was never to be rebuilt on the ancient site beside the sea. By the beginning of the seventeenth century, however, the new town built in the hills was adjudged handsome by Georges Sandys when he visited it in 1611.

The continuity of the tradition is unbroken from the fourth century down to the present, first having been kept alive by Christians and later, since at least 1611 when Georges Sandys visited the place, by the Muslims. The very earliest shrine we know about, that visited by Paula, sought to reproduce the house of the widow, by building a tower *(turricula)*, and is surely to be related to the "upper chamber," הָעֲלִיָּה of 1 Kings 17:

19 (Vulgate, *coenaculum*). By the sixth century it had been equipped with the bed on which Elijah lay and the marble trough in which the widow made bread. The location of the shrine was at the southern gate of the city, since the prophet came from the south. There is little reason to doubt that the present-day Wely-el-Khŭdr, beside the Sidon-Tyre road, marks at least approximately the location of the ancient shrine.

It will be interesting to see how far the results of excavations at Sarafand confirm the profile of the city's history as it has appeared through the eyes of those who were drawn to it because of the tradition of the miracles of Elijah. But whether or not these paths to the city's history will be found to coincide or even meet, it cannot be gainsaid that the ancient miracle stories have contributed materially to the history of an important Phoenician site. And the miraculous events, kept alive by chapel and church, provided for the people of the city a source of pride and a common bond of folk memory that served to make Sarepta something more than it otherwise would have been. Certainly Tyre and Sidon were more prominent as political entities, but for the faithful over a span of fifteen centuries Sarepta held an aura of wonder and miracle which the two greater neighbors did not possess. This distinction was the gift of the miracles that are as deeply rooted in the body of human experience as the need for food in a time of famine and the desire for life in a time of sickness and death.

NOTES

[1] Excavations made in June and July, 1969, by the University Museum of the University of Pennsylvania under the direction of the writer disclosed a Roman harbor built in about the first century A.D. and used with modifications for several centuries (see *AJA*, 74 [1970], p. 202). In April, May, and June, 1970, excavations were continued and disclosed evidence of occupation through the Hellenistic, Iron, and Late Bronze Ages. I wish to express my thanks to Pierre Proulx, S.J., a member of the staff of the 1970 expedition, for his valuable suggestions on the subject of this paper and for some additional references.

[2] Papyrus Anastasi I, published by A. H. Gardiner, *Egyptian Hieratic Texts*, Series I, Part I, . . . (Leipzig: J. C. Hinrichs, 1911), p. 22*-23*. The name of Sarepta appears as *D̲-r-p̲-t*, which W. F. Albright vocalizes as *D̲a-ar-pá-ta* (*The Vocalization of the Egyptian Syllabic Orthography* [New Haven: American Oriental Society, 1934], p. 42,) and W. Helck as *s̲a-r-pu-ʾu-ta₂(Die Beziehungen Ägyptens zu Vorderasien im 3. und 2. Jahrtausend v. Chr.* [Wiesbaden, 1962], p. 329).

[3] Translation of John A. Wilson in *ANET* [3], p. 477.

112/Understanding the Sacred Text

4 Translation of A. Leo Oppenheim in *ANET*[3], p. 287. See also D. D. Luckenbill, *The Annals of Sennacherib* (Chicago: The University of Chicago Press, 1924), col. ii, lines 41-45.

5 R. Borger, *Die Inschriften Asarhaddons, Königs von Assyrien, AfO*, 9 (1956), 49:16, where the name appears as URU*Ṣa-ri-ip-tu*. Note should be made of the mention of Zarephath in Obadiah 20, but the date is so disputed that it adds little to the history of the site.

6 C. Müller, *Geographi Graeci minores* (1855-1861), vol. 1, p. 78; *Callimachus, Hymns and Epigrams; Lycophron* . . ., trans. A. W. Mair, Loeb ed. (Cambridge: Harvard University Press, 1960), lines 1296-1300.

7 *Pliny's Natural History*, trans. H. Rackham, Loeb ed. (Cambridge: Harvard University Press, 1942), 5.76.

8 *Berytus*, vol. 9 (Beirut: The American University Press, 1948-1949), pp. 45-49.

9 *Achilles Tatius*, trans. S. Gaselee, Loeb ed. (Cambridge: Harvard University Press, 1917) 2.17.1-3.

10 J. Rougé, ed., *Expositio totius mundi et gentium* (Paris: Éditions du Cerf, 1966), pp. 164-165.

11 *Scriptores Historiae Augustae*, trans. D. Magie, Loeb ed. (Cambridge: Harvard University Press, 1932), vol. 3, p. 188.

12 Carmina, 17.16, *PL*, vol. 58, col. 723. I am indebted to Professor Robert E. A. Palmer for his aid in translating quotations from Latin poets.

13 Fabii Planciadis Fulgentii, *Mythologiarum*, Book 2.15, in *Auctores mythographi Latini* (1742), p. 693.

14 As quoted by Hadrian Reland, *Palestina ex monumentis veteribus illustra*, vol. 3 (1714), p. 985.

15 *Life of St. Martin*, PL, vol. 88, col. 381. The wine of Sarepta is also mentioned by Corippus of the sixth century, *Corpus scriptorum historiae Byzantinae*, ed. B. G. Niebuhr, vol. 17 (Bonn: 1836), pp. 189-190.

16 *Idrîsii Palaestina et Syria*, ed. J. Gildemeister (1885). p. 12. *The Pilgrimage of Joannes Phocas*, p. 10, in the publications of the Palestine Pilgrims' Text Society (hereafter abbreviated as PPTS), vol. 5.

17 R. Grousset, *Histoire des Croisades* (Paris: Librairie Plon, 1935), vol. 2. p. 806.

18 Guy Le Strange, *Palestine under the Moslems* (London: Palestine Exploration Fund, 1890; reprinted, Beirut, 1965), p. 531, from *Muꞌjam al-Buldân*, ed. Wüstenfeld (1866), iii. 382.

19 *Livre des deux jardins, ou histoire des deux règnes"* [*Nur ed-Din et de Salah ed-Din*], *Historiens occidentaux (ou orientaux) des croisaides* (l'Academie des Inscriptions et Belles-Lettres), vol. 4, p. 308.

20 For commentary on this passage see James A. Montgomery, ed. H. S. Gehman, *A Critical and Exegetical Commentary on the Book of Kings*, ICC (New York: Charles Scribner's Sons, 1951), pp. 294-298. The motifs and their relation to the Ugaritic literature have been studied by Leah Bronner, *The Stories of Elijah and Elisha as Polemics against Baal Worship* (Leiden: Brill, 1968), pp. 82-85, 119-122.

21 An attempt to classify the miracle stories of the Old Testament was made by the writer in "Motifs of Old Testament Miracles," *CQ*, 27 (1950), pp. 97-109.

22 *Jewish Antiquities*, trans. H. St. J. Thackeray and Ralph Marcus, Loeb ed. (Cambridge: Harvard University Press), vol. 5 (1934), pp. 744-749, Book 8. 320-327 (8.13.2-3).

[23] Louis Ginzberg, *The Legends of the Jews* (Philadelphia: The Jewish Publication Society of America), vol. 4 (1936), p. 197; vol. 6 (1945), p. 318, n. 9. For another text with this tradition see J. P. Brown, *The Lebanon and Phoenicia* (Beirut: The American University Press, 1969), p. 166. I am indebted to J. Pairman Brown for several of the references to Sarepta.

[24] C. H. Kraeling, *The Synagogue, The Excavations at Dura-Europos*, Final Report 8, pt. 1 (1956), pls. 31, 63, pp. 135-137, 143-150.

[25] *Itinerary from Bordeaux to Jerusalem*, in PPTS, vol. 1, pp. 15-16. See also PW, vol. 9 (1916), col. 2355, "Itinerarien," by Kubitschek.

[26] *The Pilgrimage of the Holy Paula*, in PPTS, vol. 1, p. 4. See also text *Corpus Scriptorum Ecclesiasticorum Latinorum* (hereafter abbreviated as *CSEL*), vol. 55, p. 313.

[27] *On the Topography of the Holy Land*, in PPTS, vol. 2, p. 16, par. 73; and *CSEL*, vol. 39, p. 147.

[28] PL, vol. 72, col. 900; and *CSEL*, vol. 39, p. 160. For a translation see *Of the Holy Places Visited by Antoninus Martyr*, in PPTS, vol. 2, p. 3.

[29] E. Honigmann, *Évêques et évêchés monophysites*, CSCO, vol. 127 (1951), p. 45.

[30] *A History of Deeds Done Beyond the Sea by William, Archbishop of Tyre*, trans. E. A. Babcock and A. C. Krey (New York: Columbia University Press, 1943), vol. 1, p. 331; vol. 2, p. 68.

[31] *Anonymous Pilgrim VI (Pseudo Beda)*, in PPTS, vol. 6, p. 49.

[32] *Fetellus*, in PPTS, vol. 5, pp. 50-51.

[33] *Theoderich's Description of the Holy Places*, in PPTS, vol. 5, p. 72.

[34] *Description of the Holy Land*, in PPTS, vol. 5, p. 63.

[35] R. Grousset, *op. cit.*, vol. 3, p. 199.

[36] *The History of Jerusalem by Jacques de Vitry*, in PPTS, vol. 11, p. 19.

[37] *The Pilgrimage of Joannes Phocas*, in PPTS, vol. 5, p. 10. See also *Rev Bib*, 29 (1920), pp. 157-159, and E. Rey, *Les colonies franques de Syrie aux XIIme et XIIIme siècles* (1883), p. 520.

[38] *A Description of the Holy Land*, in PPTS, vol. 12, p. 13.

[39] *Secrets for True Crusaders to Help Them to Recover the Holy Land*, in PPTS, vol. 12, p. 25. Marino Sanuto's map has the name of Caput fii Raphaelis at Sarafand. F. C. Rey has suggested that Raphaelis may have been a corruption for Ras Naby-Elias *(Arch. de l'Or. Lat.*, vol. 2 [1884], p. 339).

[40] *John Poloner's Description of the Holy Land*, in PPTS, vol. 6, pp. 30 and 32.

[41] Georges Sandys, *Sandys Travells, Containing an History of the Original and Present State of the Turkish Empire . . .*, 6th ed., (London, 1670), Book 3, p. 166.

[42] *Ibid.*

[43] *Mémoires du Chevalier d'Arvieux . . .*, par le R. P. Jean-Baptiste Labat, vol. 2 (1735), p. 4.

[44] Richard Pococke, *A Description of the East and Some other Countries* (London, 1745), vol. 2, pp. 84-85.

[45] *Biblical Researches in Palestine* (1874), vol. 2, p. 475.

[46] See note 25.

[47] See note 27.

[48] See note 28.

[49] See note 31.

[50] See note 32.

[51] See note 16.

[52] See note 34.

[53] See note 33.

[54] T. Tobler, Descriptiones Terrae Sanctae . . .(1874), p. 183 [IV.24].

[55] See note 38.

[56] See note 39.

[57] Thomas Wright, Early Travels in Palestine (Leipzig: J. C. Hinrichs, 1848; reprinted, New York: KTAV, 1968), p. 142.

[58] Guide-Book to Palestine, in PPTS, vol. 6, p. 39.

[59] See note 40.

[60] R. G. Goodchild, "The Coast Road of Phoenicia and its Roman Milestones," Berytus, 9 (1948-1949), pp. 91-127.

[61] The Middle East, Hachette World Guides, 1966, pp. 239-240.

[62] E. Klostermann, Eusebius Werke, III.1 (Leipzig: J. C. Hinrichs, 1904), p. 163.

[63] See note 27.

[64] R. T. O'Callaghan, in DBS, vol. 5, cols. 702-703.

[65] PG, vol. 87.3, 3636D.

[66] E. Honigmann, Traditio, 5 (1947), p. 153. After the Crusades Sarepta was the seat of bishops of the Latin rite. Le Quien names five bishops of Sarepta in the thirteenth and fourteenth centuries: Radulphus, Bartholomaeus, Jacobus, Wenceslaus, and Nicolaus (Le Quien, Oriens Christianus in quatuor patriarchatus digestus [1740], vol. 3, col. 1340).

The Synoptic Apocalypse: Matthean Version

by F. W. Beare

The so-called "synoptic apocalypse" with which this article is concerned consists primarily of the thirteenth chapter of the Gospel According to Mark, which is reproduced almost in its entirety in Matthew, with additions, some omissions, and with editorial alterations of varying degrees of significance (Matt. 24:1–44). It is found also in a radically altered form, somewhat reduced in compass, in Luke 21:5–34. This article will be devoted chiefly to the content and distinctive features of the Matthean version. As the generally accepted theory of the priority of Mark has again come under challenge in recent years, it may be stated at the outset that the writer still finds no substantial reason to abandon that position and continues to find evidence to support it in almost every pericope.

In its Matthean form the greater part of the Markan apocalypse is reproduced, to a large extent verbatim and in the same order, but with some important additions. More significant than all the internal differences, however, is the fact that it is incorporated by Matthew into a much more comprehensive discourse, including masses of non-Markan material, which is devoted to the general theme of judgment. This in itself involves a radical diminishing of the importance of the apocalyptic section in the total structure of the Gospel. The Markan apocalypse is the only sustained discourse of the earliest Gospel and it is given as the totality of the farewell address of Jesus to his disciples. It is put before us as an esoteric revelation communicated not even to all the disciples but to an inner circle of four, on the eve of the passion. For Mark, then, it is presented as the climax of Jesus' teaching ministry.[1] It culminates in the appeal: "Take heed, watch; for you do not know when the time will come. . . . Watch therefore — for you do not know when the master of the house will come . . . and what I say to you I say to all: Watch" (Mark 13:33, 35, 37). In the Matthean version it is still included in the farewell address of Jesus, but now only as part of a much larger totality, and then not as the culmination of all. The commands to take heed and to watch (βλέπετε, γρηγορεῖτε) are retained and given even greater emphasis in some ways, but they no longer carry the final message. The culmination now comes in the impressive picture of the Last Judgment (25:31–46).

The following outline of synoptic relationships will show at a glance the reduced importance of the Markan apocalypse in Matthew's treatment. The Markan parallels amount to only 34 out of a total of 136 verses in the discourse in Matthew.

THE FIFTH DISCOURSE OF MATTHEW, WITH PARALLELS

[In this outline, the elements of the Matthean structure are indicated as follows: Mk, for passages reproduced from Mark without change of substance; Mk^e, for passages drawn from Mark, but with editorial changes which affect the substance; Q, for non-Markan passages which have parallels in Luke; and M, for passages that are peculiar to Matthew. It is not assumed that Q and M are unitary documentary sources.]

Part 1. The Coming Retribution on Israel

Matthew 23:1–3	M		
4	Q		Luke 11:46
5	M		
6–7a	Mk^e	Mark 12:38b–39	20:46; cf. 11:43
7b–22	M	[Matt. 23:14, weakly attested, i.e., an assimilation to Mark 12:40]	[with Matt. 23:13 cf. Luke 11:52]
23	Q		11:42
24	M		
25–26	Q		11:39–41
27–28	M		[with Matt. 23:27 cf. Luke 11:44]
29–31	Q+M		11:47–48
32–33	M		
34–36	Q		11:49–51
37–39	Q		13:34–35

Part 2. The Apocalypse

Matthew 24:1–42		Mark 13	Luke 21:5–36 [17:22–37]
		Introduction	
(a) 24:1–2	Mk^e	13:1–2	21:5–6
(b) 3	Mk^e	3–4	7

The Discourse Proper

(The numerals I to VI indicate the main sections of the Markan apocalypse)

I.	4–8 Mk	5–8	8–11
II.	9–14 Mkᵉ+M	9–13	12–19
III.	15–22 Mk	14–20	20–24
IV.	23–25 Mk	21–23	
	26–28 Q		17:23–24, 37
V.	29–31 Mk+M	24–27	21:25–27
VI.	(a) 32–36 Mk		
	(b) 37–41 Q		17:26–27, 34–35
	(c) 42 Mkᵉ	35a	

Part 3. Parables of the Parousia and the Last Judgment

Matthew 24:43—25:46

24:43–51 Q		Luke 12:42–46
25:1–13 M	[with Matt. 25:13	
	cf. Mark 13:35a]	
14–30 Q		19:12–27
31–46 M		

The relative importance attaching to the apocalypse in the Matthean structure is further reduced by the fact that even the entire discourse in which it is incorporated is itself only one of the five major collections of sayings in which Matthew presents the teachings of Jesus, so that the evangelist does not seem to have placed more importance on this section than the others.

The Matthean discourse,[2] like the apocalypse which it includes, is related in all its parts to the Parousia of the Son of man, though this particular expression — never employed at all by the other evangelists — is not always used. The woes pronounced upon the scribes and Pharisees (chap. 23) are concluded by a general warning that the reckoning for all the innocent blood that has been shed on earth from the slaying of Abel onward (including that of the Christian martyrs of the coming years) is to be exacted of them, and that, within that very generation (vv. 34–36). No agent of this summary vengeance is indicated, but the evangelist undoubtedly has in mind the execution of judgment by the Son of man at his coming (cf. 24:29–30, 34). The lament over Jerusalem issues in an anticipation of one "who comes in the name of the Lord" (23:39). This at least hints at a return of Jesus, no longer to be rejected but to receive a triumphant welcome, even from this city that has murdered the prophets and stoned God's envoys and rebuffed Jesus in all his yearning love. The apocalypse itself, in its Matthean form, is specifically set forth under the headline of "the sign of your Parousia and of the end of the age" (τὸ σημεῖον τῆς σῆς παρουσίας καὶ

συντελείας τοῦ αἰῶνος – 24:3) — a distinctive Matthean recasting of the vague words of Mark, "What shall be the sign when all
these things are to come to pass?" (τί τὸ σημεῖον ὅταν μέλλῃ
ταῦτα συντελεῖσθαι πάντα; — Mark 13:4).[3] The same event is
spoken of as "the Parousia of the Son of man" (24:27), as "the
[unknown] hour in which your Lord comes" (v. 42), or "hour in
which the Son of man comes" (v. 44). Twice it is expressed under
the figure of a master coming to call his slaves to account for their
conduct during his absence (24:46, 50; 25:19); once under the
figure of a bridegroom arriving for his wedding breakfast (25:10);
and finally, the Son of man is pictured as enthroned in glory, to
judge by kingly authority all the nations of the earth (25:13 ff.).

There are few passages in the Gospels that the reader of our time
finds less congenial than this apocalypse. Not only is the imagery
strange, but even with the best will in the world it is hard to extract
any kind of enlightenment or inspiration for our own life or the life
of the church from it, without an arbitrary and even violent herme-
neutic transposition. More than that, many critical scholars would
now deny that any substantial part of the apocalypse is an utterance
of Jesus himself, and this skepticism is not based upon any desire to
relieve Jesus of the error of anticipating the end of the world within
the generation that witnessed the fall of Jerusalem. (On any approach, we cannot relieve Jesus of the burden — if such it is — of
this error.) But we are left with the task of discovering what all this
pattern of apocalyptic expectation and warning meant to the evangelists, and in particular what it meant to Matthew and to the
church in and for which he wrote. We must assume that he did not
incorporate it in his Gospel as an incomprehensible, much less as
an uncongenial, fragment of a tradition that was now without life.
It ought to be recognized as a fundamental principle of criticism
that "the redactors of the gospels retained nothing in their narrative
that was useless to their churches."[4] Even if we find all this material
quite useless to ourselves and our contemporaries, we have still to
ask what it meant to Christian readers of the late first century, with
the presupposition that to them it was full of significance.

Further, it is not a primary concern for us to distinguish what
elements, if any, may be regarded as authentic words of Jesus, or
to frame hypotheses about other contexts in which they might have
been spoken by him with a different point of interest. In any case,
the readers of the Gospel were not intended to hear from Matthew

a report of words which Jesus spoke some fifty, sixty, or seventy years earlier to a group of disciples on the Mount of Olives, but rather what the Lord of the church, now endued with "all authority in heaven and on earth" (Matt. 28:18), had to say to his followers in the troubled days through which they were actually passing or as they faced the prospect of worse tribulations in the immediate future.[5] Matthew, like his fellow evangelists, does not merely transmit an unaltered and unalterable tradition; he interprets and applies it and even supplements it to meet the needs and circumstances of his own time.

The Markan apocalypse, though it came to Matthew in the form of a sustained discourse, is obviously a composite structure shaped by Mark out of a number of fragments of tradition, which were not all attached at their coining to the same place and circumstances. Some sections of it may have come to Mark in composite form (as, for instance, vv. 14–20), and some of it may have been collected by him as isolated sayings without context. Whatever the earlier history of its component parts, it came to Matthew in the form of a unitary discourse and he would not dream of distinguishing secondary elements from primary. We are therefore justified in excusing ourselves from a detailed analysis of the Markan structure and shall merely set forth in summary fashion a view that will be fairly representative of recent studies.[6] We shall then be in a position to look more closely at the Matthean construction.

Mark has framed for his discourse a double introduction, both parts of which are artificial. The naïve exclamation of an unnamed disciple: "Look, Teacher, what wonderful stones and what wonderful buildings!" is nothing more than a setting constructed for the saying of Jesus: "Do you see all these great buildings? There will not be left here one stone upon another that will not be thrown down" (vv. 1–2). This "biographical apophthegm" (Bultmann) or "pronouncement-story" (V. Taylor) was probably formed independently of the apocalypse, with which it has in fact a very tenuous relationship. The discourse appears to speak of a profanation of the temple (at least, that is the surface meaning of the cryptic words of v. 14a), but does not so much as hint at its destruction. The second part (vv. 3–5b) is loosely linked to the first, in that the prediction gives rise to the question of the four disciples: "When will this be, and what will be the sign when all these things are to be accomplished?" Unlike the first part, this is obviously not self-contained and can only have been framed, probably by Mark himself, to introduce the reply of Jesus. In effect, the phrase "all these things" does not look back to the prophesied destruction of the temple but forward to the events and signs of the end time which the discourse will describe.

The discourse proper falls into six sections, most of which are themselves composite.[7] (I) In 5*b*–8, beginning with the warning, "take heed that no one leads you astray," we have predictions of the coming of messianic pretenders, and then, incongruously, of "wars and rumors of wars" (v. 7), of international conflicts, earthquakes, and famines (v. 8), and the declaration that this is only "a beginning of birthpangs."

II. In vv. 9–13 we have a number of sayings about persecution, with trials before various authorities, and beatings (v. 9); then after the aside of v. 10 ("the gospel must first be preached to all nations"), the theme of persecution is resumed with the promise that the Holy Spirit will speak in them and for them when they make their defense (v. 11). This is followed by predictions of bitter family divisions and betrayals (v. 12) and of a universal hatred of Christians as such ("for my name's sake" — v. 13*b*). The section ends with the appeal to hold firm despite all these terrible experiences, for salvation depends on enduring to the end (v. 13*c*).

III. The third section (vv. 14–20) may be the nucleus around which the entire discourse has been built. A situation will arise that demands precipitous flight. It is described in cryptic terms, borrowed from the Book of Daniel: "When you see the abomination of desolation ($\tau\grave{o}$ $\beta\delta\acute{\epsilon}\lambda\upsilon\gamma\mu\alpha$ $\tau\hat{\eta}\varsigma$ $\grave{\epsilon}\rho\eta\mu\acute{\omega}\sigma\epsilon\omega\varsigma$, Dan. 11:31; 12:11; cf. 9:27, LXX) standing where he ought not to be (let the reader understand), then let those who are in Judea flee to the mountains" (v. 14). There will not be a moment to spare, even to fetch a cloak (vv. 15 f.). It will be dreadful for women with child and for those with infants (v. 17), and they must pray that it will not take place in winter (v. 18). This will be the worst time of terror that the world has ever known or ever will know (v. 19; cf. Dan. 12:1*b*). If it were long continued, not a soul would survive, but for the sake of his elect the Lord will bring it to an early end (v. 20).

IV. The following section (vv. 21–23) can hardly have originated as a sequel to III. Days of hasty flight, under the threat of extermination, are not the time for would-be messiahs to gather a following. The theme of vv. 5*b*–6 is taken up again. If they are told that

Christ has somewhere appeared on earth again (related to 2 Thess. 2:2?), they must not believe it. Impostors will indeed appear and will even work miracles wonderful enough to deceive the very elect, if that were possible. The term "elect" is the catchword that has brought about the association of IV with III (and with V). The section ends with a renewal of the warning: "Take heed!" The forewarning given by Jesus should put them on their guard against deception.

V. In vv. 24–27 comes the climax of the apocalyptic drama. Reverting to the tribulation ($\theta\lambda\hat{\iota}\psi\iota\varsigma$) of vv. 19–20, Jesus now predicts that it will be followed by catastrophic occurrences in the heavens, with the overthrow of the astral deities (αi $\delta\upsilon\nu\acute{\alpha}\mu\epsilon\iota\varsigma$ αi $\acute{\epsilon}\nu$ $\tau o\hat{\iota}\varsigma$ $o\mathring{\upsilon}\rho\alpha\nu o\hat{\iota}\varsigma$ — v. 25); and then will come the Son of man in heavenly glory with his angelic train (v. 26) and he will send out his angels to gather together his elect from all over the universe (v. 28).

VI. The last section (vv. 28–37) forms the conclusion to the whole discourse. It is a medley of parables and fragments of parables and injunctions, with little internal unity, "somewhat artificially compiled by the aid of catchwords."[8] The parable of the fig tree continues in a way the answer to the question of verse 3. It does not in itself suggest that the time is near or the hour unknown, but only that it will be very near when the portents appear. The next verse, however, declares that it will not be delayed beyond the span of the current generation. The solemn declaration of verse 31 appears to be an independent logion (a companion-piece to Matt. 5:18?), which owes its place here to the linkword "pass away" ($\pi\alpha\rho\acute{\epsilon}\lambda\theta\eta$, $\pi\alpha\rho\epsilon\lambda\epsilon\acute{\upsilon}\sigma o\nu\tau\alpha\iota$, $\pi\alpha\rho\acute{\epsilon}\lambda\theta\omega\sigma\iota\nu$). It may reflect a desire of Mark to dispel some doubts about the fulfillment of the Parousia-hope. The avowal of ignorance of the day and hour, even on the part of "the Son" (v. 32 — the only absolute use of the title in Mark) has something of the same purpose. The promise is sure, even though the date of fulfillment is uncertain. The following verses base renewed injunctions to watchfulness on the very fact of the uncertainty of the time. And at the end the evangelist breaks away from the fiction of a private discourse, which only four disciples were privileged to hear, and makes it clear that Jesus speaks to all his followers: "What I say to you, I say to all, Watch!"

Matthew takes over Mark's twofold introduction, but makes some not insignificant alterations. The very first words are rephrased to emphasize the abandonment of the temple by Jesus, in keeping with the sentence pronounced in 23:38, "Your house is left to you" (ἰδοὺ ἀφίεται ὑμῖν ὁ οἶκος ὑμῶν). Mark's unemphatic circumstantial clause ἐκπορευομένου αὐτοῦ ἐκ τοῦ ἱεροῦ is replaced in Matthew by the principal clause ἐξελθὼν ὁ 'Ιησοῦς ἀπὸ τοῦ ἱεροῦ ἐπορεύετο. The departure from the temple is given a deliberate emphasizing, even the aorist of the participle adds to the impression of finality. Jesus is not merely going out of the temple, on this occasion as on others; he has left it forever and is going on his way to complete his mission. Again, Matthew takes the vividness (according to his wont) out of the Markan picture of an unnamed disciple expressing his astonishment at the size of the stones and the grandeur of the buildings, and he puts it much more flatly: "his disciples came to him to show him the buildings of the temple." The artificiality of the setting is not thereby diminished — after the stormy scene of the temple cleansing, the confrontation with the authorities, the challenges and counter-challenges, the questions and answers, they are proposing to him a sightseeing tour of the buildings. As if he had never seen them before! More significant is Matthew's abandonment of the fiction of a private communication to a select group of four. Now it is "the disciples" that question Jesus and hear his discourse in reply. We still have the unmediated transition to the Mount of Olives, and the retention of the element of privacy (κατ' ἰδίαν) for the communication, though this has lost its point once the circle of auditors is enlarged. As is usual in Matthew, οἱ μαθηταί are not merely the twelve or even some broader group of immediate followers, but the representatives of the Christian believers of the evangelist's time — "la figure stylisée des questionneurs chrétiens de l'église matthéenne."[9]

The question itself is given a precision which it lacks in Mark. The first part: "When shall these things be?" would seem to bear solely upon the prophecy of the destruction of the temple. The second part presupposes that this destruction will have eschatological significance and will be simultaneous with, or directly related to, the Parousia of Jesus and the end of the age. This is not rooted in anything that Jesus has said earlier in the Gospel, nor can it be regarded as a spot-reaction to the prophecy. It surely reflects a conviction that arose in the church only after Jerusalem was captured and the temple wrecked. It is here, rather than in the prediction itself, that we are led to perceive a *post eventum* outlook. Whatever

view we take of the time of Mark (whether before or shortly after
the fall of Jerusalem), there can be little doubt that by the time
Matthew wrote, the destruction of the temple belonged to the
past — perhaps as much as thirty years had gone by — and it is
most remarkable that it should still be possible for a Christian
writer to link it so closely with the Parousia of Jesus as Son of man
and with the end of the age. For a short period after the fall of the
city the reverse is true. Such an event might well provoke an outburst of apocalyptic fever and agitate men's minds with renewed
hopes and fears that the end of all things was close at hand (cf. the
effects of the fall of Rome to Alaric in 410 on the Western world).
But thirty years later, or even ten or fifteen years later, if we are
inclined to date Matthew around 80–85, the first tremors of expectation would surely have faded and it would be hard to imagine
that there would be no temporal gap between the destruction of
the temple and the appearance of the Son of man to bring the age
to its appointed end. Yet as Schmid points out, though "a distinction, which is not at all clear in Mark 13:4, is made with complete
clarity in verse 3, between the destruction of the temple and the
end of the world at the Parousia, yet no temporal division of the two
events is presupposed. The association between them is seemingly
even more explicitly expressed than in Mark."[10]

The first section of Mark's discourse is employed by Matthew
with no change in substance and scarcely any in wording. The additions of ὁ Χριστός (v. 5), of ὁρᾶτε (v. 6), and of πάντα (v. 8) are
hardly significant, and any other slight alterations are stylistic. It
has been argued that the change from ὅταν . . . ἀκούσητε to
μελλήσετε . . . ἀκούειν (v. 6; Mark 13:7) contributes to a shift
in the whole emphasis of the passage from the present circumstances
to the future,[11] but this is not convincing. The interest of both
evangelists is the same, and we may presume that the same dangers
were threatening in their very different circles — that Christians
may be led astray by impostors, claiming that in them Christ has
come to earth again; that they may be thrown into panic by a succession of disasters (wars, earthquakes, famines) and may take these
for the onset of the last judgment itself. "Don't be led astray by
impostors! Don't be frightened! Keep your heads!" The aim all
through is not to whip up a waning interest in the last things, or
to revive a fading hope, but to damp down an apocalyptic excite-
ment which the evangelists feel to be a continuing danger. There

is a good deal to be said for the view that in this discourse apocalyptic materials current in the tradition are employed to counteract
an over-absorption in apocalyptic fears and delusions.

When we come to the second section of the Markan schema, we
find major deviations in Matthew, not only in wording but in substance. Most of the Markan material has already been used by
Matthew in his mission charge (10:17–22), where it is reproduced
almost verbatim. There he has applied it to a mission formally restricted to Jews (10:5 f.). Now he makes it clear that he is thinking
of the Gentile mission and of the damaging effects of persecution
by hostile pagans. There is no mention of Sanhedrins or of synagogues, of floggings, of trials before rulers, or of the promised aid
of the Spirit. From the Markan section he retains only the opening
phrase παραδώσουσιν ὑμᾶς (εἰς), the prophecy of universal hatred
of Christians, and the warning that salvation is only for those who
stick it out to the end, along with the ineptly placed saying about
the preaching of the gospel to all nations, which he transfers, appropriately, to the end of the section. The whole Markan picture of
trials and punishments is summed up in the words: "they will deliver you up to tribulation (εἰς θλῖψιν, anticipating the θλῖψις
of vv. 15, 29 = Mark 13:19, 24), and will put you to death" (v. 9a),
and to this he attaches directly the prophecy of universal hatred
with a significant addition — Mark's "hated by all men" becomes
"hated by all nations." He has used the same clause without the
addition in 10:22, where he takes it to mean "hated by fellow-Jews."
He then introduces three verses (10–12) which describe the inward
deterioration of the Christian communities. Persecution and hatred
do not stimulate men to a higher and more refined spirituality.
"Many will then renounce their faith (σκανδαλισθήσονται) and
betray one another and hate one another" (v. 10, peculiar to
Matthew). Verse 11 is almost a doublet of verse 5 (cf. also v. 24)
and reflects the deep concern of Matthew over the success which
has attended the false prophets (cf. also Matt. 7:15 ff.). Verse 12,
again peculiar to Matthew, describes a general moral deterioration
of the Christian society — increasing lawlessness (ἀνομίαν) and a
widespread cooling of love (for Christ? or for fellow-Christians? or for
both? — cf. Rev. 2:4). Matthew gives expression to deep pessimism
over the conditions and prospects of Christianity as he observes it.
To hold firm to the end is hard enough in the face of external pres-
sures — the hatred of one's neighbors, persecution, and death; it is

all the more difficult when the faith and love of one's fellow-Christians is crumbling, and many of them are turning back to lawless ways. Yet the church is still called to her task of evangelizing the world, and this will be accomplished before the end of the age. "This gospel of the kingdom will be preached in all the world (ἐν ὅλῃ τῇ οἰκουμένῃ) for a witness to all the nations, and (only) then will the end come" (v. 14). The words are in large part borrowed from Mark, but they are given clarification and more specific pointing with respect to the Gentile mission by the Matthean additions. "The gospel" is defined as "this gospel of the kingdom"; Mark's πρῶτον is made more precise by the substitution of "then will the end come"; the future κηρυχθήσεται is substituted for Mark's δεῖ κηρυχθῆναι, and "to all the nations" is expanded to emphasize still more strongly the scope of the future mission by the addition of the phrase "in all the world." Matthew is anticipating the commission of the risen Christ (28:19). His words do not suggest, however, that he anticipates the *conversion* of the world (cf. 7:14). The gospel will be preached in all the world "for a witness" to all the nations — probably with the thought that in the great day of judgment their unbelief will not be excused by ignorance.

The third Markan section is taken over by Matthew with only minor changes (vv. 15–22). The source of Mark's reference to "the abomination of desolation" is given as "Daniel the prophet," and the vague ὅπου οὐ δεῖ is changed to the interpretative ἐν τόπῳ ἁγίῳ (v. 15). Minor changes of phrasing are made in the injunctions to flee (vv. 17–18), and the plea that the flight may not be in winter (v. 20) is supplemented by the puzzling μηδὲ σαββάτῳ, that it may not fall on a sabbath day. Are the Matthean churches still observing the Jewish regulation that limited a sabbath day's journey to about eight hundred yards? The changes in the prophecy of the "great tribulation" are stylistic.

What is meant by τὸ βδέλυγμα τῆς ἐρημώσεως and by a flight of Judeans to the mountains? The reader is bidden to understand (ὁ ἀναγινώσκων νοείτω, a clear indication that this part of the apocalypse at least has been transmitted in a written source; how can it be supposed that a reader of the Book of Daniel is meant?), but what is he to "understand"? Surely that more is meant than meets the eye and that "Judea" is not to be taken literally, as a geographical expression. The flight of the Judean rebels to the hills in the Maccabean days is of course in the writer's mind, though he does not think of the escaping followers of Jesus as forming guerilla bands for armed resistance. The story of the Seleucid persecution provides him with a picture of how the power of the state could go about enforcing apostasy from the worship of the one living and true God, and he retains the local setting in Judea, but only as part of his imagery. The dwellers in "Judea" of the oracle will then be Christians who live anywhere in the world (i.e., in the Roman empire) where they may be exposed to organized state pressure, backed by the threat of execution, to force them into apostasy.

Let us keep it clearly in mind that neither Mark nor Matthew is given to copying woodenly a source which no longer has meaning for him or has only an antiquarian interest. Even if Mark is making use of a "fly sheet" which had been published some years earlier, and for the benefit of Jews or Christians of Judea, he will understand it as referring to something which still lies in the future and which threatens Christians of every region. As "Judea" must have the wider reference and "the mountains" will not be the hill country to which Mattathias rallied his guerilla bands, so "the abomination of desolation" will not be a statue of Zeus or Jupiter — or of the emperor — to be set up in the temple. Christian readers of the second generation would not be deeply concerned with a pagan profanation of a temple which had been more deeply profaned by the impiety of its own worshipers and had now (in the time of Matthew if not already of Mark) been reduced to ruins. It might be added that such an interpretation would make nonsense of the whole passage. If things had reached the point at which Jerusalem and its temple were already in the hands of the legions, it would be far too late for people to flee to the hills, with or without their cloaks.

The passage, whether in Mark or in Matthew, appears to rest upon a Christian anticipation that the Roman authorities were planning to enforce the worship of the emperor on all the inhabitants of the empire. Such an anticipation is clearly enough reflected in the Apocalypse of John (especially chap. 13). So far as we know, such drastic measures were not introduced until the time of Decius (A.D. 250), and we have no evidence that they were contemplated in the first century. But for such fears to be entertained it is not necessary that they should be justified by anything on the contemporary political horizon. The Book of Daniel provided all the justification that was needed.

For it must be kept in mind that the Christian reader of the first century was not equipped with the modern critical understanding of the Book of Daniel. He never imagined that "the abomination of desolation" and its accompanying disasters were descriptions of what had happened more than two centuries earlier in the time of Antiochus Epiphanes (167–163 B.C.). At the end of the book he could read: "But you, Daniel, shut up the words, and seal the book, until the time of the end" (LXX, actually ἕως καιροῦ συντελείας — Dan. 12:4). He would naturally conclude that the setting up of the abomination belonged to the future — to "the time of the end." In his own circumstances, he would understand it as the setting up of altars and images here, there, and everywhere for the cult of the emperor. But when he sees such preparations being made, he is not to wait until he is actually haled to the place of sacrifice and bidden to offer his portion of incense on the altar. He must flee to whatever place of refuge he can find with the utmost haste, not even delaying to get his little treasures from his house (τὰ ἐκ τῆς οἰκίας αὐτοῦ) or even to fetch a cloak. Life under such conditions would involve indescribable hardships; if the ordeal were prolonged, none would survive.[12]

Section IV of the Markan apocalypse is taken over by Matthew almost verbatim (vv. 23–25) and is supplemented by a passage which deals with false reports of a reappearance of Christ in secrecy. Here the emphasis is not on the warning against impostors who may be clever enough to deceive the very elect, but on the thought that the coming when it does take place will be no more secret than the lightning-flash that fills the whole sky, or the carcass that quickly draws hordes of vultures (vv. 26–28). These verses have close parallels in Luke, again in an apocalyptic context, but in a different part of his Gospel (Luke 17:23–24, 37).

In section V (vv. 29–31), Matthew again follows Mark very closely, but makes two significant additions. For the first and only time, we are told of the "sign" of the Parousia which the disciples had asked for at the beginning, but the nature of this sign is not divulged. Its appearance will cause consternation. "Then will appear the sign of the Son of man in heaven, and then all the tribes of the earth will mourn" (v. 30). This brings a new element into the picture. In Mark the coming of the Son of man finds effect only in the gathering of the elect; here in Matthew, the strong suggestion is made that to the inhabitants of earth in general the day of his

coming is a day of wrath. This double aspect of "that day" belongs
to the pattern of Christian expectation. See, for instance, the opening
and closing of the Apocalypse of John: "Behold, he is coming with
the clouds, and every eye will see him . . . and all tribes of the earth
will wail on account of him" (1:7), and "Behold, I am coming soon,
bringing my recompense, to repay everyone for what he has done. . . .
Surely I am coming soon. Amen. Come, Lord Jesus" (22:12, 20).
The same double aspect is seen in the words of Paul in 1 Thessalonians 5:1–4. The second addition of substance is the phrase μετὰ
σάλπιγγος μεγάλης (v. 31). The sounding of a trumpet is a standard feature of apocalyptic imagery; in Paul also it is specifically
attached to the descent of the Lord from heaven and the gathering
of the elect into his presence (1 Thess. 4:16 f.), or to the instantaneous
transformation of our mortal bodies at the resurrection (1 Cor.
15:51 f.). Its introduction by Matthew at this point is merely an
incidental borrowing from the general stock.[13] The change of
phrasing in 31c brings the mixed Markan phrase more or less into
conformity with such Old Testament passages as Deuteronomy
30:4 — ἐὰν ᾖ ἡ διασπορά σου ἀπ᾽ ἄκρου τοῦ οὐρανοῦ ἕως ἄκρου
τοῦ οὐρανοῦ, ἐκεῖθεν συνάξει σε κύριος ὁ θεός σου. The phrase
ἀπ᾽ ἄκρου τῆς γῆς ἕως ἄκρου τῆς γῆς is also found in LXX but
there seems to be no instance of the Markan combination of γῆ
and οὐρανός.

In section VI Matthew follows Mark for the first five verses
(32–36) with scarcely the change of a syllable, but from that point
on he strikes out on his own, reflecting his use of Mark only by the
retention of part of a single verse (v. 42 = Mark 13:35a), and even
that he is compelled to alter by reason of the radical change he has
made in the context. In Mark, the clause makes a hortatory conclusion to a fragmentary parable — probably, indeed, a conflation
of fragments of two or even of three parables — concerning a master
who entrusts certain responsibilities to his servants during a temporary absence. Nothing is said of the duties appointed for the
others, but everything is concentrated on the charge to the door-
keeper that he is to keep awake. This is then generalized into a
charge to all: "Keep awake, then; for you do not know when the
master of the house is coming."[14] Matthew has replaced these
somewhat incoherent parable fragments by two groups of sayings
which make no reference to a house or its master, and he must
therefore change Mark's "master of the house" to "your Master."

The injunction is not particularly appropriate to the illustrations which Matthew has chosen to bring together here (the people of Noah's time, heedless of the approaching disaster; the sudden division among pairs, at their usual tasks in the field or at the mill); but at all events it becomes the theme for the series of parables which is to follow.

There is a certain absurdity in treating the remainder of the discourse, consisting of four parables and the dramatic depiction of the last judgment, as an "epilogue" or "supplement" to the apocalypse (so in Aland's *Synopsis Quattuor Evangeliorum*, and in many of the major commentaries), seeing that the so-called supplement is much longer than the discourse. Not only that, but it can hardly be questioned that in the mind of Matthew the ultimate interest is focused not on the apocalyptic portents, but on the issues of the day when all the nations are gathered before the throne of the Son of man. It is only because we attribute too much importance to the priority of Mark that we can even think of the long non-Markan conclusion to the discourse in Matthew as a mere "supplement" to the apocalyptic section which he has taken over from Mark. For as we have indicated above, in Matthew the apocalypse is a *section*, and not at all the weightiest section, of a much broader collection of sayings bearing on the last things.

A remarkable feature of the apocalypse is that in it nothing is said of any activity of Jesus in the intermediary period that must elapse before his coming in glory as the Son of man.[15] There is no suggestion that he will be with his followers in their tribulations or (in the Matthean version) that his Spirit will be with them even at the most critical moment. They are sustained only by the hope that at his coming they will be among the number of those whom the angels will gather from the four quarters of the earth. The same holds true of the series of parables which Matthew puts before us here. The emphasis is on the *absence* of the master.[16] He is away from home while his overseer attends faithfully to his duties of supervision, or abuses his temporary authority (24:45–51). The bridegroom is off the scene while the ten maidens await his arrival, all of them falling asleep (25:1–13). He has gone on a journey while his servants employ at their discretion the money which he has entrusted to them (25:14–30). Even in the judgment scene, he is absent in person until he arrives for judgment, even though he recognizes kindnesses done to the least of his brethren as done to himself

(25:31–46). There is no hint of the assurance which will be given in the final commission: "Lo, I am with you always, to the end of the age" (28:20). Certainly there is the conviction that all that is to come is decreed by God and under his control, and that the end will be glorious; but until the day of triumph dawns, the followers of Jesus must simply endure and attend faithfully to their duties. Whatever we may read elsewhere in the New Testament, there is in all this discourse simply no thought of an experience of communion with Jesus in this life, or of a promise that he will be present to help and comfort them. The focus is wholly upon his appearance in judgment at the end of the age, and upon the accounting which they will then have to render to him with its consequences for eternal punishment or eternal life. And one can hardly fail to feel that for Matthew the emphasis is on the awful consequences of failure rather than on the blessedness of immortality reserved for those who are found faithful.

NOTES

[1] This climactic effect is even more pronounced if we accept the thesis of E. Trocmé that the Gospel of Mark originally ended with chapter 13 and that the passion narrative is a supplement (*La formation de l'évangile selon Marc* [Paris: Presses Universitaires de France, 1963]). E. Schweizer, in rejecting this thesis, also rejects the thought that Mark 13 is climactic, on the ground that in the rest of the Gospel, references to the Parousia and the signs which are to precede it are extremely sparse (*The Good News According to Mark*, tr. Donald H. Madvig [Richmond: John Knox Press, 1970], p. 262).

[2] I take it that Matthew himself sees this last of his major discourses as including chap. 23 along with chaps. 24 and 25, in spite of the transitional narrative-cum-dialogue passage (24:1–3) which introduces the apocalypse. It may be noted that Josef Schmid, even though he distinguishes six major discourses by treating chap. 23 alone as the fifth, nonetheless concedes that the omission of the story of the widow's mite (Mark 12:41–44) and the absence (following chap. 23) of the stereotyped rubric which follows each of the other discourses, are indications that the evangelist "wants chapters 23–25 to be understood as a great unity" (*Das Evangelium nach Matthäus*, Regensburger Neues Testament, vol. 1, 5th ed. [Regensburg: Pustet, 1956], pp. 333, cf. 24). We might add that his insertion of the lament over Jerusalem at this point where it is not at all coherent with its context ("En effet, ces trois versets ne sont pas exactement dans le ton de ce qui précède et les suit immédiatement," P. Bonnard, *Évangile selon saint Matthieu*, CNT [Neuchatel: Delachaux et Niestlé, 1963], p. 343), seems intended to link the sevenfold denunciation of the scribes and Pharisees with the prophecy of the destruction of the temple.

[3] How can anyone imagine this to be a secondary reworking of the clear Matthean phrase?

[4] Bonnard, *op. cit.*, p. 147.

[5] Attempts are indeed made to "vindicate the eschatological discourse" (G. R. Beasley-Murray, *Jesus and the Future* [New York: St. Martin's Press,

1954], chap. 4). All such attempts are bound to assume that Jesus predicted not only his own death and resurrection but his coming in power and glory as "the Son of man." I must confess that I find it impossible to imagine that he entertained any such view, unless one is prepared to base it on the hypothesis that he was insane. How could any person in his senses be persuaded that he would at some future time descend to earth from heaven, with or without cloud-chariots and hosts of angels?

[6] Cf. my remarks in "Sayings of the Risen Jesus in the Gospel Tradition: An Inquiry into their Origin and Significance," in *Christian History and Interpretation: Studies Presented to John Knox*, ed. W. R. Farmer *et al.* (New York: Cambridge University Press, 1967), pp. 178 ff.

[7] The sixfold division of the Markan apocalypse adopted here is that of Vincent Taylor, *The Gospel According to St. Mark* (London: Macmillan, 1959), p. 500. In another analysis, he associates certain parts with one another to reduce this to four groups (Additional Note E, sec. 3, pp. 638 ff.).

[8] V. Taylor, *op. cit.*, p. 519.

[9] P. Bonnard, *op. cit.*, p. 345.

[10] J. Schmid, *op. cit.*, p. 335.

[11] G. Strecker, *Der Weg der Gerechtigkeit: Untersuchungen zur Theologie des Matthäus*, FRLANT, 82 (Göttingen: Vandenhoeck and Ruprecht, 1962), p. 44; cf. p. 239.

[12] This whole interpretation is deeply indebted to E. Haenchen, *Der Weg Jesu* (Berlin: A. Töpelmann, 1966), pp. 443–450. A similar approach is favored by P. Bonnard, *op. cit.*, p. 351. Note especially his remark that "les v. 19 à 22 montrent bien qu'ils s'agit d'une catastrophe cosmique dépeinte poétiquement dans les termes de la vie palestinienne."

[13] Cf. B. Rigaux, "La seconde venue de Jésus," in *La venue du Messie: Messianisme et eschatologie*, by É. Massaux *et al.*, Recherches bibliques, 6 (Bruges: Desclée de Brouwer, 1962), p. 215: "L'imagerie apocalyptique . . . postule la même interprétation que les textes semblable de Paul et de l'Apocalypse. Ce sont des moyens littéraires dont la teneur réelle nous échappe. Ce n'est pas trop de dire qu'ici une démythisation . . . est nécessaire."

[14] J. Jeremias, *The Parables of Jesus*, trans. S. H. Hooke, rev. ed. based on the 6th German ed. (New York: Charles Scribner's Sons, 1963), pp. 53–58.

[15] Cf. E. Schweizer, *op. cit.*, p. 267: "it is necessary to observe that in this passage Jesus has no vital role in the period between Easter and the end of the world (in contrast to those passages where the exalted Lord is the center of faith), except that his preaching is remembered and his coming is anticipated." See also the remarkable note of E. Haenchen, *op. cit.*, p. 434, note 1.

[16] See the comments of H. J. Cadbury on "the motif of an absentee master" in the parables, in *Jesus: What Manner of Man?* (New York: The Macmillan Company, 1947), pp. 42 ff. He suggests that behind this "recurrent feature" lies an aspect of the authentic teaching of Jesus involving "the notion of an absentee God," and goes on to say: "Like the apocalyptic term *parousia*, they remind us that normally we are on our own and alone. For long intervals we have no contact with the one to whom we are responsible. He is in a distant country and there is no certainty that he will return soon. Our business is to live as we should, but without him. Normal rectitude, fidelity, diligence, are expected of us and not emergency behavior. . . . This absence goes far beyond the intermittent dullness of contact to which even the mystics confess. It is frankly non-mystical, and holds out no promise of a realized experience of God in this life" (p. 45).

The Transfiguration in Mark: Epiphany or Apocalyptic Vision?
by Howard Clark Kee

A dominant view of the transfiguration in modern scholarship is that formulated a half century ago by Dibelius,[1] who treats this pericope in his chapter on mythology. He sketches the Christ-myth utilized by Paul, in which the divine Son voluntarily gave up his heavenly place and in obedience to the divine will accepted first humiliation as a human being and then the fate of death. In consideration of his total obedience, God exalted him as *kyrios* and gave him a new heavenly status. Dibelius sees this myth more clearly expressed in the transfiguration story than in any other unit of the gospel tradition. In it, according to Dibelius, Jesus is revealed as Son of God and an epiphany takes place in which the disciples see Jesus' future glory.

Siegfried Schulz, in his compendium of *Redaktionsgeschichte*, *Die Stunde der Botschaft*, reaffirms Dibelius's position, and adds that this pericope, which is of hellenistic-Jewish origin, is a "scarcely to be surpassed witness for the hellenistically understood divine sonship which is understood in terms of (divine) essence."[2]

On this basis, the story of the transfiguration has been thought of as a kind of archetypal epiphany story, along with the Walking on the Water (Mark 6:45–52) and the two Feedings (Mark 6:30–44; 8:1–10).[3] It is assumed that, no matter what the source of the tradition underlying Mark's account (9:2–8), the evangelist's aim in telling the story is to show that in this moment the true divine nature of Jesus was disclosed:[4] the "incognito of the God-man."[5]

Apart from the lack of exegetical evidence for Mark having spliced together in the transfiguration account two wholly disparate elements — display of eschatological glory and metaphysical transformation[6] — which we shall consider below, it is doubtful that the term "epiphany" has a sufficiently precise meaning to illuminate meaningfully the history-of-religions background of this Markan pericope. Ἐπιφανεία in hellenistic writers refers to the appearance of gods or lesser divinities to men, whether waking or in dreams.[7] They appear in order to aid their favorites or to punish their enemies,[8] or in association with a cult in connection with which they are evoked by hymns.[9] Originally used of earthly appearances of divine beings in human forms, the term came to be applied to men who exhibited divine characteristics or for whom divine powers were claimed, e.g., the Ptolemies,[10] the Seleucids,[11] and Antony,[12] who sought to identify himself with Hercules and especially with Dionysus. In biblical usage, ἐπιφανεία is limited to theophanies, as in Genesis 35:7 and Deuteronomy 33:2–7, or to manifestations of divine power coming to someone's aid.[13] Similarly, Philo uses the term with the connotation of fame or splendor of God, revealed to men. In the New Testament, the word is a late, largely Deutero-Pauline (1 Tim. 6:14; 2 Tim. 4:1, 8; Titus 2:13) term for the "appearing" of the exalted Christ, rather vaguely awaited in the future rather than expected imminently, as in the Pauline and Synoptic traditions. Significantly the use of ἐπιφανεία is a correlate of the tendency of the later New Testament tradition to speak of Jesus as God (Titus 2:13, προσδεχόμενοι τὴν μακαρίαν ἐλπίδα καὶ ἐπιφά-νειαν τῆς δόξης τοῦ μεγάλου θεοῦ καὶ σωτῆρος ἡμῶν, Ἰησοῦ Χρι-στοῦ) in a way that the Synoptics and Paul never do. Linked as it is with the hellenistic concept of divinization in later New Testament writings, it is perhaps significant that the term is not used in the Synoptic form of the so-called epiphany stories. But more important than the use of the *term* is the question whether the *concept of diviniza-tion* implicit in the later use of ἐπιφανεία is present in the Synoptic accounts of the transfiguration.[14] Or to turn the question around, is there a concept documented in the literature of the first century A.D. which provides a more appropriate and illuminating background against which to understand the transfiguration story than the notion of epiphany?

I

In seeking an answer to this last question, we must examine in some detail both the larger setting in which Mark has placed the transfiguration story and the specifics of the narrative itself.

Bultmann classifies the pericope as a legend and suggests that it may have been a resurrection appearance story placed back into the lifetime of Jesus, as "a heavenly ratification of Peter's confession."[15] He thinks that the names of Moses and Elijah were added in keeping with the law of folklore which supplies names for originally anonymous persons, and that the mention of the uncertainty and fear of the disciples is evidence of the author's ineptitude in dating the post-resurrection story back into the ministry of Jesus. Although Bultmann, in discussing the transfiguration narrative, refers to the theophany granted to Moses on Mount Sinai, he does not think Exodus 24 influenced Mark appreciably, if at all, and he does not explain in what sense he sees a theophany in the transfiguration account. In the text of Mark, the climax of the narrative is not in the metamorphosis of Jesus and the radiance of his clothing, but in the heavenly voice. There, however, we read only of the divine voice and not of a vision of God experienced by Jesus or the disciples. It is not at all clear, therefore, in what sense this story can be spoken of as a theophany.

If we were to consider the theophanic or epiphanic disclosure of Jesus to the disciples as the main point of the story, we should expect some manifestation of his powers as a divine being. Instead, apart from the radiance of his garments and his being named as "Son," all that we read in Mark is the instruction, "Hear him" (9:7). Unless we have decided in advance that Son of God means for Mark that Jesus is a divine being in human disguise or that the term connotes divine nature, there is no detail in the narrative which would compel that conclusion. It is significant that Peter, after witnessing the radiant garb and the conversation with Elijah and Moses, addresses Jesus, not as *kyrios*, but as rabbi (9:5). According to Mark, Jesus remains for Peter the teacher; he is not transformed or revealed as a divine being.

Mark is centrally concerned, therefore, to define in dialogical fashion — raising questions which he wants his readers to answer for themselves (see Mark 1:27; 4:41; 8:27; 12:10) — what it means to say that Jesus is the Christ.

Peter's affirmation that Jesus is Messiah (8:29), followed as it is by his rejection of the notion of Jesus' suffering and the sharp rebuke that he accordingly receives from Jesus (8:32–33), is intended to show that there is a wide gap between asserting that Jesus is Messiah and the awareness of what his messiahship involves. It is not adequate or accurate to say with Rudolf Otto[16] and a large number of Anglo-Saxon commentators that in Mark we see the combining of the Son of man and the Suffering Servant traditions. The motifs combined by Mark are Son of man and Son of God. The major issue at stake, as Mark sees it throughout his Gospel, is the authority of Jesus as the instrument by which God will establish his Rule.

Mark makes clear that for him the terms *Christos* (the Davidic King) and Son of God are synonyms. This is in part apparent from the title of the book where the terms "Christ" and "Son of God" stand in synonymous parallelism: Ἰησοῦ Χριστοῦ υἱοῦ θεοῦ,[17] but it is clearly implied in the question about Christ being both David's son and his lord (12:35–37), and it is explicitly stated in the question addressed to Jesus by the high priest in 14:61, "Are you the Christ, the Son of the Blessed?" The use of Son of David as a designation for Jesus' kingly role is likewise implicit in the acclaim of the Palm Sunday crowd, "Blessed is the kingdom of our father David that is coming" (11:10). Mark establishes links between Jesus' miracles and the titles "Son of David" and "Christ" at 10:47–48, where Bartimaeus beseeches Jesus to heal him of his blindness, addressing him as Son of David; similarly, at 1:34, if we follow the well-attested reading αὐτὸν Χριστὸν εἶναι. Another set of synonyms is represented by the implicit link between Jesus as Christ and as Son of man in Mark's version of the synoptic apocalypse, where the subject shifts from Christ (13:20) to Son of man (13:26). The identity of these terms becomes explicit in Jesus' response to the high priest's question whether or not he is the Christ: he replies in 14:62, "I am, and you will see the Son of man seated at the right hand of the power [i.e., God] and coming with the clouds of heaven." The tie among these clustered terms is thus evident: Christ, the kingly descendant of David, is awaited as the Son of man.

The question which Mark wants to illumine by his Gospel as a whole moves beyond the merely christological to the related question about the nature of the kingdom whose coming Jesus announces (Mark 1:15). The issue may be stated thus: By what process does Jesus, in whose ministry of healings and exorcisms the powers of the kingdom are proleptically present and the binding of the strong man is already under way, achieve the full realization of his kingly power? The disciples expect a quick and easy achievement of kingship, with the result that they object to Jesus' predictions of suffering and begin to jockey for positions of privilege in the kingdom situation (10:35–37). The threefold passion predictions (8:31; 9:31; 10:33 ff.) are obvious to any reader of Mark, but less frequently noticed is the fact that each of these is followed by (1) a call to share in the suffering of discipleship and then by (2) a power-play on the part of the disciples. The depth of their incomprehension continues without modification throughout the rest of Mark, right up to the events of the Gethsemane, the hearing before the Sanhedrin, and the crucifixion. The disciples cannot grasp that suffering must precede triumph. The clearest statement of the necessity for suffering follows the request of the sons of Zedebee in Mark 10; there Jesus is reported as declaring that the manner of gaining kingly power among the Gentiles, lording it over others and exercising authority over them through sheer power, is wholly inappropriate to the coming of God's kingdom. It requires suffering and the giving of one's life (10:45). Why suffering is necessary is never explained, but *that* it is necessary to the working-out of God's plan is assumed, as it is generally in apocalyptic literature. In the opening chapters of Daniel, his sufferings and those of his companions are *necessary* to prove their moral merit and to demonstrate their fidelity to Israel's God in the face of opposition from the pagan ruler (cf. Dan. 2:28 and Mark 13:7). The point of Daniel is that faithful endurance of suffering leads inevitably to divine vindication.

The coming of Elijah, which in Mark may refer to John the Baptist or to Jesus himself (9:11–13), is described as (1) necessary (δεῖ) and (2) as the first in a series of divinely determined events (πρῶτον), the program for which has already been laid down in Scripture (καθὼς γέγραπται). If we consider ἐποίησαν as simple past tense, it must refer to John; but if it is regarded as a prophetic word, it could point to Jesus' suffering. For Mark's literary stance in narrative, that would lie in the future, but from his personal historical perspective, it would have occurred in the past. As has often been noted, Mark links closely the death of Jesus and that of John the Baptist. The first hint of this is in the pericope about fasting (Mark 2:18 ff.): John's disciples fast while Jesus' do not. When Jesus (=the bridegroom) is taken away from them, they will fast, just as John's disciples fast (since their eschatological figure has been taken from them?). The point is made unequivocally in 6:14–29, where the death of John is linked with the appearance of Jesus, described by Herod as John raised from the dead. The final link is forged in 9:12*b*, widely recognized as a Markan insertion in older tradition,[18] where the suffering of Elijah is directly associated with the suffering of the Son of man. As the passage now stands, what is described in the apocalyptic scheme of Mark 9:9–13 is the coming and suffering of Elijah, and the "setting at nought" (KJV) of the Son of man (ἐπὶ τὸν υἱὸν τοῦ ἀνθρώπου). The reader — and in terms of Mark's literary strategy, Jesus' hearers — might seem to be left in doubt as to the outcome of this somber predictive pronouncement.

Once more we must look at Daniel to see how the promise of deliverance is given as a means of offsetting the prospect of suffering. For Daniel, the hope of deliverance is held out through reports of visions of the end time when the kingdom is given to "one like a son of Man." It is true that the phrase, son of man, seems to have meant for Daniel no more than a human being in contrast to the horrendous beasts who represented the earthly kingdoms in Daniel's scheme of the ages. But by the beginning of the first century A.D., and perhaps somewhat earlier, Son of man came to be used by Jewish apocalyptic writers as a designation for a redemptive figure of the End Time. Although the failure to find the *Similitudes* of Enoch among the Enochian fragments from Qumran has been interpreted as proving that the *Similitudes* are Christian, the fact is that there is nothing distinctively Christian about the Son of man passages in Enoch. Their use of Son of man as a redemptive title is therefore inadequate ground for treating them as of Christian origin. Mark's joining the term "Son of man" with other apocalyptic elements is evident in that the coming of the Son of man in glory is predicted in Mark 13:14–25 in words which are drawn chiefly from Daniel, but also with phrases echoing eschatological or apocalyptic passages out of Isaiah, Ezekiel, and Joel. The apocalyptic climax in which the Son of man appears "coming in clouds" (13:26) is taken over directly from Daniel.

II

But what has the transfiguration story to do with this? What connections might it have with apocalyptic, or what apocalyptic purpose could Mark have intended the story to serve? To answer this question, we must examine in some detail the text of Mark's narrative of the transfiguration.

καὶ μετὰ ἡμέρας ἕξ — Eduard Schweizer is correct in suggesting a link between the scene of Moses' receiving the Law on Mount Sinai (Exod. 24) and Jesus' confirmation as Son on the unnamed mountain in Palestine.[19] Moses had to wait six days; on the seventh the voice of God came from the cloud. Similarly, it is on the seventh day — "after six days" — that the voice comes to Jesus acknowledging him as Son. It seems most unlikely that this time reference is an historical recollection, since the scene itself is not historical, even if one can imagine some historical kernel or experience lying in the dim background of this Markan narrative construct.

The disciples who accompany Jesus are the inner core, among the first four chosen according to Mark, and those to whom the fullest explanation was offered of the meaning of Jesus' death and resurrection (10:35–45; 13:3; 14:33; 16:7). Since Peter is to be the prime witness of Jesus' future vindication, it is fitting that he be present for this anticipation of the glory of Jesus.

Although conjectures have been made as to the identity of the mountain — Tabor and Hermon are among the favorite guesses — there is no point in inquiring, since the fact that it is a mountain is all that matters. The parallel with the experiences of Moses and Elijah in their respective confirmation as God's agents also occurred on mountains (Exod. 24:15; 1 Kings 19:11). The fact that it is not a public event but a private disclosure is in keeping with Mark's literary and theological scheme of keeping the explanations of Jesus' words and actions for the inner circle of his followers (4:34; 6:31; 7:33; 9:28; 13:3; $\kappa \alpha \tau \grave{\alpha}$ $\mu \acute{o} \nu \alpha s$ 4:10).

$\mu \epsilon \tau \alpha \mu o \rho \phi \acute{\omega} \theta \eta$ is simply stated, not explained. The reader has no indication of the nature of the transformation, apart from the radiance of the clothing which is naïvely but vividly described in the second half of verse 3. From the Moses-tradition we do have precedent for this borrowed radiance which results from coming into the presence of God. In Moses' case, it was his face that shone and it continued to shine after he left the mountain, while the brilliance of Jesus' appearance was only a passing phenomenon. There is also precedent, however, in Jewish apocalyptic for the radiance of those who come into God's presence. Daniel 12:3 describes the rewards of the faithful as follows:

> And those who are wise shall shine like the brightness of the firmament,
> And they that turn many to righteousness as the stars for ever and ever.

The Syriac Apocalypse of Baruch is even more explicit (51:1–3):

> And it shall come to pass, when that appointed day has gone by, that then shall the aspect of those who are condemned be afterward changed, and the glory of those that are justified. For the aspect of those who now act wickedly shall become worse than it is, as they shall suffer torment. Also as for the glory of those who have now been justified in my Law, who have had understand-

ing in their life, and who have planted in their heart the root of wisdom, then their splendor shall be glorified in changes, and the form of their face shall be turned into the light of their beauty, that they may be able to acquire and receive the world which does not die, which is then promised to them. When therefore they see those, over whom they are now exalted, but who shall then be exalted and glorified more than they, they shall be respectively transformed, the latter into the splendor of angels, and the former shall yet more waste away. . . .

This theme of the clothing of the righteous in white in the eschaton is familiar from the Johannine Apocalypse (Rev. 7:13–14), but the specific combination of eschatological glory for the righteous and the precedent of Moses' radiance are found in Paul (2 Cor. 3:7–18, where μεταμορφόω is also used). The effulgence of the righteous in the kingdom of the Father is also affirmed in Matthew 13:43, where their shining is compared with the sun. There is no evidence, therefore, that the glistening garb of Jesus and the metamorphosis is intended to convey that he underwent a fundamental change so that his concealed divine nature became disclosed for the moment. Rather, the radiance is connected with "borrowed glory" as our cliché has it, just as Moses shone when he stood in the presence of God. If one insists on a theophany here, it was a private disclosure to Jesus of which we learn nothing from Mark, and of which the sole effect discernible by the disciples was the glowing of Jesus' clothing. The central meaning of the whole incident in Mark's account was disclosed at a later point in the pericope: in the voice which came from the cloud, as God's voice had come to Moses from the cloud (Exod. 24:16). The only thing that can be inferred from the radiance is that Jesus was seen as entering proleptically into the eschatological glorification that Jewish apocalyptic expected the righteous to share in. It is evident in what follows, however, that Jesus is not represented by Mark as merely one among many righteous who enter the age to come, but as one who has a unique eschatological role.

The two figures who appear to Jesus, Moses and Elijah, have often been described as embodying the Law and the prophets. Most recently R. Grob has repeated this interpretation, but he provides no justification beyond the simple assertion.[20] It is no accident that Elijah is first named, since he seems to have had first place in eschatological expectations, among the prophets, the rabbis, and apocalypticists. Furthermore, Elijah was not numbered among the prophets of the Nebi'im, and the narratives concerning him were included not in the prophetic portion of the canon but in the

Writings. It is not as prophet out of Israel's historic past that Elijah appears, but as messenger of the End Time, in keeping with Malachi 3 and 4. In addition to the role of Elijah in reconciling fathers and children and thereby assuaging the divine wrath, we learn from Ecclesiasticus 48:10 that he will restore the tribes of Israel. But in the expanded Hebrew version (or original?) of Ecclesiasticus, there is a triplet which extends still further the description of Elijah. The first two lines read:

> Blessed be he who sees you and dies;
> Blessed will he be who, before he dies, will see you.

The third line has been restored by R. Smend as follows:

> Blessed are you yourself, for you live on.

Elijah is accordingly asserted to be the one who will inaugurate the new age, but who himself lives forever. Conleth Kearns, in the *New Catholic Commentary*,[21] proposes that this and other additions to the book, many of which significantly modify the eschatological outlook, have their closest affinity with Jubilees and the *Similitudes* of Enoch, the latter of which Kearns dates to the first quarter of the first century B.C. The additions to Ecclesiasticus he thinks are of Essene origin, and come from Qumran.

In the text of the Assumption of Moses as we know it (in chapters 9 and 10), Taxo (= the Restorer) seems to have the function assigned by Malachi to Elijah: he is of the tribe of Levi and promotes righteousness in a form which is reminiscent of Daniel, including fasting, entering a cave, and announcing his willingness to accept martyrdom. Then God's kingdom will be established, Satan will be destroyed, God will go forth in judgment, seismic and cosmic disturbances will occur, idolatry will be extirpated, and Israel exalted. While one cannot be certain that the author of the Assumption of Moses had Elijah in mind, the role here described seems to be an elaboration of what Malachi foresaw for Elijah.

As summarized by Billerbeck and Jeremias, the rabbinic tradition expected Elijah to bring about penitence in Israel, to reassemble the scattered of the nation, to settle disputed points of the law, ritual, and biblical exposition.[22] If Elijah is to be linked with Levi, then it is perhaps significant, as Jeremias hints, that Levi is the one who identifies the Messiah for Israel (Test. Levi 2:10) if we follow Charles's *a*-text, or who reveals the mysteries of redemption if we follow the other two main text traditions.

Still more significant is the Apocalypse of Elijah — admittedly available only in a late Coptic version, but from its affinities with Revelation, apparently as early as the first century A.D. Revelation 11 seems to be able to presuppose familiarity with an apocalyptic expectation which is embodied by John in his Apocalypse and which is attested in the Apocalypse of Elijah. According to the Apocalypse of Elijah, Enoch and Elijah do battle in the end time with the anti-Christ and defeat him, an eschatological task that matches well with Taxo's in the Assumption of Moses. Jeremias's theory of a suffering Elijah, by contrast with Elijah's apocalyptic role, is wholly conjectural and rests almost solely on an (unwarranted) inference from Mark 9.

The evidence thus points to the conclusion that Elijah was considered in first-century Judaism as an almost exclusively eschatological figure. There is no hint of his being numbered among the prophets, but his roles in relation to the establishment of God's Rule are manifold, and all of them crucial. It is in this history-of-religions background that we must look for light on the meaning of Elijah as one of the companions of Jesus on the mount of transfiguration.

What are we to infer about the significance of Moses here? The roles of Moses are so numerous and so varied that it would be impossible within the scope of this paper to summarize them or even to enumerate them. But at this point in Mark's narrative, there is no hint of Moses as law-giver, such as we find implied in the Q tradition and especially in Matthew's version of the so-called Sermon on the Mount. Mark does comment critically on Jewish interpretation of the Law, but he does so without engaging in direct critique of Moses. The authorization for divorce which Moses gave is seen as a concession to the hardness of Israel's heart rather than as a failure on the part of Moses (Mark 10). But in the transfiguration pericope there is only one clue given to the meaning of Moses: the allusion to Deuteronomy 18:15, ἀκούετε αὐτοῦ (9:7). From it one can only conclude that Mark wants to present Jesus as the eschatological prophet whose coming Moses had announced. If Jesus is a second Moses for Mark, it is not as giver of the New Law but as fulfiller of the promise of the Prophet. We now know from the Qumran Florilegium[23] how burning was the hope of the Prophet's coming. Presumably the Deuteronomic prophet was also connected with Jesus by Mark or his tradition, as it was in Acts 3:22 f.

III

Although Elijah and Moses were linked in Jewish eschatological tradition by their having both been translated (as was Enoch), Moses had a role not shared with Elijah that suggests another aspect of meaning for his presence at the transfiguration. Wayne Meeks[24] has shown that in both rabbinic and Samaritan tradition, Moses was understood to have been enthroned at Sinai — or in heaven which he reached via Sinai — as God's vice-regent. The language of the rabbis is so bold as to read מֹשֶׁה אִישׁ הָאֱלֹהִים in Deuteronomy 33:1 as Moses, a man, god, since his being a god is proved by his shining face. But inasmuch as the term is used of angels and other heavenly beings, we should not read simple apotheosis into the rabbis. Meeks concludes with justification that Moses was portrayed in some of the rabbis as enthroned as God's vice-regent when he received the Law at Sinai. Is there any hint of a kingly function or an enthronement in the details of the transfiguration narrative?

More than twenty years ago, Harald Riesenfeld, in his doctoral dissertation, *Jésus transfiguré*, investigated the connections between the details of Peter's proposal about erecting booths and the eschatological significance of Succoth in first-century Judaism.[25] Although his conclusions were so weighted down with debatable Scandinavian theories about enthronement ceremonies that the book's major theses never found wide acceptance, Riesenfeld did make a good case for an eschatological meaning of the booths. And as for the Feast of Booths, Barnabas Lindars has shown that Psalm 118, a central passage in the Succoth liturgy, was understood eschatologically by Judaism before the Christians took it over as one of their favorite prooftexts.[26] Proto-apocalyptic texts such as Ezekiel 37:27 and Zechariah 14:9–11 predict the dwelling of Yahweh in Jerusalem when his rule is established, and Zechariah 14:16 explicitly associates this final victory with the annual observance of the Feast of Booths.

What then is the meaning of Peter's proposal to build booths, and why is it treated by Mark as lacking in understanding? The analogy between Peter's confession, which is followed by his rejection of the idea of Jesus' suffering, and Peter's proposal, which is dismissed as uncomprehending and fearful, is quite precise. Peter was right in affirming that Jesus was the Christ; he is right in sensing that the eschatological end is being enacted in the conclave of Moses, Elijah, and Jesus. He was wrong in rejecting Jesus' prediction that the path to kingship must necessarily (δεῖ) lead through suffering and death, and on the mount of transfiguration he wants once more (as in Mark 8:32) to bypass this indispensable factor, the cross. We have already noted earlier in this essay that each of the predictions of the passion is followed by an implicit or explicit proposal of a shortcut to the kingdom that does not pass through suffering. Luke's instincts are therefore correct in identifying the subject of the conversation of the three redemptive figures as Jesus' *exodus*, although the introduction of this detail nearly converts the scene into a seminar.

The disciples are set straight, or at least the attempt is made to set them straight, on who Jesus is and what God's purpose for him is in what follows. In 9:7 we come closest of all to a theophany, although the presence of God is evident only by the voice, not by sight. Hence it is a *theophony*, or more elegantly, a *theoepeia*.[27] The details match quite precisely the experiences of Elijah and Moses, as already noted. Now, however, in contrast to the heavenly voice addressed only to Jesus on the occasion of his baptism, the declaration is made to the inner circle of the disciples: Οὗτός ἐστιν ὁ υἱός μου ὁ ἀγαπητός, ἀκούετε αὐτοῦ.

υἱὸς τοῦ θεοῦ is to be understood, as Georg Fohrer points out in *TWNT*,[28] of the Jewish king, not because he gained the essence of the divine when he was enthroned or because he was physically begotten by God, but because he was the agent of the divine will. It was on this ground that he received a share in the dominion, the possessions, and the heritage of God. The term "son" was taken over from the ancient Near Eastern, especially Egyptian, ritual, in which the divine sonship of the king was proclaimed, but the significance of the title was closely linked with the concept of Israel as God's son. The covenant with Israel at Sinai has its echoes in the election of and covenant with the house of David, chosen to be the instruments of God's rule over his people. Later Judaism, Lohse reminds us,[29] was chary of using "Son of God," except in direct quotations of Scripture, since the term was liable to carry the misunderstanding of a physical divine sonship. At Qumran, 1QSa 2.11 f. has been read as "until God begets the messiah,"[30] but the crucial consonants are missing. The allusion may be to Psalm 2:7, but it could as well be to Isaiah 66:9, where God causes the Messiah to be born. In the same series of articles on υἱός, Schweizer[31] states flatly that the title υἱὸς τοῦ θεοῦ is never used for θεῖος ἀνήρ, and concludes that the term is not to be clarified on the basis of hellenistic

Judaism. Peter Wülfing von Martitz[32] similarly finds no links between υἱὸς τοῦ θεοῦ and θεῖος ἀνήρ in the literature of the late classical world.

The only appropriate background against which the term is to be understood is that of the Jewish kingship, here viewed in respect of eschatological fulfillment. Jesus' enthronement, which was announced to him at baptism, is now seen proleptically in the apocalyptic vision granted to the inner circle of his followers.

The eschatological aspects of Jesus' kingship are underlined in the phrase, ἀκούετε αὐτοῦ, which as we have noted derives from Deuteronomy 18, where the coming of the prophet like Moses is announced. The sudden disappearance of the heavenly figures shows that the vision is at an end. Matthew's term for the scene at this point is appropriate: τὸ ὅραμα. M. Sabbé has pointed out, however, that τὸν λόγον in 9:10 is used in precisely the same sense in the LXX version of Daniel 10:1, where "word" and "vision" appear in parallel construction.[33] Indeed the whole of Daniel 10 is relevant to the transfiguration scene: the appearance of the heavenly visitors; the companions who are fearfully aware that a vision is occurring but who cannot comprehend it; the radiant appearance of Daniel as he receives the vision (λόγος ἀπεκαλύφθη); the change which subsequently occurs in his appearance, although in Daniel the change is for the worse. Finally Daniel is left alone (v. 8). His vision concludes with words which are perhaps echoed in Mark 9:9, where it is decreed that the vision (ἃ εἶδον) is not to be disclosed until after the resurrection of the Son of man. As Daniel 10:14b phrases it, "The vision is for days yet to come." Although the details common to Daniel 10 and Mark 9 function in different ways in Mark than they do in Daniel, each has its counterpart in the other account, and the whole picture which they form has the same aim: to give assurance to the righteous undergoing suffering that God will effect vindication in spite of Satanic opposition and that the rule of God will ultimately triumph.

IV

Thus the transfiguration scene is not a theophany *to*, nor an epiphany *of*, Jesus, but a proleptic vision of the exaltation of Jesus as kingly Son of man granted to the disciples as eschatological witnesses.[34]

Why is it placed here? Would it not have been sufficient to have the prophetic words of Jesus in 8:38; 13:26; and 14:62 that announce Jesus' coming as Son of man? Mark seems to have thought not. Therefore, in addition to the promises, he employed the literary device of an apocalyptic vision in order to convey the message of assurance to the disciples, well before Jesus' death, in which God guaranteed that beyond the passion was the victory. In keeping with Mark's theory of the gradual unfolding of the nature of Jesus' messianic role, the disciples, like the companions of Daniel, do not grasp what is going on. This is the case even though the transfiguration narrative is followed immediately by the prediction of the passion, which is placed in the sequence of events determined by God, in keeping with apocalyptic convention: Elijah *must* come δεῖ ἐλθεῖν; the Son of man *must* suffer (8:31) and be ἐξουδενηθῇ (9:12). Mark declares that Elijah has already come (9:13), and has been treated in a way that the first Elijah expected (1 Kings 19:2, 10), but did not experience. Mark has already described the fate of the forerunner in 6:14–29. He wants his reader to be as convinced of the future vindication of the Son of man as he is of the death of John. Accordingly the great eschatological enthronement is previewed in the most vivid and compelling manner known to Mark: an apocalyptic vision.

This interpretation of Mark 9 has implications for the ending of Mark: just as the disciples were fearful and uncomprehending during the vision, so they were throughout the events of the passion. One might say that Jesus need not have had misgivings about the disciples' telling anyone the meaning of the vision until after the Son of man had risen from the dead. In Mark's portrait of them and of the events that they witnessed, there was little likelihood of their revealing anything. It was only after the Son of man had risen that they themselves understood the vision, the passion, and the coming enthronement of the Son of man.

NOTES

[1] M. Dibelius, *Die Formgeschichte des Evangeliums*, 3rd ed., with Supplement by G. Iber (Tübingen: J. C. B. Mohr, 1966), p. 232. See also the English translation *From Tradition to Gospel*, trans. B. L. Woolf (New York: Charles Scribner's Sons, 1934), pp. 267–275. Dibelius describes the transfiguration story as the clearest example of the Christ-myth. On the wide acceptance of this view, see W. Marxsen, *Introduction to the New Testament*, trans. G. Buswell (Philadelphia: Fortress Press, 1968), p. 137. Also, W. G. Kümmel, *Introduction to the New Testament*, trans. A. J. Mattill, Jr. (Nashville: Abingdon Press, 1966), p. 67.

[2] S. Schulz, *Die Stunde der Botschaft* (Hamburg: Furche Verlag, 1967), p. 57.

[3] M. Dibelius, *Die Formgeschichte* . . ., p. 64.

[4] F. Hahn, *The Titles of Jesus in Christology*, trans. Harold Knight and George Ogg (New York: World Publishing Co., 1969), pp. 300–302, 334–337.

[5] S. Schulz, *op. cit.*, p. 57.

[6] So Hahn, following Lohmeyer, "Die Verklärung Jesu nach dem Markus-Evangelium," *ZNW*, 21 (1922), pp. 185–215.

[7] P-W, Suppl. IV (Stuttgart: J. B. Metzler, 1963), cols. 269–279.

[8] *Ibid.*, cols. 293–297.

[9] *Ibid.*, col. 304.

[10] *Ibid.*, cols. 308 ff.

[11] Cf. the chosen epithet of Antiochus IV: Ἐπιφανής (=θεὸς ἐπιφανής).

[12] Antony sought to promote the notion of his identification with Dionysus. See Lily Ross Taylor, *The Divinity of the Roman Emperor* (Middletown, Conn., n.d.), pp. 102 ff. According to Plutarch (*Life of Alexander*, 67), Alexander in his time had made the same effort at identification with the god Dionysus.

[13] R. Bultmann, *TWNT*, vol. 9, pp. 10–11.

[14] Pfister, in P-W, *loc. cit.*, mentions the following as examples of epiphanies in the New Testament: the appearances of angels in the infancy stories; the appearances at the empty tomb; the conversion of Paul; also John 12 (the voice from heaven); Matthew 16:12 ff. (although only a reference is made to a revelation at an unspecified time and by an unspecified means, no account of the revelation is given other than the truth that was conveyed through it); 2 Corinthians 4:4; 1 Thessalonians 4:13 (a reference to the Parousia is made in v. 15); and the transfiguration narrative. But apart from the revelatory element, there is no common factor in these stories. One of these seems not to refer to a distinct event at all (2 Cor. 4:4), unless the incarnation itself is thought of as "event." But in that case epiphany is a broad term which covers appearances of divine persons and of supernatural beings (such as angels), revelation, parousia, incarnation — all of which seem to have in common nothing more than the general notion of supernatural disclosure. Such a vague concept is of little service as an analogical basis for interpreting the transfiguration account.

[15] R. Bultmann, *The History of the Synoptic Tradition*, trans. J. Marsh (New York: Harper & Row, Publishers, 1968), pp. 259–261.

[16] R. Otto, *Kingdom of God and Son of Man*, trans. B. L. Woolf (London: Lutterworth, 1943), pp. 237–261; V. Taylor, *The Person of Christ in the New Testament* (London: Macmillan Co., 1954), p. 181; R. H. Fuller, *The Mission and Achievement of Jesus*, Studies in Biblical Theology, 12 (Naperville, Ill.: Alec R. Allenson, 1954), pp. 55–64; but see also R. H. Fuller, *Foundations of New Testament Christology* (New York: Charles Scribner's Sons, 1965), p. 130.

[17] Nearly all the textual variants include the two elements: Christ and Son of God.

[18] E. Schweizer, *The Good News According to Mark*, trans. Donald H. Madvig (Richmond: John Knox Press, 1970), pp. 185–186. E. Lohmeyer, *op. cit.*, pp. 182–183; Sherman E. Johnson, *The Gospel According to St. Mark*, Harper's New Testament Commentaries (New York: Harper and Row, Publishers, 1960), pp. 158–159.

[19] E. Schweizer, *op. cit.*, pp. 181–182.

[20] So D. E. Nineham, *St. Mark*, The Pelican Commentaries (Baltimore: Penguin Books, 1963): "Moses and Elijah will have been seen as the two great representatives of the Law and the Prophets" (p. 235). But cf. E. Lohmeyer, *Das Evangelium des Markus*, Meyer Kommentar (Göttingen: Vandenhoeck & Ruprecht, 15th ed. 1959), p. 175, especially note 4, where Johanan ben Zakkai is quoted. R. Grob, *Einführung in das Markusevangelium* (Zürich: Zwingli Verlag,

1965), p. 130. Similarly, V. Taylor, *The Gospel According to St. Mark* (London: Macmillan Co., 1953), p. 390.

[21] C. Kearns, "Ecclesiasticus," in *A New Catholic Commentary on Holy Scripture* (London: Thomas Nelson and Sons, 1969), pp. 546-551.

[22] H. L. Strack and P. Billerbeck, *Kommentar zum Neuen Testament aus Talmud und Midrasch* (Munich: C. K. Beck), vol. 4, part 2 (1924), pp. 764-798. J. Jeremias, art. 'Ηλ[ε]ίας, *TDNT*, vol. 2, pp. 928-941.

[23] J. Allegro, "Further Messianic References in Qumran Literature," *JBL*, 75 (1956), pp. 174-187.

[24] W. Meeks, "Moses as God and King," in *Religion in Antiquity*, ed. J. Neusner (Leiden: Brill, 1968), pp. 354-371.

[25] Harald Riesenfeld, *Jésus transfiguré: L'Arrière-plan du récit évangelique de la Transfiguration de Nôtre Seigneur*, ASNU, 16 (Lund: Gleerup, 1944).

[26] Barnabas Lindars, *New Testament Apologetic* (Philadelphia: The Westminster Press, 1961), pp. 112, 169-174.

[27] These terms were suggested to me by my colleague, Professor Gregory Dickerson, of the Bryn Mawr College Greek Department.

[28] G. Fohrer, art. "υἱός" *TWNT*, vol. 8, p. 352.

[29] E. Lohse, *ibid.*, pp. 358-363.

[30] Morton Smith, " 'God's Begetting the Messiah' in IQSa," *NTS*, 5 (1958-1959), pp. 218-224.

[31] E. Schweizer, *TWNT*, vol. 8, pp. 364-395, especially p. 378.

[32] W. von Martitz, *ibid.*, pp. 335-340, especially 339 f.

[33] M. Sabbé, "La redaction du récit de la Transfiguration," in *La Venue du Messie*, Recherches Bibliques, 6 (Louvain, 1962), p. 69.

[34] On the apocalyptic background of this narrative, see Maria Horstmann, *Studien zur markinischen Christologie: Mk 8:27-9:13 als Zugang zum Christusbild des zweiten Evangeliums*, Neutestamentliche Abhandlungen, N.F. 6 (Münster: Aschendorff Verlag, 1969), p. 135.

Forms, Motives, and Omissions in Mark's Account of the Teaching of Jesus

by Morton Smith

For as long as I can remember, Professor Enslin has been outstanding in the Society of Biblical Literature for — among other things — his habit of asking pertinent questions. It is therefore as a tribute to his persistently inquiring mind that I offer here not a solution, but a problem.

The problem can best be approached from the history of *Formgeschichte*. The founders of that school set out to write a description and history of the literary [1] forms in the Gospels, but almost immediately became involved in a study of the motives which had produced these forms. Its objectives thus divided, the school achieved neither: we have as yet no definitive history of even so obvious a form as the miracle story, nor has the material in the Gospels been fully and convincingly classified according to the motives which produced it. We have, however, had full classifications of the material by literary form, and when the results of these are examined, a remarkable fact appears: *to an amazing extent the groups yielded by literary classification coincide with the groups yielded by classification according to motive.* That is to say, if one takes all the examples of a single literary form, then it usually happens that the great majority of them shows the influence of a single motive or group of motives. This is a fact which, a priori, would not be expected. Why should not every form have been used to serve many different motives? To this question we shall return later. At the moment the thing to be emphasized is the point that, to a quite amazing extent, particular motives and particular literary forms go together.

This does not mean that all, for example, of the sayings attributed to Jesus are to be explained by reference to a single motive. Of course, the simplest literary forms are common property and may reflect a great variety of concerns. But even in the

155

use of the simplest forms there is often an astonishing unanimity, and, in general, the more complex the form the more likely it is to be associated with few motives or with only one.

These generalizations can be illustrated conveniently by the following account of the various sorts of Markan tradition about Jesus' teaching.[2]

I

First of all, there are general statements that Jesus taught or preached. They are few, short, and abstract: "He went preaching in their synagogues everywhere in Galilee" (1:39). "Another time he taught by the sea" (4:1). "He went round the villages teaching" (6:6b). "Crowds again came to him and, as he was accustomed, he again taught them" (10:1b). These and their like are all summaries, stopgaps. They do not actually conclude or introduce the stories they follow or precede, they never refer to any specific teaching,[3] no stories nor even consequences follow from the vague teaching they refer to in general terms. They are put in to represent Jesus as a wandering preacher, the model of the wandering preachers of the apostolic age.

This motivation is particularly clear in the first instance of the type, 1:14f. "After John was handed over, Jesus came into Galilee preaching the gospel of God: The time is fulfilled and the kingdom of God is at hand, repent and believe in the gospel." The anachronism by which Jesus is made a preacher of the gospel has often been noticed.[4] Another anachronism is probably the word "repent." Mark, at least, has no stories about Jesus' preaching repentance, nor does he represent his followers as penitents. The peculiar message of the Jesus of Mark is not, "Repent," but, "Follow me." The preaching of repentance should lead to baptism, but we hear almost nothing of Jesus' baptizing (John 3:22; 4:1; cf. 4:2),[5] and the specific reference of "*the* Baptist" as a title suggests that the baptism of repentance was a mark of John's practice as opposed to that of Jesus. At any rate, the evangelist's motive in these verses — to make Jesus a preacher of the apostolic gospel — is clear.

The same motivation appears in the casual references to Jesus' teaching when there is no teaching to refer to — in the synagogue at Capernaum, before the feeding of the five thousand, and so on. But these instances, and other sorts of passages in which the same motive appears, are not here in point. Here attention must be limited to the groups of passages in which like form and like motive go together. The first of these groups, then, is that composed of the short, abstract, summary statements, not connected with their contexts, and intended to represent Jesus as a wandering preacher of the gospel of the apostolic age.

II

A second sort of tradition about Jesus' teaching, one which recurs again and again through the Gospel, is the appended explanation. The form is easily recognized: At the end of a story the disciples ask Jesus about the meaning of what he said or did, or the question is implied by their astonishment or obvious failure to understand, or even by their expressed anger or objection, which indicates their misunderstanding. Then Jesus explains, and the explanations, curiously enough, are either moralizing exposition of what has already been said, or obviously serve the apologetic interests of the early church.

As examples of moralizing exposition appear the explanation of the parable of the sower (4:13ff.) ; the two explanations of the saying, "Nothing from without a man, going into him, can defile him, but the things which come out of a man are those which defile him" (7:15) ; the emphatic restatement of the rule on divorce (10:11f.) and of the saying on the salvation of the rich (10:24bf.) ; and the rebuke of the disciples' anger at James and John by the teaching that, in the Christian community, rulers must serve (10:42ff.).

The apologetic statements include the first explanation of teaching in parables (4:11f.) ; it is to fulfill the prophecy of Isaiah, "That seeing they may see and not perceive." This explains not only why Jesus taught in such an obscure fashion, but also why the Jews did not believe him — a serious difficulty, as shown by Romans 9ff. The outburst at the disciples' failure to understand the saying about leaven (8:17ff.) quotes a similar passage ("Having eyes ye see not") and uses it as an excuse for the disciples — their failure, like that of the Jews, was necessary to fulfill prophecy. Whatever exegesis be adopted for the saying on Elijah [6] which is appended to the story of the transfiguration (9:12f.), it certainly is apologetic in motive and intended to answer a difficulty created by the scribes' teaching about Elijah.

Sometimes the difficulty which needed explanation was one which arose out of Jesus' own sayings. Thus that about the camel and the needle's eye came to be followed by a question with the reassuring answer, "All things are possible with God" (10:27). We have already seen that the stupidity of the disciples required an appended apology; in the same way Peter's denial was excused by making him contradict Jesus' general prophecy (that the disciples would abandon him) and making him subject to a special prophecy (that he would do worse, 14:30). On the other hand, the objection and the answer appended to the anointing in Simon's house are perhaps [7] not really an apology for the woman, but an excuse for the diversion of funds from the church's charities to its administrative expenses (14:4ff.). Finally, a special form of apologetic is encouragement: why do Christian exorcists fail to budge some demons? Insufficient prayer (9:29). What will be the reward of those who have left all to follow Jesus? A hundredfold with persecutions in this world, and in the world to come eternal life (10:29f.). Thus apologetics and moral exposition account for all the appended explanations in the Gospel, except 13:5-37, where the form has been expanded to constitute almost a whole chapter of apocalyptic material. One should note that the one exception as to motive goes with the one striking variation of the form.

One noticeable feature of these appended explanations, including that in chapter 13, is that they are so often represented as secret. This undoubtedly reflects the practice of a church which made a sharp distinction between the more and the less advanced (cf. Heb. 5:11ff.; 1 Cor. 3:1ff.). Here again the Jesus who taught his moral regulations and explanations of difficult texts (in secret, to the closed circle of the church) could well have been the projection backward of the Christian teacher of a later generation, in this instance not the wandering preacher but the incipient bishop. The contrast between the more and the less advanced serves also an apologetic purpose against other Christian groups. Here, it says, is the true teaching which was privately revealed to the closest followers; accept no substitutes.

III

In sharp contrast to the appended explanations stand the appended sayings, sayings which have been tagged onto or, rarely, inserted into stories, but which stand so free from the context that the story remains apparently complete after their removal. The remarkable thing about these sayings is that they do *not* explain. They are almost all hard sayings, either hard in form, epigrammatic, or hard in content, severe, obscure, doctrinally difficult,[8] or both. "I came not to call the righteous, but sinners" (2:17b). "All things shall be forgiven the children of men . . . but he who blasphemes against the Holy Spirit has no forgiveness forever" (3:28f.). Measure for measure (4:24b). "There are some of those standing here who shall not taste death till they see the kingdom of God come in power" (9:1). "If your hand offend you, cut it off" (9:43). "He who does not receive the kingdom of God as a child will not enter it" (10:15). "The Son of man came not to be served, but to serve, and to give his life a ransom for many" (10:45). These examples are enough to suggest the range of variety and also the characteristics which these *logia* have in common. They are particularly characterized by the antithesis and therefore particularly dear to the existentialists, who may have sometimes mistaken literary form for philosophic content. The fallacy would appear at once if one were to argue that "The spirit is willing, but the flesh is weak" (14:38b) necessarily implies such an absolute antithesis of spirit and flesh as was made by some Gnostics. But the antithesis between new wine and old bottles (2:22), between gaining the world and losing one's life (8:36), may be equally rhetorical.

The motive which has determined the placement of these sayings in Mark is obvious — it was the desire to explain them by attaching them to stories or larger sayings which they seemed to fit. Often this end was happily achieved and the saying fits so well that only analogy with other examples of the type enables us to notice the joint. Sometimes the attachment was less fortunate and the saying is patently out of place. This is especially apparent when a string of such sayings has been inserted as a block, e.g., in the middle of the parables (4:21ff.) and at the ends of chapters 8 (35ff.) and 9 (40ff.). The common motive here was evidently to put in Jesus' mouth these admired sayings which were circulating in the community and which were a part of the Christian preacher's store of proverbial wisdom. Some of them (e.g., measure for measure) were probably some centuries older than Jesus himself.

IV

In a very few passages Mark reports directly, with only the scantiest of narrative frames, teaching which he attributes to Jesus. These passages are the parables in chapter 4, the three prophecies of the passion in chapters 8, 9, and 10, the parable of the vinedressers and perhaps the question on the Son of David and the attack on the scribes, in chapter 12, and the saying, 8:34. This saying really belongs to the previous class of hard sayings (it stands at the head of a list of such sayings). Among the other members of this group, the coincidence of motive and form is illustrated most strikingly, of course, by the three almost identical prophecies of the passion. But it is also remarkable that *all* the parables (except, just possibly, that of the sower) deal with the kingdom, a theme which is conspicuously absent from other literary forms, e.g., the miracle stories and, as far as direct reference goes, the conflict stories. The question on the Son of David and the attack on the scribes are both unique as to form and both are polemic against the same group. The absence of sermons is a surprising characteristic which Mark, except for chapter 13, shares with the earliest rabbinic literature.

V

Finally, there is the teaching embedded in the stories. Here the obvious distinction is that now generally recognized; it involves stories told for their own sake, stories told merely to introduce teaching, and stories told for the kerygmatic or liturgical importance of the action reported. Admittedly, the distinctions are not perfectly clear. In some instances miracle stories have been made over to serve as vehicles for teaching; the paralytic let down through the roof (2:1-12) and the man with the withered hand (3:1-5) are clear cases. In other instances it is possible that sayings have generated stories (e.g., 9:35-37) or that stories have degenerated into reports of teaching (the question on the Son of David, mentioned above). Even allowing for such exceptions, however, the stories told for their own sake (miracle stories) are examples of a single, recognizable form and contain a notable series of sayings on faith (meaning *trust*) not found elsewhere. The stories told to introduce teaching again exemplify a single, distinct form and this form is used principally for the conflict with Judaism, expressed in disputes with Jewish authorities and in contrasts of Jesus' teaching with Jewish law. Here, however, is found the most considerable variety of content shown by any form other than the saying. Some stories stand only on the verge of conflict (so 3:31ff.; 10:17-23) ; there is even one "harmony story" (12:28-34) ; and in a few the doctrine introduced is not connected with the conflict with Judaism (10:35-40). Finally, the stories told because of the kerygmatic or liturgical importance of the action they recount are not so clearly examples of a single literary form and contain relatively little teaching, so that for the most part they fall outside the purview of this article. What teaching they do contain, however, with constant emphasis on the fulfillment of prophecy, has obviously been shaped by the early church's interpretation of Jesus' career.

CONCLUSIONS

If the above account is correct, Mark has preserved or created traditions about the teaching of Jesus in a number of different literary forms, and for the most part each of these forms is at the service of one particular set of motives or concept of Jesus. It must be emphasized that this coincidence of content, motive, and form is not absolutely unvarying; in particular there is considerable variety in the content and motivation of the isolated sayings and of the teaching embedded in stories (apart from the miracle stories) . But when all exceptions are allowed for, it remains a fact that throughout Mark, with a surprising consistency, certain literary forms are associated predominantly with certain themes of content or motive, and vice versa. In particular: *the brief, general statements* about Jesus' teaching make him a wandering preacher of repentance, but elsewhere in Mark he never preaches repentance; indeed, he rarely preaches at all and Mark has none of his sermons except the Little Apocalypse. *The appended explanations* make him a different sort of teacher, an authority for the closed Christian group, concerned with exposition of its moral rules and explanation of its doctrinal difficulties. *The free logia* are so epigrammatic that it is difficult to determine their original sense. If, as seems probable, there were once collections of them, then the content of these collections seems to have been determined at least as much by literary as by doctrinal or historical criteria, and any sharp, antithetical saying was a likely candidate for inclusion. *The sayings embedded in stories* differ according to the types of story. In the miracle stories the teaching is practically limited to a remarkably uniform series of statements on the relation between trust and healing. The conflict stories again show Jesus as the teacher and apologist of the developed church, this time in its public relations with competing groups. For the stories of the life and passion, by contrast, Jesus is a cult figure, the predestined sacrifice by whose blood the new covenant was to be instituted, and what teaching there is in these stories explains the prophetic determination of the events and their symbolic significance. In contrast to all this material where the teaching is incidental, Mark has very few *traditions which report Jesus' teaching directly* and in isolation: the four parables (all of the kingdom), the three prophecies (all of the passion), and the two pieces of polemic (both against the scribes) are all there is to find, except for the apocalypse in chapter 13. It seems likely that, for the final editor, the most important *teaching* of Jesus, at least, the most important one he wished to present fully in his Gospel, was that apocalypse.

PROBLEM

This summary suggests two answers to the question why, in Mark, literary forms and motives coincide so remarkably. Either the teaching was determined, and largely generated, by the content of the literary form (as in the stories of the passion and the miracle stories), or even by the literary form itself (as in the antithetical sayings); or the peculiar form is the work of a single editor with a single set of motives (as in the summary statements and, perhaps, most of the appended explanations). But even taken together, these answers do not seem wholly sufficient to explain the facts.

The problem, why more direct teaching material was not reported, must take into consideration the letters of Paul, *whose comparative neglect of Jesus' teaching matches Mark's and may have some historical connection with it.* When Paul does appeal to Jesus' teaching, his appeal is to authority rather than content (1 Corinthians 7:10).[9] Similarly for Mark, Jesus is a lay figure, a symbol of authority, to which practices or doctrines, for which authority is desired, are referred. Mark is not interested to preserve all his utterances, either as a system of teaching, or as a record of his personality. Of all the things he said, the church represented by Mark wants only those which provide assurance for its hopes, authorization for its doctrines or practices, and answers to the questions which are in dispute among its members. These are the uses of authority, and it seems likely that Mark preserved whatever he found useful. Therefore the bulk — if any — of Jesus' teaching would seem to have been either unknown to Mark, alien to the concerns of the church for which he wrote, or deliberately withheld by him from presentation in his Gospel. Why?

APPENDIX: THE TEACHING MATERIAL
AND REFERENCES TO TEACHING
IN MARK, CLASSIFIED BY FORM

(It is difficult, in many stories, to decide which sayings should be considered "teaching," which not. Here most of the dubious have been excluded. Further, it has seemed best for the purpose of this paper—a study of the relation of motives to the forms which the material now has in the Gospel—to treat sayings whenever possible as parts of the stories to which they are now attached.)

I. General statements about teaching or preaching:

A. Summaries: 1:14f., 38f.; 2:13; 4:1; 6:6b; 10:1.

B. References to teaching on specific occasions, when the content of the teaching is not reported: 1:21f., 27; 6:2, 34; 14:49.

C. References to teaching, in introductions or conclusions to reports of the material taught: 4:2, 33f.; 8:31; 9:31; 10:32; 11:17f.; 12:35.

D. References to teaching by the apostles: 3:14; 6:12, 30.

II. Appended explanations:

A. Moralizing: 4:13-20; 7:18f.; 10:11f., 24b, 42-44.

B. Apologetic: 4:11f.; 7:20-23; 8:17-20; 9:12f., 29; 10:27, 29f.; 14:6-9, 30.

C. 13:5-37.

III. Sayings:

2:17b, 21f., 27, 28; 3:27, 28f., 35; 4:9, 21, 22, 23, 24a, 24b, 25; 6:4; 7:9-13, 14f.; 8:34, 35, 36, 37, 38; 9:1, 40, 41, 42, 43-48, 49, 50a, 50b, 50c; 10:15, 23, 25, 31, 45; 11:23, 24, 25; 12:10f.; 14:21, 25, 38a, 38b.

IV. Teaching reported with minimal narrative frame:

A. Parables: 4:2-8, 26-29, 30-32; 12:1-9.

B. Prophecies of the passion: 8:31; 9:31; 10:33f.

C. Polemic against the scribes: 12:35-37, 38-40.

V. Teaching reported in stories: [10]

A. Miracle stories: 1:44*; 2:10; 3:4; 4:40; 5:34, 36; 7:27; 9:19, 23; 10:52; 11:22b.

B. Conflict stories and other stories of teaching: 2:10, 17*a*, 19, 20*, 25f.; 3:4, 23, 24-26*, 33, 34*; 7:6ff.; 8:12, 15; 9:35, 37, 39; 10:5-9, 14, 18*, 19, 21, 39f.; 11:17, 33; 12:17, 24f., 26f., 29-31, 34, 43f.; 13:2.

C. Other: 8:30, 33; 9:9; 14:18, 20, 22, 24, 27f., 41, 48f., 62.

NOTES

[1] "Literary" is not to be understood in the narrow sense in which "literary composition" is opposed to pre-literary tradition, but rather in the wide sense in which "the miracle story," "the saying," "the parable," "the conflict story," etc. can be described as different "literary forms."

[2] A complete list of the teaching material and references to teaching in Mark, classified by form, is given as an appendix to this article. The sections of the article numbered I to V should be read as commentaries on the corresponding sections of the appendix.

[3] The parables have a separate introduction, 4:2.

[4] E.g., J. Weiss, *Das älteste Evangelium* (Göttingen: Vandenhoeck & Rupprecht, 1903), p. 29; J. Wellhausen, *Das Evangelium Marci* (Berlin: G. Reimer Verlag, 1903), p. 8.

[5] On the differences between Jesus and the Baptist, see W. Grundmann, *Jesus der Galiläer* (Leipzig: J. C. Hinrichs, 1940), pp. 40f. and 66.

[6] It is possible that the story of the transfiguration once concluded with the disciples' failure to understand the resurrection of the dead (9:10). This was later interpreted as a failure to understand the resurrection of the Messiah and an explanation was appended, beginning with the objection, "But the scribes say that Elijah must come first," the reasoning being: If Elijah comes first and restores all things to order, then the Messiah, coming into a world already restored to subjugation to God, will not be put to death nor, consequently, rise. Jesus' reply paraphrases the Old Testament basis for this objection, then opposes to it another prophecy, and resolves the contradiction by denying the apostles' interpretation of the passage on Elijah. It might be translated, "So Elijah, coming first, restores all things, does he? If so, how is it written, etc." Indication of a question by repetition of a statement is frequent in the Talmuds.

[7] *Perhaps*, because this interpretation is contradicted by, "But me ye have not always."

[8] Sometimes these sayings are so difficult that explanatory sayings have been appended to them, e.g., 7:18f., 20ff.; 10:27.

[9] This makes it doubtful whether he is appealing to the historical Jesus (as we should say) or to the Lord teaching in the church. Certainly when he says (1 Cor. 11:23f.), "I received from the Lord . . . that the Lord Jesus . . . said," it appears the first 'Lord' was not precisely identical with the second. But cf. 1 Corinthians 8:5f. In any event, what the Lord Jesus said has ceased to be teaching and has become a liturgical formula. See further my article, "The Reason for the Persecution of Paul," in *Studies in Mysticism and Religion Presented to Gershom G. Scholem* (Jerusalem, 1967), pp. 261ff.

[10] At least the items starred were probably at one time independent *logia*.

The Ending of the Gospel According to Mark in the Ethiopic Manuscripts

by Bruce M. Metzger

Previously published statements concerning the ending of the Gospel According to Mark in Ethiopic manuscripts are inadequate, confused, and contradictory. If one begins by consulting Tischendorf's monumental eighth edition of the Greek New Testament (1869–1872), he is told that two manuscripts of the Ethiopic version, designated *aeth*^m *et*^a, lack Mark 16:9-20 and replace the passage with the following (commonly called the shorter ending of Mark):

Et quum perfecissent dicere omnia quae praecepit Petro et suis, et postquam apparuisset iis dominus Iesus ab ortu solis usque ad occasum, dimisit eos ut praedicarent evangelium sanctum, quod non corrumpitur, in salutem aeternam.

If one asks, however, what and where these two Ethiopic witnesses are, he finds no ready answer. When he consults Tischendorf's list of sigla in the preface to the edition, he discovers that *aeth*^m *et*^a are not included. Turning to Caspar René Gregory's volume of *Prolegomena* to Tischendorf's eighth edition, he is disappointed once again, for this thesaurus of information is also silent concerning the identity of the two manuscripts. Eventually, however, if one is fortunate enough to look into Samuel Prideaux Tregelles's *Greek New Testament*, Part I (London, 1857), he will discover that Tischendorf undoubtedly derived his information concerning the two Ethiopic manuscripts (with the Latin rendering of the shorter ending) from this earlier edition, but then neglected to supply even the meager information given by Tregelles concerning the manuscripts. In the Introduction to his edition Tregelles states that a few notes which Thomas Pell Platt made while collating manuscripts for his edition of the Ethiopic New Testament (London, 1827–1830) had been placed in his hands, and that "aeth" followed by a letter or a number refers to individual manuscripts collated by Platt.[1] Platt's edition, however, includes no reference to variant readings, nor does it provide the text of the shorter ending, and therefore the evidence

167

cited first by Tregelles and subsequently taken over by Tischendorf cannot be checked.

In 1881, F. J. A. Hort stated, on the authority of a certain Dr. Wright, that the shorter ending Πάντα δέ . . . σωτηρίας is found "in at least several Æthiopic MSS continuously with v. 8, and followed continuously by vv. 9-20, without note or mark of any kind."[2] Which manuscripts they are, however, and more precise information as to their number are questions to which no answer is provided.

In 1889 William Sanday, on the basis of collations of twelve Ethiopic manuscripts made by D. S. Margoliouth and edited by A. C. Headlam, stated[3] that three Ethiopic manuscripts in the British Museum (namely codd. Add. 16,190, Or. 509, 513) omit the longer ending (Mark 16:9-20), and that seven other manuscripts (namely Or. 510, 511, 512, 514, 516, 517, 518) conclude the Gospel of Mark with the words: *et omne quod imperavit Petro et iis qui ejus erant perfecte narravit et posthac apparuit iis dominus Jesus ab ortu solis ad occasum et misit eos praedicatum evangelium sacrum incorruptibile ad salutem aeternam. Amen. Amen.* Here for the first time reference is made to specific Ethiopic manuscripts that can be identified and checked. When the present writer made such a check, however, it turned out that the three manuscripts which are said to omit verses 9-20 in reality contain the passage. Furthermore, an examination of the seven manuscripts disclosed that, instead of replacing the longer ending with the shorter ending, these witnesses actually contain both the shorter and the longer ending. So confused — and confusing — are the data supplied by Sanday that a subsequent scholar, investigating the endings of Mark's Gospel, inferred from an analysis of Sanday's complete list of the twelve manuscripts that only one (namely Or. 507) contains the longer ending[4] — whereas (as was just stated) seven of the manuscripts present the longer ending (after the shorter ending).

Although during the years several scholars[5] have drawn attention to the contradiction between the statements of Hort and of Sanday, nothing has been done to ascertain the true state of the evidence. In fact, in the most comprehensive *apparatus criticus* ever to be assembled for Mark's Gospel, that drawn up by S. C. E. Legg and published at Oxford in 1935, the reader is still told that three Ethiopic manuscripts omit 16:9-20. Although Legg provides no information as to the identity of the three manuscripts, the fact that he prints the same

Latin rendering of the shorter ending as that found in Sanday's apparatus of 1889, suggests clearly enough the origin of the (mis)-information.

In order to make a beginning of ascertaining more fully and more accurately the evidence for the ending(s) of the Gospel According to Mark in Ethiopic, the present writer combed through catalogues of collections of Ethiopic manuscripts located in many libraries and museums of Europe and America, and also wrote to curators of uncatalogued collections inquiring about the presence of Ethiopic manuscripts of the Gospel According to Mark. In a few cases it was possible to examine the manuscripts themselves; in most cases arrangements were made to secure photographic reproductions of those folios that, according to information given in the catalogues, contain the ending of Mark's Gospel. Thanks are due to Dr. Donald Davies, formerly of Lincoln University, who very kindly put at my disposal photographs of the ending of Mark's Gospel in fifteen manuscripts that he had examined in 1968–1969 at various monasteries and libraries in Ethiopia. I must also express my gratitude to Father Gebre Medhim Yohannes, a student from Addis Ababa at Princeton Theological Seminary, for valuable assistance in interpreting several lexical forms and syntactical constructions in the shorter ending.

In what follows one will find first a list of sixty-five manuscripts, belonging to about thirty different collections, arranged alphabetically by country in which they are located. For all of them except nos. 51, 60, and 64, photographs, photostats, or microfilms of the ending of Mark's Gospel are on deposit in the Theological Seminary Library, Princeton, New Jersey. Information concerning dates, either approximate or precise, is given on the authority of the scholar (usually the cataloguer of the collection) whose name, within parentheses, follows the date. In order to facilitate consultation of the fuller descriptive accounts of the manuscripts, an alphabetic listing of catalogues is also provided. In the case of a few manuscripts (notably those photographed in Ethiopia) no library or shelf number is assigned; according to Davies they are identified by the priests or the curators in charge as the oldest copy or copies in the several collections.[6] After the lists of manuscripts and catalogues are brief comments on several of the more noteworthy manuscripts. These comments are followed by the Ethiopic text of the shorter ending; this is given in the form that is common to the two oldest Ethiopic manuscripts of Mark which present the shorter ending (nos. 6 and 23 below). The apparatus and the English translation are keyed to the Ethiopic text by superscript roman letters. In the apparatus significant variant readings are provided with an English rendering, but variants that involve only orthographic details (such as the interchange of guttural letters) are cited without an English rendering.

LIST OF ETHIOPIC MANUSCRIPTS
CONTAINING THE GOSPEL ACCORDING TO MARK

AUSTRIA

1 = Vienna, Österreichische Nationalbibliothek, MS. Aeth. 10; xviii cent. (Rhodokanakis); photograph.
2 = Vienna, Österreichische Nationalbibliothek, MS. Aeth. 25; xviii cent. (Rhodokanakis); photograph.

ETHIOPIA

3 = Abba Garima, east of Adowa, MS. 1; ca. A.D. 1000 (Davies); photograph.
4 = Abba Garima, east of Adowa, MS. 2; xi–xii cent. (Davies); photograph.
5 = Abba Garima, east of Adowa, MS. 3; xi–xii cent. (Davies); photograph.
6 = Addis Ababa, National Library; A.D. 1343 (Davies); photograph.
7 = Asmara; A.D. 1468 (Davies, who writes "copied by David Buxton in 1947 at Maryam (?) near Asmara"); photograph.
8 = Daga Estefanos, Lake Tana; A.D. 1550 (Davies); photograph.
9 = Debra Bizen, east of Asmara; A.D. 1473 (Davies); photograph.
10 = Debra Damo, northwest of Adigrat; A.D. 1429 (Davies); photograph.
11 = Debra Maryam, Lake Tana; xiv–xv cent. (Davies); photograph.
12 = Haik, Lake Haik; A.D. 1494 (Davies); photograph.
13 = Kebran, Lake Tana; A.D. 1429 (Davies); photograph.
14 = Lalibela-Ashetin; A.D. 1468 (Davies); photograph.
15 = Lalibela-Emmanuel; A.D. 1429 (Davies); photograph.
16 = Lalibela-Medhani Alem; A.D. 1429 (Davies); photograph.
17 = Ura Kidani Miheret; xvi cent. (Davies); photograph.

FRANCE

18 = Paris, Bibliothèque nationale, d'Abbadie MS. Éthiop. 2; xviii cent. (Conti Rossini); microfilm.
19 = Paris, Bibliothèque nationale, d'Abbadie MS. Éthiop. 47; xviii cent. (Conti Rossini); microfilm.
20 = Paris, Bibliothèque nationale, d'Abbadie MS. Éthiop. 82; xix cent. (Conti Rossini); microfilm.
21 = Paris, Bibliothèque nationale, d'Abbadie MS. Éthiop. 95; xix cent. (Conti Rossini); microfilm.
22 = Paris, Bibliothèque nationale, d'Abbadie MS. Éthiop. 112; xix cent. (Conti Rossini): microfilm.

23 = Paris, Bibliothèque nationale, MS. Éthiop. 32; xiii cent. (Zotenberg); microfilm.
24 = Paris, Bibliothèque nationale, MS. Éthiop. 33; xvii cent. (Zotenberg); microfilm.
25 = Paris, Bibliothèque nationale, MS. Éthiop. 34; xviii cent. (Zotenberg); microfilm.
26 = Paris, Bibliothèque nationale, MS. Éthiop. 35; xv cent. (Zotenberg); microfilm.
27 = Paris, Bibliothèque nationale, MS. Éthiop. 36; xviii cent. (Zotenberg); microfilm.
28 = Paris, Bibliothèque nationale, MS. Éthiop. 37; xix cent. (Zotenberg); microfilm.
29 = Paris, Bibliothèque nationale, MS. Éthiop. 38; xvii cent. (Zotenberg); microfilm.
30 = Paris, Bibliothèque nationale, MS. Éthiop. 39; xvi cent. (Zotenberg); microfilm.

GERMANY

31 = Munich, K. Hof- and Staatsbibliothek, kön. Aeth. 25; (date unknown); microfilm.
32 = Münster/Westf., Institute für neutestamentliche Textforschung; without shelf-mark; (date unknown); photograph.

GREAT BRITAIN

33 = Cambridge, University Library, MS. Add. 1165; xvi cent. (Ullendorff and Wright); microfilm.
34 = Cambridge, University Library, MS. Or. 1802; xviii cent. (Ullendorff and Wright); microfilm.
35 = Edinburgh, National Library of Scotland, MS. 1894; "no later than end of fourteenth century" (Laing);[7] microfilm.
36 = London, British Museum, MS. Add. 16,190; xviii cent. (Dillmann); microfilm.
37 = London, British Museum, MS. Or. 481; latter half of xvii cent. (Wright); microfilm.
38 = London, British Museum, MS. Or. 507; xv cent. (Wright); photograph.
39 = London, British Museum, MS. Or. 508; latter part of xvii cent. (Wright); microfilm.
40 = London, British Museum, MS. Or. 509; xviii cent. (Wright); microfilm.
41 = London, British Museum, MS. Or. 510; "Dated A.D. 1664–1665, but apparently written A.D. 1667–1668" (Wright); microfilm.
42 = London, British Museum, MS. Or. 511; xvii cent. (Wright); microfilm.
43 = London, British Museum, MS. Or. 512; xvii cent. (Wright); microfilm.
44 = London, British Museum, MS. Or. 513; xvii cent. (Wright); microfilm.
45 = London, British Museum, MS. Or. 514; xvii cent. (Wright); microfilm.
46 = London, British Museum, MS. Or. 515; A.D. 1675–1676 (Wright); microfilm.
47 = London, British Museum, MS. Or. 516; xvii cent. (Wright); microfilm.
48 = London, British Museum, MS. Or. 517; xvii cent. (Wright); microfilm.
49 = London, British Museum, MS. Or. 518; A.D. 1655 (Wright); microfilm.
50 = London, British Museum, MS. Or. 519; xvii cent. (Wright); microfilm.
51 = London, Library of British and Foreign Bible Society, MS. VI (formerly MS. A); (date unknown); consulted May, 1970.
52 = Manchester, John Rylands Library, MS. Eth. 27; xviii cent. "from the

royal scriptorium at Gondar" (Frank Taylor, Keeper of Manuscripts, letter dated 5 May 1970); microfilm.
53 = Oxford, Bodleian Library, MS. Bruce 76 (olim X); xviii cent. (Dillmann); microfilm.
54 = Oxford, Bodleian Library, MS. Bruce 78 (olim XII); xviii cent. (Dillmann); photostat.
55 = Oxford, Bodleian Library, MS. Aeth. c.1; "probably end of the 15th century" (Ullendorff); photograph.
56 = Oxford, Bodleian Library, MS. Aeth. c.2; xv cent. (Ullendorff); photograph.

IRELAND (EIRE)

57 = Dublin, Chester Beatty Library, MS. 911; xix cent. (Cerulli); microfilm.
58 = Dublin, Chester Beatty Library, MS. 912; xviii cent. (Cerulli); microfilm.

ITALY

59 = Vatican City, Library, MS. Eth. 4; xix cent. (Grébaut and Tisserant); microfilm.
60 = Vatican City, Library, MS. Eth. 25; xv cent. (Grébaut and Tisserant); microfilm of entire manuscript at Claremont, Calif. (International Greek New Testament Project).
61 = Vatican City, Library, MS. Eth. 107; xix cent. (Grébaut and Tisserant); microfilm.
62 = Vatican City, Library, MS. Eth. 270; xviii–xix cent. (van Landschoot); microfilm.

UNITED STATES OF AMERICA

63 = Princeton, University Library, Garrett MS. 78 (Dep. 1470), ca. A.D. 1650; photostat.
64 = New York, Pierpont Morgan Library, MS. 828, A.D. 1401; consulted May, 1970.

UNION OF SOVIET SOCIALIST REPUBLICS

65 = Leningrad, M. E. Saltykov-Shchedrin State Public Library, Efiop. 17 (Turayev 25), xix cent. (Turayev); microfilm.

CATALOGUES AND DESCRIPTIONS OF ETHIOPIC MANUSCRIPTS
(Containing Copies of Mark's Gospel)

Abbadie, Antoine Thompson d', *Catalogue raisonné de manuscrits éthiopiens appartenant à Antoine d'Abbadie* (Paris, 1859).
Cerulli, Enrico, "I manoscritti etiopici della Chester Beatty Library in Dublino," *Atti della Accademia Nazionale dei Lincei*, Anno CCCLXII, *Memorie*, Classe di scienza morali, storiche e filologiche, Ser. VIII, vol. XI, fasc. 6 (1965).
Conti Rossini, Carlo, "Notice sur les manuscrits éthiopiens de la collection d'Abbadie," *Journal asiatique*, Sér. dix, vol. XIX (1912), pp. 551-578; xx (1912), pp. 5-72 and 449-494.

[Dillmann, August], *Catalogus codicum manuscriptorum orientalium qui in Museo Britannico asservatur*; Pars tertia, *Codices Æthiopicos amplectens* (London, 1847).

Dillmann, August, *Catalogus codicum manuscriptorum Bibliothecae Bodleianae Oxoniensis*; Pars VII, *Codices Aethiopici* (Oxford, 1848).

Grébaut, Sylvain, and Tisserant, Eugene, *Codices Aethiopici Vaticani et Borgiani* . . ., 2 vols. (In Bybliotheca Vaticana, 1935–1936).

Laing, David, "A Brief Notice of an Ancient MS. of the Four Gospels, brought from Abyssinia . . .," *Proceedings of the Society of Antiquaries of Scotland*, VIII (Edinburgh, 1871), pp. 52-55.

Lantschoot, A. van, "Inventaire sommaire des MSS Vaticans éthiopiens 251–299," *Collectanea Vaticana in honorem Anselmi M. Card. Albareda*, I (Città del Vaticano, 1962), pp. 453-512.

Rhodokanakis, Nicolaus, "Die äthiopischen Handschriften der k. k. Hofbibliothek zu Wien," *Sitzungsberichte der kaiserlichen Akademie der Wissenschaften in Wien*, philos.-hist. Kl., Bd. 151, Abh. 4 (1906).

Turayev, Boris, "Efiopskiya rukopisi v. S.-Peterburgye," *Zapiski Vostochnavo Otdeleniya, Imperatorskoye Russkoye Arkheologicheskoye Obshchestvo*, XVII, II-III (1906), pp. 115-248.

Ullendorff, Edward, *Catalogue of Ethiopian Manuscripts in the Bodleian Library*, vol. II (Oxford, 1951).

Ullendorff, Edward, and Wright, Stephen G., *Catalogue of Ethiopian Manuscripts in the Cambridge University Library*. With a Contribution by D. A. Hubbard (Cambridge, 1961).

Wright, William, *Catalogue of the Ethiopic Manuscripts in the British Museum Acquired Since the Year 1847* (London, 1877).

[Zotenberg, Hermann], *Catalogue des manuscrits éthiopiens (gheez et amharique) de la Bibliothèque nationale* (Paris, 1877).

Among the manuscripts included in the preceding list, mention may be made of two or three that are, for one reason or another, especially noteworthy.

An exceptionally fine copy of the Four Gospels, profusely illustrated,[8] is the Pierpont Morgan Library MS. 828 (no. 64 above). According to information contained in a colophon (fols. 205ᵛ — 206ᵛ), the vellum manuscript was written and illuminated in A.D. 1400–1401, during the reign of David I (1382–1411) of Ethiopia, by a scribe whose name has been deleted, for a granddaughter of King Amda Seyon (1314–1344) whose name before she became a nun was Zir Gānēlā. In the opinion of Patrick W. Skehan, who has provided a detailed account of the canon tables and of the cycle of illuminations, which deal with the life of Christ, "the manuscript is noteworthy in all its parts; and in respect of the illuminations it is to a considerable extent unique, and in general intensely interesting."[9]

The Vatican MS. Eth. 25 (no. 60 above) is of interest because it was utilized in the preparation of the first printed edition of the Ethiopic New Testament.[10] This was produced at Rome in 1548–

1549, two volumes in quarto, by the brothers Valerius Doricus and Ludovicus of Brescia,[11] who worked under the supervision of Tasfā-Ṣeyōn (= Sion), who assumed the Latin name Petrus,[12] an Ethiopian monk, born (according to the inscription on his monument at Rome)[13] "beyond the tropic of Capricorn" of noble parents. Well-versed in many languages, he was assisted by his two brothers, who were also monks, Tensea Wald, or Paulus, and Zaslask, or Bernardus. The second volume, which contains the Epistles of Paul, includes in Ethiopic and Latin the following note to the reader: "Fathers and Brethren, be pleas'd not to interpret amiss the faults of this edition: for they who compos'd it could not read [Ethiopic]; and for ourselves we know not how to compose. So then we help'd them, and they assisted us, as the blind leads the blind; and therefore we desire you to pardon us and them."[14]

What appears to be the oldest dated Ethiopic manuscript that contains the shorter ending is in the National Library of Addis Ababa (no. 6 above). According to Davies, a colophon indicates that the manuscript came from Haik and was copied no later than A.D. 1343. The oldest undated manuscript that contains the shorter ending is no. 23 above, a manuscript in the Bibliothèque nationale in Paris which Zotenberg dated in the thirteenth century but which Grébaut thought was copied in the third quarter of the fourteenth century.[15] As was mentioned earlier, the text of the shorter ending is identical in these two manuscripts and is given below.[16] Antedating these two manuscripts are three copies of the Gospels at the monastery of Abba Garima (nos. 3, 4, and 5 above), the oldest of which Davies dates on palaeographical grounds at approximately A.D. 1000, a date independently confirmed by Jules Leroy.[17] These three contain the traditional ending of Mark; that is, verses 9-20 follow immediately after 16:8.

THE SHORTER ENDING OF MARK'S GOSPEL
(following 16:8 and preceding verses 9-20)

[a] ወኩሎ ፡ [b] ዘአዘዘ ፡ [c] ለጴፕሮስ ፡ [d] ወለእሊአሁ ፡ [e] ፈጺሞሙ ፡ [f] ነገሬ ፡ [g] ወእምድኅሬዝ ፡ [h] አስተርአየ ፡ [i] ሎሙ ፡ [j] ኢየሱስ ፡ [k] ወእምሥራቅ ፡ [l] ዐ‍ሐይ ፡ [m] እስከ ፡ [n] ምዕራብ ፡ [o] ፈነዎሙ ፡ [p] ይስብኩ ፡ [q] በወንጌል ፡ [r] ቅዱስ ፡ [s] ዘኢይማስን ፡ [t] ለመድኃኒት ፡ [u] ዘለዓለም ።

APPARATUS CRITICUS[18]

The text above is read by MSS. 6 9 13 23, except that in 6 the first word is erroneously pointed ወ ፡ ኵሎ. The other manuscripts present the following variant readings: b] om 11 / ዘአዘዞሙ "which he commanded them" (masc.) 32 / ዘአዘዞን "which he commanded them" (fem.) 31 35 / ዘአዘዘ "which he commanded" 39 / በከመ ፡ አዘዘ "as he commanded" 42 / አዘዘ pr ዘ sec. man. 38 c] om ለ 32 d] om ወ "and" 7 / ወለእሊዓሁ 31 38 46 53 57 61 65 (add ለእለ ፡ ምስሌሁ "who were with him" 38) / ወለእሊአሁሰ 18 ef] om 65 e] pr ወ "and" 7 38 53 / ፈጸሞን (fem.) 31 57 / om ሙ 14 34 / ወፈጸሞም 53 g] om ዝ 39 41 56 / ወእምዝ 20 47 57 (om ወ 48) / ወእምዝ ፡ እምድኅረዝ 34 / ወእምዝ ፡ ድኅረ 46 hi] አስተርአዮሙ 19 32 42 46 47 48 57 62 65 (om ሙ 61) j] pr እግዚእ "the Lord" 9 10 12 17 18 19 20 29 31 32 33 34 35 37 38 (sec. man.) 39 41 42 43 44 45 48 49 50 51 52 53 56 57 62 63 64 65 / pr እግዚእነ "our Lord" 46 47 / add ክርስቶስ "Christ" 12 / ለአርዳኢሁ "to his disciples" 46 47 65 k] om ወ 7 9 10 14 17 18 19 22 31 32 33 34 35 37 39 41 42 43 44 45 47 48 49 50 51 52 53 56 63 l] ፀሐይ 23 m] pr ወ "even" 10 12 17 19 22 26 29 34 39 41 44 63 n] ነየረብ 33 (om ነ 61) / ምዕራቢሃ "the going down of it" 46 47 / om 57 / ምኵራብ "sanctuary" (or "synagogue") 30 o] pr ወ 10 19 32 44 45 46 48 56 57 p] add ወይምሀሩ "and to teach" 19 (ወይምሐሩ 17) / add ውስተ ፡ ኵሎ ፡ ፍጥረት "into all creation" 46 q] በወንጌል 32 / om በ "by" 62 r] add ለሕይወት "life" 46 stu] om 57 t] ለሕይወት "life" 65 / ለመድኅኒት 55 / pr ወ "and" 30 46 / add ለሕይወት "life" 32 38 50 (pr ወ "and" 38 50) u] add አሜን "amen" 12 14 18 22 33 38 39 42 50 63 / add አሜን አሜን "amen, amen" 41

TRANSLATION

[a]And all things [b]which he commanded[19] [c]Peter [d]and those who were his, [e]they finished [f]telling, [g]and after this [j]Jesus [h]manifested himself [i]to them; [k]and from the rising [l]of the sun [m]as far as [n]the west [o]he sent them [p]to preach [u]eternal [t]salvation[20] [rq]by the holy Gospel, [s]which is incorruptible.

COMMENTS

The manuscripts that contain the shorter ending in Ethiopic, as also those in Greek[21] and Coptic,[22] present a number of variant readings, some of which deserve comment. The manuscripts that have the greatest number of differences from the basic text are nos. 32, 46, and 57.

The original translator into Ethiopic misunderstood the sense of the opening sentence of the shorter ending, Πάντα δὲ τὰ παρηγγελμένα τοῖς περὶ τὸν Πέτρον συντόμως ἐξήγγειλαν ("And all that had been commanded [them] they reported briefly to Peter and his companions"). Besides missing the meaning of συντόμως, as well as the idiom involved in τοῖς περὶ τὸν Πέτρον, the latter phrase is construed as the object of παρηγγελμένα rather than of ἐξήγγειλαν. Several scribes sought to make amends. Since the masculine form ፈጸሙ ("they finished") is not grammatically congruent with the preceding subject (the women at the tomb, 16:8), in manuscripts 31 and 57 the verb is given in the feminine form.[23] Similarly the suffix "him" attached to the word translated "which he had commanded" is altered in manuscripts 31 and 35 to "them" (feminine).

The shorter reading "Jesus" (attested by all the known Greek, Latin, Coptic, Syriac, and Armenian[24] witnesses) is expanded in about half the Ethiopic manuscripts by prefixing "the Lord," and two manuscripts (nos. 46 and 47) further append the possessive pronoun, so as to read "our Lord Jesus." One manuscript (no. 12) reads "the Lord Jesus Christ." Instead of "manifested himself to them," manuscripts 46, 47, and 65 read "manifested himself to his disciples." After "he sent them to preach," two manuscripts add "and to teach" (nos. 17 and 19).

In view of the tradition that during the second half of the fifth century Christianity was introduced into Ethiopia by the "Nine Saints," who seem to have been Syrian monks, it is appropriate to raise the question whether the Ethiopic version of the shorter ending was translated from Greek or Syriac. In favor of a Syriac original is the agreement of the two versions in misconstruing the sense of the opening sentence in Greek (though the Syriac correctly uses the feminine form for the final verb): ܚܠܦ ܕܝ ܗܢ ܐܝܠܝܢ ܕܐܬܦܩܕ ܠܗܢܘܢ ܕܥܡ ܦܛܪܘܣ܃ ܒܠܝܠܐܝܬ ܐܘܕܥ ("And all that had been commanded to those who were with Peter they [fem.] reported

briefly"). Furthermore, it can be argued that the use of the preposition ⲛ in the Ethiopic ("he sent them to preach *by* the holy Gospel")
somehow reflects the preposition ⲋ in the Syriac, ܐܘܫܕ ܝܚܫ
ܪܟܘܣܢ ܪܟܐܘܐܝܢ ("he sent through them [lit. by their hands[25]]
the holy proclamation").

On the other hand, it is altogether possible that each version
independently misconstrued the opening sentence of the Greek text,
and the presence of the same preposition in both, though curious,
is without much weight, since its employment differs in the two
versions. More important is the circumstance that the Syriac as
given by White[26] has nothing that corresponds to the clause in the
Ethiopic rendered "manifested himself to them," an expression
that clearly reflects one form of the Greek text — for after Ἰησοῦς
the seventh-century uncial manuscript 099 adds ἐφάνη αὐτοῖς
and Ψ reads ἐφάνη. It appears, therefore that the Ethiopic version
of the shorter ending rests upon a Greek *Vorlage*.[27]

In conclusion it will be appropriate to draw together several data
that have emerged from the preceding discussion of the manuscripts
which have been studied.

1. In eighteen of the sixty-five Ethiopic manuscripts that were
examined the text of Mark 16:9-20 follows directly after verse 8
(nos. 1, 2, 3, 4, 5, 8, 15, 16, 21, 24, 25, 27, 28, 36, 40, 54, 59, and 60).
These manuscripts range in age from the three oldest known copies
(nos. 3, 4, and 5) to two copies transcribed in the nineteenth century (nos. 28 and 59).[28]

2. All of the remaining forty-seven manuscripts contain the
shorter ending, which stands immediately following 16:8 and preceding verses 9-20. In nine of these manuscripts (nos. 12, 14, 18,
22, 33, 39, 42, 50, and 63) the word "amen" occurs between the
shorter and the longer endings ("amen, amen" in ms. 41). Three
manuscripts leave part of a line vacant after the shorter ending and
before verse 9 (nos. 13, 56, and 64), and one (no. 64, the highly
decorated copy in the Pierpont Morgan Library) has a line of deco-
ration between the two endings.

3. Despite statements in various *apparatus critici* to the contrary,
no Ethiopic manuscript is known that ends the Gospel of Mark
with the concluding words of 16:8,[29] or that ends the Gospel with
the shorter ending.

NOTES

[1] Unfortunately Platt preserved only the most desultory account of the several manuscripts which he had consulted. For a list of the manuscripts, with several more or less inconclusive guesses as to their identity, see Samuel Prideaux Tregelles in vol. 4 of Thomas H. Horne's *An Introduction to the Critical Study and Knowledge of the Holy Scriptures*, 13th ed. (London: Longmans, Green & Co., 1872), p. 318, note 2. Tregelles states that for the Gospel of Mark Platt made use of two Ethiopic manuscripts; was one of the two no. 51 in the list below (the manuscript was formerly designated "A")?

[2] "Notes on Select Readings," in Westcott and Hort, *The New Testament in the Original Greek* [vol. 2], *Introduction [and] Appendix* (London: Macmillan Co., 1881; 2d ed. 1896), p. 38. The Dr. Wright referred to must be William Wright, the scholar who prepared the *Catalogue of the Ethiopic Manuscripts in the British Museum, Acquired Since the Year 1847* (London, 1877). The catalogue, however, makes no reference in any of the descriptions of Ethiopic manuscripts to the sequence of the endings of Mark's Gospel.

[3] *Appendices ad Novum Testamentum Stephanicum* . . . (Oxford, 1889), p. 195; cf. p. 182, note 1.

[4] Clarence R. Williams, *The Appendices to the Gospel According to Mark; A Study in Textual Transmission* (= *Transactions of the Connecticut Academy of Arts and Sciences*, vol. 18 [New Haven: Yale University Press, 1915]), pp. 396 f.

[5] E.g., H. B. Swete, *The Gospel According to St. Mark*, 3rd ed. (London: Macmillan, 1909), p. cvii, note 3, and Williams, *op. cit.*, p. 397.

[6] The numbers "1," "2," and "3" identifying the three manuscripts from Abba Garima (nos. 3, 4, and 5 in the list) were assigned by Davies.

[7] Laing's date, as George F. Black points out, is doubtless too early ("Ethiopica and Amharica," *Bulletin of the New York Public Library*, 32 [1928], p. 458).

[8] For other examples of illuminated Ethiopic manuscripts, see Otto A. Jäger and Liselotte Deininger-Englhart, "Some Notes on Illuminations of Manuscripts in Ethiopia," *Rassegna di studi etiopici*, 17 (1961), pp. 45-60. See also the article mentioned in note 17 below.

[9] "An Illuminated Gospel Book in Ethiopic," in *Studies in Art and Literature for Belle da Costa Greene*, ed. Dorothy Miner (Princeton: Princeton University Press, 1954), pp. 350-357; the quotation is from p. 350. The text of most of the colophon is printed by Grébaut in *Journal asiatique*, 213 (1928), pp. 141-146. One of the most striking illuminations is the full-page miniature (fol. 14ʳ) which depicts the scene of the crucifixion but without the body of Christ on the cross. According to Cerulli the absence of the human figure of Christ may reflect the contemporary Ethiopian Gnostic heresy of the so-called Mikaelites (see *New Catholic Encyclopedia*, 5 [New York, 1967], p. 591, with fig.). For another miniature in the manuscript, see P. A. Underwood, "The Fountain of Life in Manuscripts of the Gospels," *Dumbarton Oaks Papers*, no. 5 (Cambridge, Massachusetts, 1950), pp. 104, 109, 117, and fig. 54.

[10] So Sylvain Grébaut and Eugene Tisserant, *Codices Aethiopici Vaticani et Borgiani*, 1 (in Bybliotheca Vaticana, 1935), p. 127.

[11] For an interesting account of early printers of Ethiopic, see Hendrik F. Wijnman, *An Outline of the Development of Ethiopic Typography in Europe* (Leiden: Brill, 1960) (reprinted from *Books on the Orient*). Wijnman indicates that he expects to publish a more detailed description of Ethiopic typography in Europe during the sixteenth century in paper no. 15 of *Publications de l'Institut historique et archéologique néerlandais de Stamboul*.

[12] For a discussion of two letters (written in Ethiopic) preserved in the

Biblioteca communale of Siena, one written by Petrus concerning his edition of the Ethiopic New Testament and the other a reply by a certain priest Giovanni to Petrus, see Ignazio Guidi, "La prima stampa del Nuovo Testamento in etiopico, fatta in Roma nel 1548–1549," *Archivo della R. Società Romana di Storia Patria*, 9 (1886), pp. 273-278.

[13] The tomb of Petrus, who died August 28, 1550, in his 42nd year, is in the Church of S. Stefano de' Mori in Rome (so Job Ludolf, *Historia Æthiopica* [Frankfurt a. M., 1691], Bk. III, ch. VII, § 26).

[14] Quoted in Ethiopic and Latin by Ludolf, *op. cit.*, p. 245; the quaint English translation of Ludolf's work is by J. P. Gent, *A New History of Ethiopia* (London, 1682), p. 263. For other information concerning Petrus and his edition, see Ludolf, *ad suam Historiam . . . Commentarius* (Frankfurt a. M., 1691), Bk. III, ch. IV; James Townley, *Illustrations of Biblical Literature*, 1 (London, 1821), p. 148, and 3, pp. 60 f.; and George F. Black, *op. cit.*, pp. 534 f.

[15] H. Zotenberg in *Catalogue des manuscrits éthiopiens (gheez et amharique) de la Bibliothèque nationale* (Paris, 1877), p. 29, and Sylvain Grébaut, "L'Age du ms. Éth. n° 32 de Paris (Bibliothèque nationale)," *Æthiops: Bulletin Geʿez*, 4 (1931), pp. 9-11.

It is notoriously difficult to date Ethiopic manuscripts on paleographical grounds; cf. Eduard König, *Neue Stüdien über Schrift, Aussprache und allgemeine Formenlehre des Aethiopischen, aus den Quellen geschöpft, comparativ und physiologisch erläütert* (Leipzig, 1877); Adolf Grohmann, "Über den Ursprung und die Entwicklung der äthiopischen Schrift," *Archiv für Schriftkunde*, 1 (Leipzig, 1918), pp. 57-87; H. Grimme, "Die südsemitische Schrift. Ihr Wesen und ihre Entwicklung," *Buch und Schrift. Jahrbuch des deutschen Vereins für Buchwesen und Schriftum*, 4 (1930), pp. 19-27; and "De Aethiopum scriptura," by S. Grébaut and E. Tisserant, *op. cit.*, pp. 33-35. For other literature on the Ethiopic alphabet and paleography, see Wolf Leslau, *Bibliography of the Semitic Languages of Ethiopia* (New York: New York Public Library, 1946), pp. 18-21 (reprinted, with additions and corrections, from the *Bulletin of the New York Public Library*, vol. 49 [1945]).

[16] Exactly the same text of the shorter ending is presented also in two other manuscripts (nos. 9 and 13), and, with one orthographic variant, in no. 55, all of the fifteenth century.

[17] Leroy dates the manuscript in the tenth to eleventh century; see his article, "L'Évangéliaire éthiopien du couvent d'Abba Garima et ses attaches avec l'ancien art chrétien de Syrie," *Cahiers archéologiques*, 11 (1960), pp. 131-143, especially p. 143, note.

[18] In the apparatus a square bracket preceded by a superscript roman letter and followed by an Ethiopic word signifies that that word replaces the Ethiopic word marked by the same roman letter in the text; add = add to the text the following Ethiopic word; om = omit from the text the following Ethiopic word (or letter); pr = place the following Ethiopic word (or letter) before the word in the text designated by the same roman letter; sec. man. = second hand.

[19] Literally "commanded him" (i.e., Peter).

[20] It is also possible to translate "salvation which is eternal."

[21] For an apparatus of the variant readings in the Greek witnesses that contain the shorter ending (namely L Ψ 099 0112 274^{mg} 579 and l^{1602}), see p.162 of Kurt Aland's "Bemerkungen zum Schluss des Markusevangeliums," in *Neotestamentica et Semitica; Studies in Honour of Matthew Black*, ed. E. Earle Ellis and Max Wilcox (Edinburgh: T. & T. Clark, 1969). Aland also gives the text of the one Latin witness (it^k) to the shorter ending (in this manuscript the Gospel ends with the shorter ending and omits vv. 9-20).

[22] For the Coptic evidence see P. E. Kahle, "The End of St. Mark's Gospel. The Witness of the Coptic Versions," *JTS*, n.s. 2 (1951), pp. 49-57.

[23] According to information provided by Father Yohannes, the official text of the shorter ending in use in the Ethiopian Orthodox Church today reads the feminine form of the verb "they finished." The remainder of the passage runs as follows: "Our Lord manifested himself to them after he had risen from the dead. And he sent them to preach, from the east as far as the west, to all creation by the holy Gospel which is incorruptible for the salvation of all the world."

[24] The Armenian tetraevangelium Etchmiadzin 303 (xii–xiii cent.) has the text of the shorter ending of Mark immediately after Luke 24:53 (for the text see Stanislas Lyonnet in M.-J. Lagrange, *Critique textuelle*; II, *La Critique rationnelle* [Paris, 1935], p. 372, and for a discussion see E. C. Colwell, "Mark 16 9-22 in the Armenian Version," *JBL*, 56 [1937], pp. 369-386, especially 379 f.).

[25] The Armenian shows the influence of the Syriac by reading *i jers noca* ("in their hands").

[26] It should be observed, however, that the Harclean Syriac text of Mark in Joseph White's edition (Oxford, 1778) is very narrowly based, being represented by only one manuscript. In order to broaden somewhat the Syriac attestation, and thereby perhaps to discover additional variant readings, the present writer collated the printed text with two other Harclean witnesses, British Museum Add. 14456 (which is a manuscript of the Peshitta version with Harclean marginalia) and University of Cambridge Add. 1903 (which is a transcript made by H. Petermann of a Harclean tetraevangelium at Damascus), but no significant variation was disclosed. As is well known, not all Harclean manuscripts contain the marginal apparatus, in which the shorter ending occurs. Unfortunately the Harclean manuscript of Matthew and Mark in the Houghton Library at Harvard University (Syriac MS. 16) breaks off at Mark 10:36.

[27] The statement made above is not intended to prejudge the moot question how far the Ethiopic version as a whole discloses traces of a Syriac *Vorlage*. Among modern discussions of what can be said in support of such a view, see Arthur Vööbus, *Die Spuren eines älteren äthiopischen Evangelientextes im Lichte der literarischen Monumente* (Stockholm, 1951), and *Early Versions of the New Testament; Manuscript Studies* (Stockholm, 1954), pp. 249-265; for what can be said against it, see B. Botte, "Orientales de la Bible (Versions); Versions éthiopiennes," *DBS*, 6 (Paris, 1960), cols. 828 f., and H. J. Polotsky, "Aramaic, Syriac, and Gə'əz," *Journal of Semitic Studies*, 9 (1964), pp. 1-10.

[28] One other Ethiopic manuscript (Vat. Eth. MS. 1) is known in which vv. 9-20 follow immediately upon Mark 16:8, but since it was copied from the printed edition published at Rome in 1548–1549 (see Grébaut and Tisserant, *op. cit.*, p. 1), it has been disregarded in the present study.

[29] According to Cerulli's catalogue of the Ethiopic manuscripts in the Chester Beatty collection, in manuscript 912 (no. 58 above) the Gospel of Mark ends at 16:8. In this manuscript, however, the last page of text (fol. 29ᵛ) ends with the word **ወኢሰሙኑሂ** and nothing follows to represent ἐφοβοῦντο γάρ, the concluding words of Mark 16:8. The recto of each of the next two folios contains a full-page miniature, the verso being blank. Since the last word in the Ethiopic text is followed by ፣ and not by ።, which the scribe uses to indicate the close of a sentence, it is certain that the manuscript in its present state is fragmentary and that originally it continued with additional textual material.

The Quest
for the
Historical Baptist

by John Reumann

John the Baptist, in fact and fiction — *wie er eigentlich gewesen war* and in Christian transformation — has long been a subject of interest to the honoree of this volume. In *Christian Beginnings* Professor Enslin outlined a position on the Baptizer which he further developed in an article in 1958 and reiterated in his life of Jesus.[1] Characteristically, his position clashes with the easy consensus holding sway over these years. Yet at many points, when the quest for the historical Baptist as a whole is carefully assessed, this position is in tune with emerging conclusions today, and strikingly ahead of its time, as independent research often is.

An "enigmatic John the Baptist"[2] is what Professor Enslin found, an independent preacher whose historical contours are scarcely discernible from our sources — Josephus is "solid . . . reporting"[3]; the Gospels, however, are tendentious; the Dead Sea scrolls, applications from which suggest "a pyramid balanced upon its apex,"[4] have been handled more with zeal than caution. It was not that John molded Jesus as a disciple. Rather Christian tradition enrolled the Baptist as a forerunner of Jesus, forged connections between the two mothers, and built up, in ever increasing detail, the story of how John had baptized Jesus — all this in order (1) to get rid of an embarrassing rival ("if you can't beat 'im, have him join you") and (2) "to fulfill the prophecy of Malachi [3:1=Mark 1:2] and thus silence Jewish criticism that the Christian claim that the 'great and terrible day of the Lord' was at hand was impossible since the divinely appointed precursor had not arrived."[5] What Jesus historically had said about a greater successor to come — the Son of man, an Elijah figure — the early church put on John's lips, to point to Jesus. But John and Jesus probably never met. If one had asked the Baptist about the man from Nazareth, he might well have replied, "Jesus . . . who?"

The soundness of much in this position — which insists that our New Testament sources, "regardless of their value for an understanding of later Christianity . . ., throw far less light than has often been imagined upon the one popularly supposed to have designated and quickened his greater successor" [6]—will be appreciated only as it is viewed in the long haul of *Täufer-Forschung* and amid the conflicting views of several recent "lives" of John.

I. LEBEN-JOHANNES RESEARCH

"Life-of-John study" lacks a chronicler like Albert Schweitzer or the many recent surveys of *Leben Jesu* books.[7] But the quest for the historical Jesus, with its distinct, though overlapping, stages of *(a)* Old Quest, *(b)* the Bultmannian "no biography" view, and *(c)* the New Quest (with its subsequent fragmentation), should provide a parallel outline. Thus study of the Baptist has been judged by Walter Wink "an adjunct to the quest for the historical Jesus," and has had, he concludes, "a far more successful issue than the quest for the historical Jesus." [8] The history of Pauline studies might also suggest some analogies to the progression in Baptist research: F. C. Baur and the Tübingen School, with the reactions it provoked; the *Religionsgeschichtliche Schule,* and then the eschatological approach to Paul, around 1900; the "main line" Liberal interpretation; the Barthian, theological, reversal; Bultmann's existentialism; the current, dominant, historical approach, varying in its degree of critical rigor; the "Anti-Tübingen" school of Heilsgeschichte; and all the old "schools" and attitudes revived under new labels.[9]

My own reading of the evidence, however, does not find that research into the life of John the Baptist has followed fully either the trends of Pauline studies or, surprisingly, the Jesus-quest. Space here permits only a few highlights from studies on the life of John, and some possible conclusions — yet enough, it is hoped, to suggest that the "broad consensus" and "substantial progress" assumed about the historical Baptist may be something of a chimera.

Hermann Samuel Reimarus, the man who raised the problem of the historical Jesus in his *Wolfenbüttel Fragments,* posthumously published by Lessing in 1774-1778, also initiated new notions about John the Baptist, when he portrayed him as a political revolutionary. David Friedrich Strauss's *Leben Jesu* (1835-1836) rejected that notion, as Strauss sought to strip off the legendary accretions from the early church and ascertain what was historical. He concluded that Jesus had been baptized by John but later outgrew his mentor, though ever honoring him; apologetic intent, to convert the Baptist's followers, colors many of the legends which arose, like Matthew 11:2-6 par. Luke 7:18-23 ("Are you he who is to come . . .?").

Other nineteenth-century "lives" deal with the Baptist in the shadow of Jesus, as we might expect. Theodor Keim, in his *Geschichte Jesu* (1867–1872), typical of the liberals who preserved historicity and psychologized what they had reconstructed, stressed the Old Testament parallels to preserve the factualness of Matthew 11:2-6 and of the baptism itself. Edersheim's *Life and Times of Jesus the Messiah* (1883) more conservatively harmonized accounts and drew on rabbinic backgrounds. Romantic speculations marked Ernst Renan's *Vie de Jésus* (1863) — with John's group we "imagine ourselves transported to the banks of the Ganges," perhaps influenced by "wandering Buddhist monks"; John and Jesus are "two young enthusiasts," in mental development John "the brother rather than the father of Jesus."[10]

Similarity to trends in *Leben-Jesu* research also appears in the twentieth century, and to schools likewise found in Pauline studies. Thus, the history-of-religions school worked its influence, at times seeking to depict John's baptism as akin to the mystery cults, but more commonly setting it within a general baptizing movement of the period (J. Thomas, *Le mouvement baptiste,* 1935) or more specifically suggesting Persian connections (Carl Kraeling, 1951). The eschatological approach of Albert Schweitzer treated the Baptist, like Jesus, in light of apocalyptic expectation — in this case, Jesus' messianic consciousness. Because he thought himself Messiah, Jesus invented the notion that John was to play Elijah to him. This "Elijanic secret" led Jesus to apply the Elijah title to John, though only cryptically, as in the language of Matthew 11:2-6.[11]

There were those who argued that John the Baptist, like Jesus, never lived (Arthur Drews). Form criticism made its entrance into Baptist studies, in a way before it came to be applied to Jesus' life. Martin Dibelius's monograph of 1911 concentrated on the sayings materials and laid a groundwork developed by Kraeling.[12] We have had a cultically-determined treatment of John by Ernst Lohmeyer in which the Baptist is understood in light of his rejection of the Jerusalem temple and its worship.[13] Reimarus's picture of a revolutionist was revived with a vengeance by Robert Eisler (John as the "chaplain to the underground"), a view found more recently in *The Interpreter's Dictionary of the Bible*.[14] Qumran has given us, if not John the Baptist as "a sort of semi-Tarzan," "living with nature in the raw," [15] at least a desert ascetic and mystic.[16] Bornkamm is to be credited with dealing with John, in accordance with the New Quest, in a kerygmatic way.[17] The Baptist's significance for Heilsgeschichte is what emerges in Walter Wink's significant *redaktionsgeschichtlich* investigation.[18] All this list says nothing of the host of pious popularizations which keep appearing, belated monographs from scholars of another generation,[19] Jewish treatments,[20] and artful reconstructions which embrace several of these trends.

As an example of the last, I cite Maurice Goguel's *Jean-Baptiste* (1928), "On the Threshold of the Gospel," a prelude to his life of Jesus (1932).[21] Goguel employed both literary and form criticism, but his concern was to reconstruct history, yet not ignoring eschatology. He stressed connections between Jesus and John, but also a break, specifically a dispute over the question of conditions for salvation — John demanded works of repentance, Jesus stressed free forgiveness. All this Goguel recovered behind an emended text at John 3:25, plus the conclusion that after the break John saw Jesus as a renegade!

It would seem, therefore, as we survey the "lives" of John that we have a number of options on the historical Baptist:
1. the traditional portrait, combining, with greater or less rigor, the biblical references and using extra-biblical data occasionally (e.g., C. H. H. Scobie);[22]
2. the "sectarian" Baptist, developed on the basis of supposed "Baptist sources" in or outside the New Testament — e.g., Mandean finds;[23]
3. John the Essene (cf. the many reconstructions utilizing Qumran documents);

4. John the ascetic (Steinmann's "desert tradition") ;
5. John the Zealot (Eisler, W. R. Farmer) ;
6. the evangelists' creation (s) *(Redaktionsgeschichte);*
7. the Old Quest continued (the lure of Jewish sources — e.g., E. Bammel).[24]

Though one might wish to agree that "research has culminated in a rather broad consensus among scholars today on the main issues of the life of John the Baptist" and that problematical points "have been brought to within the range of but a few possibilities," [25] I should regard it as more prudent to conclude that:

1. There has been and is a quest — old, new, and mixed — for the historical Baptist;

2. Surprisingly, the Bultmannian "no biography" view does not much appear, as Wink has noted: ". . . ironically, while the quest for the historical Jesus had its messengers of defeat, the quest for the historical John had none." [26]

3. Scholars sometimes think they can be sure on John when they know they were not on Jesus (e.g., Goguel!) ; yet,

4. All the hazards of the quest for the historical Jesus exist in the search for the history of John, and then some: conflicting sources, canonical and beyond; tendentiousness in sources; the unsettling role of form and redaction criticism; problems of *religionsgeschichtlich* background; the theology of the early Christian church; *plus the fact that,* if we take seriously the possibility of the Baptist provenance for some of the materials (as many scholars named above do), what we have in the New Testament is *separated* from historical actuality *both by Christian usage and by (earlier) Baptist use.* It is as if we were trying to recover the historical Jesus from traditions filtered through a second, later disciple community of another faith, say Islam (save that the separation in time from the event is shorter). If in the Gospels, to use R. H. Lightfoot's oft misunderstood phrase, we hear, in the case of Jesus "little more than a whisper of his voice," [27] then in the case of the Baptist we have only an echo (or echoes) of his whisper. In short, there is more diversity in modern studies about the Baptist than assumed, more optimism than warranted about recovering knowledge of him historically, and more reason to suspect we cannot throw real light on him than even in the case of Jesus.

II. CARL KRAELING AND JOHN ROBINSON

For further assessment here I choose portraits of John by Carl Kraeling and, in a series of articles, by John A. T. Robinson,[28] both to be considered in light of *Redaktionsgeschichte* as injected into the quest for the Baptist by Walter Wink. Kraeling's book has been adjudged by Wink to be "the finest monograph on John the Baptist which has yet appeared," the "finest fruit" of the quest.[29] Robinson's sometimes historicizing reconstruction can be said to be one of the most stimulating of the examinations since the Qumran finds, and typical in several ways of current trends reflected in more popular presentations. In addition, at certain points these two treatments stand in sharp contrast, and both of them need to be reexamined in light of the new element which Wink stresses, of inquiring precisely what each source (like Q) or each evangelist has made of John the Baptist.[30]

Kraeling wrote too early to make much use of the Dead Sea scrolls. The book stands much as delivered in lecture form in 1946. A comment inserted into the Foreword (p. x) suggests the scrolls promise "to enrich our knowledge of the background against which John's life and work developed" but do not "change or effect radically the picture." Some twelve years later Professor Kraeling wrote me that if he were contemplating a new edition or writing afresh, he "would indeed wish to revise . . . in light of the Qumran evidence."[31] Perhaps his reassessments would have come particularly in seeking *religionsgeschichtlich* influences closer at hand, in Palestine, at Qumran, than more remotely in Iran and the Mandeans. Robinson, on the other hand, writing in 1957, was able to assume a widely accepted hypothesis of "an actual historical connexion between John the Baptist and the Qumran Community"[32] and undertook to test this theory by seeing how far it could be pushed. Thus, "John the Baptist by John the Bishop," as any full-scale monograph resulting from his investigations might be called, would result in a portrait which takes the New Testament statements as reputable (until evidence arises to the contrary) and reckons with Qumran as a real influence at points. Yet one does well always to recall the extensive debate over similarities and differences between Qumran and John.[33]

As Robinson pictures him, John the Baptist was born of aging parents in a priestly family in the hill country of Judea. It is as an ascetic prophet with a baptism of repentance, however, that John appears in the Jordan valley. How can we explain this change? Kraeling had suggested that John went up to Jerusalem to follow in his father's footsteps and seek priestly ordination, but that "what he saw . . . at Jerusalem" [34] in a secularized priesthood so disgusted him, compared with the piety amid which he had grown up, that he turned his back on priesthood and withdrew to the desert. Robinson and others suggest, on the other hand, in light of the scrolls, that John was reared at Qumran; hence Luke 1:80, "he was in the wilderness to the day of his manifestation to Israel." But John, when he does emerge into history, has broken with Qumran. The reason for the break, Robinson feels, was over eschatology: the Baptist believed the eschatological moment nearer than even the Qumran people did. "Now the ax is laid to the root of the trees" (Matt. 3:10, par. Luke 3:9) ; and so he went forth to summon men to a baptism of repentance.

In this period baptism was "in the air." John derived his practice, however, neither from proselyte baptism nor Jewish ablutions, Robinson thinks, but from Qumran, though John also adapted it. Qumran's initial baptism, whereby "to enter into water" [1 QS 5. 13] means to "enter into the covenant" and the community [5. 8], was given new emphasis by John, he says, as a decisive break from one's past, but both Qumran and John stress need for prior repentance and envision a further baptism still to come. We may contrast Kraeling's view, stressing Mandean rites and the "river of fire" in Persian eschatology, though allowing a strong element of originality with John.[35]

John's movement, according to Robinson, may have been called "the way of righteousness" (Matt. 21:32). Against the background of Qumran, one may speculate that this movement, like Qumran, aimed at making atonement for the sins of Israel. Thus, Jesus would have associated himself with John's baptism to identify himself, not so much with transgressors, as with a redemptive group. And if Qumran spoke of expiating iniquity "through the anguish of the refining furnace," then it would be natural for Jesus to speak of his baptism of suffering.[36] If Qumran expected this Suffering Servant ideal to be embodied in an individual, then John the Baptist, Robinson goes on, could have spoken John 1:33f., pointing to an individual after him baptized with the Spirit, not knowing precisely who or what was to come, but only that his baptism was to force the eschatological issue, to set the last things in motion by his water-baptism of some individual, the coming one, who would purge sin and baptize with the Spirit.

John's limited knowledge of things further emerges, according to Robinson, in connection with the "Elijah title." According to the Synoptics (Mark 9:11ff., par. Matt. 17:9-13; Matt. 11:14), Jesus called John "Elijah." According to the Fourth Gospel, the Baptist denied he was Elijah (1:21). However, the Fourth Gospel, Robinson insists, is not to be set aside here because of alleged anti-Baptist polemic. For even in the Synoptics the Baptist never claims to be Elijah, and the only person popular opinion was identifying as Elijah was Jesus, not John (Mark 6: 15; 8:28).

As Robinson reconstructs it, the Fourth Gospel (and here he differs from many exegetes) is quite correct in summarizing John's view. The Baptist thought that he himself was merely a voice, Jesus was Elijah (as common opinion held), and after Jesus-Elijah would come God himself. But Jesus reworked this view of the Baptist. Matthew 11:14 is said to be a carefully laid clue: "If you are willing to accept it, he [John] is Elijah," Jesus says; "he who has ears to hear, let him hear." The solemn form of this statement, plus the words "if you are willing to accept this," alert us that Jesus was saying something new, something that John himself never suspected. "Are you the Coming One?" John had asked, the Mighty Judge who baptizes with fire, are you Elijah? No, Jesus says, I am not, but you, John, are Elijah, who is to come — "if you are willing to accept it." [37] Jesus is here revealing a "Baptist secret" or an "Elijah secret," which even John himself had not grasped. And in equating John with Elijah and with the messenger of Malachi 3:1 and 4:5, Jesus is making for himself a staggering claim, for the sequel to Elijah *redivivus* in Malachi is not Messiah — Jesus probably never did use that term — but the *yom Yahweh;* Jesus connects his coming with the Day of the Lord and all that means. Thus Jesus' identification of the Baptist as Elijah was something radically new. We misread, first, because we know the outcome (Jesus = Christ, therefore John = Elijah) and, second, because Mark 1:2 prematurely gives the answer away in a gloss to that theological prologue — some "spoil-sport," as Robinson calls him, long ago interpolated Malachi 3:1 into the Isaiah quotation which Mark originally wrote.

Jesus, Robinson holds, had once been a disciple of John and worked with him for a while. There was thus a Judean ministry (cf. Goguel), which only the Fourth Gospel relates (3:22-30). Here the temple cleansing fits, precisely the thing in an Elijah program; cf. Malachi 3, where the messenger prepares the way by purifying the temple. Jesus' question to the priests and scribes about the origin of John's baptism (Mark 11:27-33) also fits better at this time, not a year or more later.[38]

This parallel ministry went on till John was arrested.[39] Then Jesus, perhaps because of too much success in Judea, went to Galilee, hailed as Elijah. But in his own thinking a change had taken place. On a decisive journey from Judea to Galilee, perhaps following the temptation struggle, Jesus decided to model himself on Servant lines, not as the "Mighty One" of John. Hence a new Galilean gospel, with which the Synoptics begin, a ministry to suffer and save, rather than to judge. And so to John's amazed emissaries came the answer, "Not I, but John is Elijah, if you will receive it; my work is along Isaianic lines, not Malachi's program." [40] But we must not assume rivalry between John's group and Jesus, Robinson cautions, for "the others" into whose labors Jesus' disciples entered at John 4:38 were not the Hellenists of Acts 8 (so Cullmann), but Baptist followers who prepared the way for Jesus.

Robinson — in thus positing (1) good historical traditions about the Baptist in the Gospels, including John's Gospel, often read at face value; (2) an early ministry of Jesus, beginning under the Baptist, in Judea; (3) Qumran connections for John, but also a break with the sect; and (4) an Elijah-secret, fashioned by Jesus — is, of course, in good company with other exegetes at each point, e.g., on (2), cf. Goguel; on (4), cf. Schweitzer. He is more independent on (1) supposed "Baptist sources" like the Benedictus (Luke 1:68-79), which Kraeling thought was a *Baptist* hymn in honor of *John* and Robinson sees as a *Christian* hymn in honor of *Jesus* now placed by Luke on the lips of Zacharias;[41] and (2) the supposed "John-the-Baptist movement" (Acts 19:1-7, the Mandeans, and all that) which Robinson tries to scotch.[42]

Kraeling agrees at times, differs at others. He assumes the existence of a "Baptist Infancy Narrative." The legendary account of John's death in Mark 6, in that it reports the Baptist's denunciation of Antipas (6:18) for divorcing his Nabatean wife to marry Herodias, "provides the one detail necessary to make Josephus' account . . . intelligible," by explaining how John's moral judgment served to align pious Jews with Nabateans and thus threatened a rebellion (*Antiquities* 18.5.2) against Herod Antipas.[43] As for the Elijah title, while cognizant of difficulties with some details, Kraeling thought it likely that Jesus, like others, saw a resemblance to Elijah in John and spoke of it, even if Matthew 11:14f. is an esoteric, intuitive saying regarding the relationship of John and Elijah.

With regard to Robinson's portrayal, Kraeling wrote me some five years before his death that he would go along with him on the Benedictus, the Elijah interpretation, and Bishop Robinson's "restraint concerning those chappies at Ephesus and the idea of using all the help I could get from Qumran in the matter of the use of baptism," but he cautioned on Robinson's use of the Fourth Gospel.[44] As for baptism, he added that "prophets are not terribly impressed by things 'in the air,' " and while Qumran may help, he would look for something more than its rite to explain John.

Professor Kraeling was thus rather generously inclined to go along with some of Bishop Robinson's hypotheses. My own inclination is to share his interest in these proposals — hence the space allotted to them here — but to question the way Qumran is sometimes much used and other times played down, and the harmonization which is made from the Gospels by stressing some verses and soft-pedaling others. Source and form criticism seem not taken with full seriousness always; there seems an easy tendency to psychologize about how John or Jesus thought, and judgments on some details seem to me unlikely, e.g., Luke 1:80 (John's youth in the wilderness, hence he was adopted by Essenes),[45] Matthew 21:32 ("the way of righteousness"),[46] and Matthew 11:14 ("if you are willing to accept it . . ."). What catches the eye particularly is that in example after example key verses such as those just cited, on which Robinson pegs his case, are labeled "redactional" by recent critics, i.e., editorial additions by the evangelist, not from any earlier source.

III. *REDAKTIONSGESCHICHTE* AND BEYOND

Precisely this element of "editorial history" or the contribution of the redactor-evangelist, a phase of Gospels-study which has emerged in the last decade and a half and which is missing in John-the-Baptist-research down through Scobie's book in 1964,[47] is the strength of Walter Wink's investigation. As is well known, Wink concentrated on what each strata of the gospel-witness says about John the Baptist. In Q he finds a twofold view of him: on the one hand, John is, in Jesus' estimate, an eschatological sign that the kingdom of God is at hand (Luke 16:16); side by side with this, his role is limited and circumscribed, he is outside the kingdom (Matt. 11:2-6, 11b). Mark presents the Baptist as Elijah who suffers, a parallel to Jesus who also suffers, according to God's plan, an inspiration to persecuted Christians. Matthew heightens features from both Q and Mark: the Baptist *is* the promised Elijah ("if you can receive it"), a "Christian martyr" who, like Jesus and the succession of prophets, meets his fate at the hands of the enemies of God; he stands *in* the kingdom (cf. 11:12f. with Luke 16:16), preaching the same kerygma as Jesus (cf. 3:2 with 4:17), yet is distinguished from the Messiah. Luke's Gospel proper (chaps. 3–24) fits the Baptist into a scheme of salvation history, inaugurating a new period as an itinerant evangelist and teacher, but *not* as Elijah. Luke 1–2 depicts him in symmetrical tandem with Jesus. The Fourth Gospel completes the "Christianization" of John: he is the ideal witness to Christ.

In all these strata, Wink notes, John the Baptist is "the beginning of the gospel," and then, taking a leap from theology to history, he concludes that this exercise in *Redaktionsgeschichte* has a *Leben Jesu* significance: the kerygma's stock phrase, "beginning from Galilee after the baptism which John preached" (Acts 10:37), is "theological expression of a historical fact, that through John's mediation Jesus perceived the nearness of the kingdom and his own relation to its coming." [48] It is, of course, precisely this which has not been, and perhaps cannot be, demonstrated *historically*, though the conclusion arises, not unnaturally, from the way Wink asks his question, in his assumption that the "proper historical significance" of John "can best be discovered by asking . . . what is the role of John the Baptist in

God's redemptive purpose?" [49] That is a question, I submit, which was asked again and again by *faith*, where John had been given a place in things by men who called Jesus the Christ or who revered John as, at the least, a martyred teacher-prophet. But it is one step (or two or more) removed from the impact John had on Jesus of Nazareth historically, and how Jesus perceived his relation to the coming kingdom. Was Jesus moved to launch his separate ministry by John's arrest (Robinson; cf. Mark 1:14) or by a doctrinal dispute (Goguel's interpretation from John 3:25) or by Jesus' particular experiences (Kraeling)? Or must we confess our ignorance biographically and psychologically?

My concern here is not whether Wink is right or not in arriving at historical bedrock — though "multiple attestation," in several sources, is one criterion for historicity in the New Quest [50] — but with the almost paralyzing implications which rigorous redaction-criticism has, or should have, when piled on top of source and form analysis, for working back to "the historical" which lies behind our Gospels. Wink has shown clearly what special features each evangelist paints in, as he portrays the Baptist. Perhaps less clearly, from Wink's analysis, we can detect the configurations of John the Baptist in Q, but one finds there already a twofold view, and some of the statements in Q already show the impact of the Christian community. Recovery of the shape of John in oral traditions behind the Q stage is even more problematical. And what if the materials about the Baptist had first passed through the same progression (oral, source, document) in circles of *Baptist* adherents who were not "Jesus men" or became so only later on, or who were Baptist *worshipers* (with a "messianology" about John) or who, at the least, had loyally followed John in his lifetime before being attracted to the man from Nazareth? It is only here and there, I think, that we can, with much confidence, put our finger on a "fact" and label it "history," less often, perhaps, than in the case of Jesus, for the quest of the historical Baptist proceeds in double jeopardy.

But these emphases — that one must proceed by laying out carefully what each evangelist says, with awareness that our Gospels are tendentious and it is often as difficult to go back behind them as it is to combine their accounts, and that the light is often brighter for understanding later Christianity than for ascertaining origins (for where beginnings are obscure, it is hard to plot trajectories of traditions, save by reverse extrapolations from the few check points visible later on) — have all been made, long since, in the case of the "enigmatic John the Baptist," long even before the word *"Redaktionsgeschichte"* was heard in our land.

NOTES

[1] M. S. Enslin, *Christian Beginnings* (New York: Harper & Row, Publishers, 1938), pp. 149-153, 155-157; "Once Again: John the Baptist," *Religion in Life*, 27 (1957–1958), pp. 557-566; copyright © 1958 by Abingdon Press. M. S. Enslin, *The Prophet from Nazareth* (New York: McGraw-Hill Book Company, 1961), pp. 41-44, 66; p. 84, n. 9.

[2] Enslin, *The Prophet from Nazareth*, p. 41.

[3] Enslin, *Religion in Life*, 27 (1957–1958), p. 557; cf. *Christian Beginnings*, pp. 150f.

[4] Enslin, *The Prophet from Nazareth*, p. 41.

[5] Enslin, *Religion in Life*, 27 (1957–1958), p. 558.

[6] *Ibid.*, p. 566; cf. *Christian Beginnings*, p. 153. Space does not permit discussion of the suggested parallel to Mark 6:14-29 in Dio Cassius, *Historiae Romanae* 66.15 (*ibid.*, p. 565), which no commentator seems to have followed up.

[7] The fullest recent account known to me is a section of Walter Wink's dissertation at Union Theological Seminary, 1963, *John the Baptist and the Gospel*, pp. 4-74, where the aim was especially to assess the historical methodology of each author. These pages were omitted for brevity in the printed version referred to below in note 18.

[8] *Ibid.*, pp. 1 and 70.

[9] Cf. B. Rigaux, *The Letters of St. Paul: Modern Studies* (Chicago: Franciscan Herald Press, 1968), pp. 5-31.

[10] E. Renan, *The Life of Jesus* (New York: Modern Library, 1927), pp. 77f., 81.

[11] A. Schweitzer, *The Quest of the Historical Jesus* (New York: Macmillan paperbacks ed., 1961), especially pp. 370-383; *The Mysticism of Paul the Apostle* (New York: Henry Holt & Co., 1931), pp. 162f., 231.

[12] M. Dibelius, *Die urchristliche Überlieferung von Johannes dem Täufer*, (FRLANT, 15; 1911). Carl H. Kraeling, *John the Baptist* (New York: Charles Scribner's Sons, 1951).

[13] E. Lohmeyer, *Das Urchristentum: 1. Buch, Johannes der Täufer* (Göttingen: Vandenhoeck & Ruprecht, 1932); more succinctly and sharply in *Lord of the Temple: A Study of the Relation between Cult and Gospel* (1942; Eng. tr. by Stewart Todd, Edinburgh: Oliver & Boyd, 1961), pp. 92-95.

[14] R. Eisler, *Iēsous Basileus ou Basileusas* (Heidelberg: 1928-1930); *The Messiah Jesus and John the Baptist* (London: 1931); W. R. Farmer, "John the Baptist," *IDB* (1962), vol. 2, pp. 955-962.

[15] The phrases are from W. H. Brownlee, "John the Baptist in the New Light of Ancient Scrolls," *Interpretation*, 9 (1955), p. 71 (-90), revised in *The Scrolls and the New Testament*, ed K. Stendahl (New York: Harper & Row, Publishers, 1957), pp. 33 (-53).

[16] Jean Steinmann, *Saint John the Baptist and the Desert Tradition* (New York: Harper & Row, Publishers, 1958).

[17] Günther Bornkamm, *Jesus of Nazareth* (New York: Harper & Row, Publishers, 1960), pp. 44-52. Walter Wink, diss., p. 68, credits him with being the first to deal with John's real significance in salvation history at the start of the kerygma; contrast Bultmann's location of the "shift in the aeons" as coming only between Jesus and Paul.

[18] Walter Wink, *John the Baptist in the Gospel Tradition* (SNTS Monograph Series, 7; New York: Cambridge University Press, 1968).

[19] Adolf Schlatter, *Johannes der Täufer*, ed. W. Michaelis (Basel: Fr. Reinhardt Verlag, 1956); this was his dissertation for the Lic. theol., written in a few weeks, while Schlatter was a gymnasium teacher. Roland Schütz, *Johannes der Täufer* (AbThANT, 50; 1967); Schütz was removed from his chair at Kiel by the Nazis in 1934 and retired in 1946; the monograph was completed in the early sixties.

[20] E.g., David Flusser, *Jesus* (New York: Herder and Herder, Inc., 1969), pp. 139, n. 24, and 157 for further literature, pointing toward a major study of John the Baptist.

[21] M. Goguel, *Au seuil de l'Évangile, Jean-Baptiste* (Paris: Éditions Payot, 1928). Much of Goguel's position appears in his *La Vie de Jésus*, Eng. tr. *Jesus and the Origins of Christianity* (New York: Harper & Row, Publishers, 1933; Harper Torchbooks, 1960), vol. 1, pp. 211f.; 2, pp. 264-279. A translation of *Jean-Baptiste* exists in the Princeton Seminary doctoral dissertation (1961) by Lawrence E. Yates, *John the Baptist: A Critical Analysis of the Monograph "Au Seuil de L'Évangile, Jean-Baptiste."* Yates criticizes Goguel for seeing John merely from a human point of view, not in the perspective of the "divine plan."

[22] Charles H. H. Scobie, *John the Baptist* (Philadelphia: Fortress Press, 1964).

[23] E.g., Hugh J. Schonfield, *The Lost "Book of the Nativity of John"* (Edinburgh: T. & T. Clark, 1929); a "Baptist cycle of tradition" behind Luke 1 (C. Kraeling; Steinmann); E. Stauffer's suggestion that Apollos brought to Ephesus a "Baptist Logos-hymn" which looms behind John 1, *Jerusalem und Rom* (Bern: Francke Verlag, 1957), p. 101.

[24] Ernst Bammel's leadership in seminars on John the Baptist at SNTS meetings at Frankfurt (1969) and Newcastle (1970) indicates his hopes for Baptist sources and even a *Leben Johannes* by careful sifting of the New Testament (e.g., the "three Q's") and Jewish and gnostic materials; for his approach, cf. "Christian Origins in Jewish Tradition," *NTS*, 13 (1966-1967), especially pp. 329f.; *Die Anfänge des Christentums in der jüdischen Überlieferung* (Erträge der Forschung, 18; Darmstadt: Wissenschaftliche Buchgesellschaft, 1971). More specifically, " 'John Did No Miracle': John 10.41," in *Miracles: Cambridge Studies in Their Philosophy and History*, ed. C. F. D. Moule (London: A. R. Mowbray, 1965), pp. 179-202; "Origen *Contra Celsum* i. 41 and the Jewish Tradition," *JTS*, 19 (1968), pp. 211-213. Pending full publication and evaluation of Bammel's exacting and often speculative work, I hope it is not unfair to record an impression that the approach here to John is similar to that of E. Stauffer to Jesus. (The paper which Bammel presented at the Newcastle seminar has now appeared in *NTS* 18 [1971], pp. 95-128.)

[25] Walter Wink, *John the Baptist*, p. ix; diss., pp. 70f.

[26] *Ibid.*, p. x; diss., p. 73.

[27] R. H. Lightfoot, *History and Interpretation in the Gospels* (London:

Hodder & Stoughton, 1935) , p. 225; for clarification on Lightfoot's allusion to Job 26:14, cf. Stephen Neill, *The Interpretation of the New Testament 1861-1961* (London: Oxford University Press, 1964) , p. 253.

[28] John A. T. Robinson, "The Baptism of John and the Qumran Community: Testing a Hypothesis," *HTR*, 50 (1957), pp. 175-191; "Elijah, John, and Jesus: An Essay in Detection," *NTS*, 4 (1957-1958) , pp. 263-281; cf. also " 'The Others' of John 4:38, A Test of Exegetical Method," *Studia Evangelica (TU*, 73 [1959]), pp. 510-515; reprinted in *Twelve New Testament Studies* (SBT 34; 1962) , pp. 11-27, 28-52, 61-66, a collection of Robinson's essays shortly after he was consecrated Bishop of Woolwich and before he entered broader theological battles with *Honest to God* (1963) . (Hereafter references to Robinson are cited by pages in *Twelve New Testament Studies.*)

[29] Walter Wink, diss., pp. 48, 62.

[30] Wink's dissertation, pp. 75ff., notes Robinson's essay of 1957 in *HTR* but does not enter into discussion of his total view; Wink's book makes reference to Robinson only in passing, p. 2, note 2; p. 45, note 3, to reject Robinson's views. Dr. Wink writes me (Mar. 30, 1971) that he "regarded Robinson's views as a later, more cautious restatement of Brownlee's," which he featured. Thus Robinson's total perspective was not treated by Wink.

[31] Postal card, Jan. 28, 1962. An earlier version of this essay, "J. A. T. Robinson's Portrait of John the Baptist," read at the 1961 SBL meeting, but never published, was kindly examined by both Professor Kraeling and the Bishop of Woolwich for descriptive accuracy. In spite of Professor Enslin's interest in the topic, I delayed publication, for further study of the quest and historical problems, until it became apparent that a happy opportunity to commit results to print would be this volume in honor of my *Doktor-Vater,* whose position foreshadows certain conclusions and reservations about lives of John to which I have been led.

[32] J. A. T. Robinson, *Twelve New Testament Studies*, p. 11.

[33] Cf. the summary by Herbert Braun, *Qumran und das Neue Testament* (Tübingen: J. C. B. Mohr, 1966) , pp. 1-29.

[34] Carl Kraeling, *op. cit.*, pp. 26f.

[35] *Ibid.*, pp. 107-118.

[36] J. A. T. Robinson, *op. cit.*, p. 21.

[37] J. A. T. Robinson, *Twelve New Testament Studies*, pp. 33ff. Robinson's reconstruction, with its distinction among three views—the Old Testament (and Judaism) , where Elijah was never thought of as a forerunner of the Messiah; the Baptist's view (once held by Jesus); and Jesus' later view—can be charted thus:

	prior stage	penultimate stage	ultimate stage
OT view:	—	Elijah the Messenger (Mal. 4:5, 3:1)	Day of Yahweh
John Baptist's view (4th Gospel) , Jesus' early view:	himself = a voice, Isaiah 40	Jesus = Elijah	God
Jesus' view:	—	John the Baptist = Elijah	Jesus = the Day of the Lord, the Christ

Luke 1:76 and Mark 1:3 reflect idea that Elijah *redivivus* prepares the way for *God Himself*. ὁ ἐρχόμενος (Matt. 11:3) is not "the Christ" but the Judge whom John expected, and equals ὁ μέλλων (11:14). It is true that some scholars (G. F. Moore, Mowinckel) claim Elijah was to be a forerunner for the Messiah. But Robinson (pp. 36f.), after examining the evidence in Malachi 3:1; 4:5; Ecclesiasticus 48:10f.; and Mark 9:11 finds no real basis for that view. Elijah as precursor and anointer of the Messiah appears first to be documented in Justin Martyr (*Dial.* 8.49; cf. A. Schlatter, *Johannes der Täufer*, pp. 35f.); the view would thus have been developed by Jesus and the early church.

[38] Robinson here reflects an idea in the book by his uncle, J. Armitage Robinson, *The Historical Character of St. John's Gospel* (London: Longman's, Green & Co., 1908), pp. 27-31, that Jesus followed a path which the Baptist had marked out for him.

[39] Robinson, *op. cit.*, p. 41. Contrast Goguel's theory that a dispute over "law vs. gospel" caused John and Jesus to split. Kraeling (*John the Baptist*, pp. 147-152) rejects Goguel's hypothesis and finds the explanation for Jesus' striking out on his own in his "experiences of the presence of the Kingdom, rather than in a break with John on a matter of principle" (p. 152), which turns out to be the reason which Robinson posited for John's break with Qumran!

[40] Robinson, *op. cit.*, p. 38; cf. the chart in note 37 above.

[41] C. Kraeling, *John the Baptist*, pp. 166-169, but allowing adaptation of a traditional Jewish hymn such as we know in the Psalms of Solomon; Robinson, pp. 48-52. Robinson sees 1:69 as the key phrase: "in the house of his servant *David*" could have applied only to Jesus, not John. Kraeling, p. 168, recognized this difficulty. Both scholars indicated in correspondence their openness to the suggestion of the late Paul Winter, that Maccabean (battle-) hymns lie behind the lyrics of Luke 1; cf. "The Main Literary Problem of the Lucan Infancy Story," *ATR*, 40 (1958), pp. 257-264; "Magnificat and Benedictus—Maccabean Psalms?" *BJRL*, 37 (1954), pp. 328-347; "The Proto-Source of Luke 1," *NovTest*, 1 (1956), pp. 184-199.

[42] Robinson, *op. cit.*, pp. 49f., note 49. The literature on Acts 19 is too extensive to cite here, let alone the problems involved, but I agree with Robinson that the "question of the existence of this Baptist sect deserves a thorough re-examination."

[43] Kraeling, *op. cit.*, pp. 66-91.

[44] Letter, January 24, 1962.

[45] Cf. H. Braun, *Qumran und das Neue Testament*, vol. 1, p. 83, and 2, pp. 20f., for a survey of the host of writers accepting this view, and for Braun's judgment that 1:80, as a redactional note, cannot bear the historical weight of this theory, and that for the further hypothesis of a break by the Baptist with Qumran there is no textual evidence.

[46] While S. V. McCasland thought it a metonym for God (*JBL*, 77 [1958], p. 229) and the *TDNT*, vol. 5, p. 86, takes it as "on the right way, on God's commission" (W. Michaelis), G. Strecker, *Der Weg der Gerechtigkeit: Untersuchung zur Theologie des Matthäus*, FRLANT, 82 (Göttingen: Vandenhoeck & Ruprecht, 1962), p. 153, is correct to see it, in light of all Matthew's uses of δικαιοσύνη , as redactional, with the meaning here, "demanding righteous conduct" (cf. my summary of the evidence in *Righteousness and Society: Ecumenical Dialog in a Revolutionary Age* [Philadelphia: Fortress Press, 1967], p. 68).

[47] So Charles E. Carlston, review, *JBL*, 84 (1965), p. 209.

[48] W. Wink, *John the Baptist,* p. 113.

[49] *Ibid.,* p. xii; Wink himself notes the irony "that redaction-criticism should direct us to conclusions regarding the historical Jesus" (p. 113, note 3).

[50] Cf. Harvey K. McArthur, "A Survey of Recent Gospel Research," *Interpretation,* 18 (1964), pp. 47f., reprinted in H. K. McArthur, ed., *In Search of the Historical Jesus* (New York: Charles Scribner's Sons, 1969), pp. 139f.; Norman Perrin, *Rediscovering the Teaching of Jesus* (New York: Harper & Row, Publishers, 1967), pp. 250f., 45f.

When Acts Sides with John

by Pierson Parker

Nearly every commentator on the Fourth Gospel notices its affinities to the Gospel of Luke. In examining these, one is likely to remark how, here and there, Luke's links with John are illustrated in Acts, too. In fact, however, Acts' notions about Jesus do not simply echo those of the Third Gospel.[1] On the contrary, over very wide areas Acts and John are closer to each other than either of them is to Luke, with traditions that Luke's Gospel either does not have at all, or which it expresses much less positively.

Jesus' career. In both John and Acts, Jesus is invariably a Ναζωραῖος (John 18:5, 7; 19:19; Acts 2:22; 3:6; 4:10; 6:14; 22:8; 26:9), not, as in Mark, Ναζαρηνός (Mark 1:24; 10:47; 14:67; 16:6). Luke's Gospel once says Ναζωραῖος (18:37), twice Ναζαρηνός (4:34; 24:19).

John the Baptist is called βαπτιστής seven times in Matthew, two in Mark, three in Luke, but never in John or Acts. In Matthew 11:14; 17:10–12, and apparently in Mark 9:12 and Luke 1:17, he is identified with Elijah. Acts has no such idea, and in John 1:21, 25 the identification is explicitly denied. In denying, further, that he is the Messiah, the Baptist uses the same phrase, οὐκ εἰμὶ ἐγώ, in John 1:20 and in Acts 13:25; and he declares that he is not ἄξιος to loosen Christ's ὑπόδημα (sing., John 1:27; Acts 13:25). Then neither John nor Acts mentions the baptism of Jesus, and this despite their intense interest in the Baptist himself.

Neither John nor Acts shows much concern for Galilee. Acts barely alludes to a "beginning from" there (10:37; cf. 12:31) and names no other northern scenes of Jesus' work. John allows less than one-sixth of its space to Galilee.[2] In neither John nor Acts does Jesus commission his disciples to work in Galilee, as he seems to do in Matthew 10:5–42; Mark 6:7–13; and Luke 9:2–7; 10:1–16.

He does very clearly expect them to work in Samaria (John

4:35–38; Acts 1:8). Further, the words Σαμαρείτης, Σαμαρεῖτις, Σαμαρία together occur in John nine times, Acts eight, but in Luke four, Matthew one time (where Jesus *forbids* work in Samaria!), and Mark none.

Jesus' own career Acts locates almost exclusively in Judea. This is asserted again and again (Acts 1:3–9; 2:14, 22; 3:11 f., 26; 4:5, 8, 10 f.; 10:36–39; 13:27–31). John, likewise, devotes more than four-fifths of its narratives to Judea and the south. Here Luke's own Gospel is much less clear. When following Mark, it usually depicts a Galilean ministry, but elsewhere it speaks, briefly, of "Judea" (5:17; 6:17; 7:17; 22:39, 53 f.).[3] Incidentally, neither John nor Acts ever names τὸ Ὄρος τῶν Ἐλαιῶν. (Acts 1:12 does have ἀπὸ ὄρους τοῦ καλουμένου ἐλαιῶνας, a phrase occurring nowhere else in the New Testament.) On the other hand, John and Acts are the only New Testament books that mention Solomon's Porch (John 10:23; Acts 3:11; 5:12).

Both John (1:34–42 ff.) and Acts (1:21 f.) indicate that Judea was where Jesus got his first disciples, that he did this while the Baptist was active, and apparently under the latter's aegis. Both add that the disciples were with Jesus *from the beginning* (John 15:27; Acts 1:22). Contrast Matthew 4:12–22, Mark 1:14–20. Here, once more, Luke's Gospel is vague. Luke 5:1–11 is sometimes read as a call of Peter by the Galilean lake, but in Luke 4:38 f. Peter is already with Jesus. Unlike John and Acts, Luke's ἀπ' ἀρχῆς (1:2) is not directly connected either to the disciples or to the era of John the Baptist.

Is the Philip of Acts 8 the apostle of 1:13, or the evangelist of 6:5; 21:8? Presumably the latter, since Acts 8:1 says the "apostles" stayed in Jerusalem, and since Peter and John were sent to follow up Philip's work. Yet this very follow-up (Acts 8:14–25) means that the apostles did *not* all stick to Jerusalem. Further, it was precisely the apostles, including Philip, Peter, and John, whom Jesus had commanded to work in Samaria (Acts 1:8). And Samaria was Aramaic-speaking, whereas the Philip of Acts 6:5 was appointed to work among speakers of Greek. *If* the Philip of Acts 8 is the apostle, he is named in Acts fifteen times, in John twelve times, but only once each in Matthew, Mark, and Luke.[4]

The Fourth Gospel treats Peter's denial much more gently than the Synoptics do (John 18:15–18, 25–27), and Acts disregards it altogether. In fact, Acts 3:13 f. has Peter accusing *others* of denying

Jesus, using the same verb ἀρνέομαι. Only John (21:11–22) and Acts (10:41) say that Peter shared a post-resurrection meal with Jesus. In contrast, Peter is evidently absent from both the meals of Luke 24 (cf. Luke 24:34), while Matthew 28 and Mark 16:1–8 describe no post-resurrection meals at all.

Neither John nor Acts recalls that Jesus cast out δαιμόνια. Acts 10:38 says that Jesus healed those oppressed ὑπὸ τοῦ διαβό-λου, which is not the same thing. (Cf. Matthew 4:24; Luke 13:16.) The Synoptics never call Jesus' miracles "signs." Mark 13:4, 22 use σημεῖα in a frightening sense, and Mark 8:11 f. roundly condemns the notion that Jesus might perform signs. Yet in both John and Acts, Jesus' wonder works *were* signs (Acts 2:22; John 2:11, 23; 3:2; 4:54; 6:2, 14, 26; 7:31; 9:16; 11:47; 12:18, 37; 20:30), and in both books these signs are proof that God was with him (John 3:2; 9:16; Acts 2:22; 10:38).

In all the Synoptics, Jewish leaders attribute Jesus' miracles to demonic power (Matthew 9:34; 10:25; 12:24, 27; Mark 3:22; Luke 11:15, 18 f.). John and Acts do not recall this; and in John, when these leaders say Jesus himself is demon-possessed (7:20; 8:48 f., 52; 10:20 f.), this is not because of his deeds, but his words. Among his opponents, in both John and Acts, Annas the high priest takes an active part (John 18:13, 24; Acts 4:6). Luke's Gospel names Annas once (3:2), but it gives him no role; and Matthew and Mark do not mention him. For both John and Acts, Isaiah 6:10 is a prophecy of Jewish rejection of Christ (John 12:40; Acts 28:27). This *may* be reflected in Luke 19:42, but elsewhere the Synoptics apply Isaiah 6:10 to Jesus' use of parables (Matthew 13:14 f.; Mark 4:12; Luke 8:10).

John and Acts both fail to mention the institution of the Eucharist at the Last Supper. Both fail to date Jesus' trial on the Passover day. Both fail to recall a formal Sanhedrin hearing — even though Luke's Gospel has one on the Passover morning (22:66–71), and Matthew 26:59 ff. and Mark 14:53 ff. describe one the preceding night.

John 17:12 agrees with Acts 1:20, that Judas's death fulfilled Scripture. Neither book mentions any supernatural portents at Jesus' own death. Contrast Matthew 27:45, 51–53; Mark 15:33, 38; Luke 23:44 f.

There is no record, in John or Acts, that Jesus forecast his resurrection. They agree, however, that the Old Testament did foretell it (John 20:9; Acts 2:25–31; 13:29–35; 17:2 f.; 26:2 f.). Luke 24:26 f. does not quite say this, and the idea is absent altogether from Mark and even from Matthew. There were many resurrection appearances, say John and Acts, over a considerable period of time (John 20:19–30; Acts 1:3; 13:31). The risen Christ was manifest not to everybody, but to a chosen few (John 14:19, 22; Acts 10:40 f.). If the Synoptics do not deny these things, neither do they assert them nearly so clearly.

Matthew and Mark do not speak of the ascension. Perhaps Luke's Gospel does at 9:51 ($\dot{a}\nu\dot{a}\lambda\eta\mu\psi\iota s$), or at 24:51$b$, but the former is ambiguous and the latter textually doubtful. In John and Acts, the ascension tradition is clear and explicit (John 6:62; 20:17; Acts 1:2, 9–11).

Jesus' teaching. Whereas Acts cites few of Jesus' words, it shares with John a good many ideas that that Gospel attributes to Jesus. Negatively, John and Acts say nothing of Jesus' teaching in parables,[5] and they never use the word $\pi a\rho a\beta o\lambda\dot{\eta}$. They never refer to riches, although $\pi\lambda o\acute{v}\sigma\iota os$, $\pi\lambda o\upsilon\tau\acute{\epsilon}\omega$, $\pi\lambda o\widehat{v}\tau os$ together occur fourteen times in Luke, four in Matthew, and three in Mark. John and Acts make no mention of adultery, whereas $\mu o\iota\chi a\lambda\acute{\iota}s$, $\mu o\iota\chi\acute{a}$-$o\mu a\iota$, $\mu o\iota\chi\epsilon\acute{\iota}a$, $\mu o\iota\chi\epsilon\acute{v}\omega$, $\mu o\iota\chi\acute{o}s$ together appear thirteen times in Matthew, six in Mark, and four in Luke. There is no hint that Jesus set aside dietary laws. In fact, Peter on the rooftop (Acts 10:14; 11:8) has never heard of such a thing. Yet the idea is at least hinted at in Luke 10:41, still more plainly in Matthew 15:1–14, and is emphatic in Mark 7:1–19.

On the positive side, among New Testament historical books only John and Acts speak of the "seed of Abraham," "seed of David," and these are their only uses of the word $\sigma\pi\acute{\epsilon}\rho\mu a$. In both books, "seed of Abraham" always means Israel, "seed of David" always Christ.[6] The verb $\pi\iota\sigma\tau\epsilon\acute{v}\omega$ occurs ninety-three times in John, thirty-eight in Acts, but only eleven in Matthew, eleven in Mark, and nine in Luke. Most of the John-Acts uses refer to believing in Christ. Constantly we are told that people believe because they have seen wonders (John 1:50; 2:11, 23; 4:48, 53; 6:30; 10:37 f.; 11:45; 12:37; 20:8, 25, 29, 31; Acts 8:13; 13:12; 17:12, 34). In Matthew, Mark, and Luke, in contrast, antecedent believing *itself* makes wonder works possible. (Cf., e.g., Matthew 15:32; 27:42.) In John 16:33 Jesus tells the disciples, "In the world you have tribulation; but be of good cheer ($\theta a\rho\sigma\epsilon\widehat{\iota}\tau\epsilon$), I have overcome the world." In Acts 23:11 he tells Paul in prison, "Be of good cheer (θάρσει), for as you have testified concerning me at Jerusalem, so you must bear witness also at Rome." Luke's Gospel does not use θάρσειν, and Matthew and Mark associate it only with healings, not persecutions. The δόξα (τοῦ) Θεοῦ (John 11:4, 40; 12:43; Acts 7:55) is not referred to in any Synoptic, although the phrase occurs sixteen times in the Epistles and Revelation. The δωρεὰ τοῦ Θεοῦ (John 4:10; Acts 8:20) is not mentioned in any other New Testament book. No Synoptic has the plural θεοί (John 10:34, 35; Acts 7:40; 14:11; 19:26), and it occurs only three times elsewhere in the New Testament. (However, Jesus in John is quoting Psalm 82:6 and talking about Judaism, whereas Acts is referring to pagan or apostate ideas.) Acts says that God raised Jesus from the dead (2:24, 32; 13:32, 34; 17:31). John says that Jesus will raise others from the dead (6:39, 40, 44, 54). No other New Testament book uses the transitive ἀνίστημι in this way, and Luke does not have it at all. John makes great use of μαρτυρέω and μαρτυρία. Acts has these, and also μαρτύριον, μαρτύρομαι, μάρτυς. Together, these "witness" words occur in Acts about four times as often, in John about six times as often, as in Luke; and Matthew and Mark have fewer still. Jesus in John, and Paul in Acts, both declare that wolves will come among the sheep to scatter and destroy (John 10:12; Acts 20:29).[7] John and Acts each has much on speaking παρρησίᾳ (John 7:4, 13, 26; 10:24; 11:14, 54; 16:25, 29; 18:20) or μετὰ παρρησίας (Acts 2:29; 4:29, 31; 28:31; cf. 4:13). The idea occurs once in Mark (8:32), nowhere in Matthew or Luke.

Several areas of teaching, in John and Acts, merit separate treatment.

The Holy Spirit. In the Synoptics, the Baptist predicts that Christ will baptize with the Holy Spirit (Matthew 3:11; Mark 1:8; Luke 3:16), but the theme is not developed. In John and Acts it is. Each of these represents the Spirit as coming *after* Christ has concluded his ministry (John 7:39; Acts 1:5, 8), and *at Christ's behest* (John 16:7, 14; Acts 2:33). Then consider the parallel ideas in these two passages:

John 3:8, 11 f.: The wind blows where it will, and you hear the sound of it, but do not know whence it comes, and whither it goes. So is every one who is born of the Spirit.... We	Acts 2:2–4, 6, 12 f.: Suddenly there came from heaven a sound as of the rushing of a mighty wind.... And they were all filled with the Holy Spirit, and began to speak ... as

speak what we know, and bear witness of what we have seen; and you do not receive our witness. . . . How shall you believe if I tell you heavenly things?

the Spirit gave them utterance. . . . And when this sound was heard, the crowd were all amazed and were perplexed, saying to one another, What does this mean?

Acts, however, dates the first coming of the Spirit at Pentecost, whereas John seems to put it on the night after the resurrection (20:22 f.) or perhaps, even, at the moment of Jesus' death, when he παρέδωκε τὸ πνεῦμα (19:30).

Eschatology. John and Acts lack the flamboyant apocalyptic language of the first three Gospels. Indeed, they devote far less space to any kind of eschatology than do Matthew, Mark, or even Luke. This very sparseness makes it the more remarkable that, when they do touch on eschatological matters, John and Acts agree so closely.

When the Synoptics foretell the coming of the Son of man, it might be argued, it has been argued, that someone other than Jesus is meant. John and Acts are unequivocally clear: Jesus himself will return (John 14:3; 21:22 f.; Acts 1:11). God, they say, appointed Christ to judge the world (John 5:22, 30; 8:15 f.; but cf. 3:17; Acts 17:31). Christ *has come* as judge (John 5:27; 9:39; Acts 10:42). There will be a general resurrection of both the righteous and the unrighteous (John 5:28 f.; 6:29, 40; 11:24; Acts 23:6; 24:15). Moreover, these are the only historical books in the New Testament that speak of "the Last Day" (John 6:39 f., 44, 54; 7:37; 11:24; 12:48; Acts 2:17; cf. James 5:3; 2 Peter 3:3; 2 Timothy 3:1). Again there is a difference, however. Acts is quoting Joel 3:1, and it seems to put the Last Day in the present moment. John gives no hint as to whether the Day is near or far.

Christology. Compare these two passages:

John 1:51: You shall see the heaven opened, and the angels of God ascending and descending upon the Son of man.

Acts 7:56: I see the heavens opened, and the Son of man standing on the right hand of God.

These are much less eschatological than Matthew 24:30 par. Mark 13:26 and Luke 21:27, or than Matthew 26:64 par. Mark 14:62 which Luke lacks. Furthermore, in John and Acts, but not in the Synoptics, the seer beholds the *heaven opened*. Acts 7:56 has other connections with the Fourth Gospel. (*a*) No Synoptic puts the phrase "Son of man" on the lips of anybody except Jesus. John 12:34 does. (*b*) In many MSS., John 3:13 agrees that the Son of man *is now* in heaven. Matthew, Mark, and Luke have nothing of the sort. (c) The Son of man of Acts 7:56 *has ascended.* John twice speaks of "the Son of man" ascending (3:13; 6:62). The Synoptics never do. (Luke 24:7 does have "Son of man" in a *post-resurrectional* context, but even there it merely recalls the pre-resurrectional 9:22, 44.)

There are other christological agreements. Οὗτός ἐστιν ὁ Χριστός (John 4:29; 7:26, 41; Acts 9:22). The phrase δι' αὐτοῦ is used of the mighty deeds of Christ, at John 1:3, 7, 10; 3:17, and at Acts 2:22; 3:16. No other Gospel does this, though it is common enough in other parts of the New Testament. Only in John and Acts do human beings call Jesus "Savior" (John 4:32; Acts 5:31; 13:23). In Luke 2:11, to be sure, angels call him that; but in Luke 1:47, the "Savior" is God. In John 1:29, 36, Jesus is the ἀμνός of God; in Acts 8:32 (as in 1 Peter 1:19), ὡς ἀμνός...οὐκ ἀνοίγει τὸ στόμα αὐτοῦ, a figure deriving from Isaiah 53:7. No other New Testament book uses it.

Christ, who is called "son" of David nine times in Matthew, three in Mark, and three in Luke, is never so styled in John or Acts. At John 7:42, Jesus' foes say that Christ must be of the "seed" of David, and in Acts 13:23 Paul says that Jesus *is.* There is a similar progression with respect to the "prophet like Moses" foretold in Deuteronomy 18:15, 18 f. John 1:21 says he is not the Baptist. In John 6:14; 7:40, the crowds say he is Jesus. In Acts 3:22; 7:37, he definitely is Jesus.

Finally, nothing in the Synoptics, not even Luke 2:32, matches the declarations of John 8:12; 9:5; and Acts 26:23, that Jesus Christ himself is light for the world.[8]

Attitudes toward surrounding culture. John and Acts often take similar stances regarding Judaism and regarding contacts with pagan life. Negatively, Elijah is named only twice in John (1:21, 25), not at all in Acts, but eight times each in Matthew, Mark, and Luke. On the other hand, of the historical books, only John and Acts name Joseph the son of Jacob (John 4:5; Acts 7:9, 13, 14, 18). Again, among the historical books, only John and Acts have the word "Israelite" (sing. in John 1:48; pl. in Acts 2:22; 3:12; 5:35; 13:16; 21:28). Only these two speak explicitly of Jewish ἔθος (John 19:40; Acts 26:3).[9] Only these refer to Shechem and Genesis 33:19, Joshua 24:32 (John 4:5; Acts 7:16). Still more striking, the expression "the Jews" occurs in John sixty-four times, Acts fifty, but in Mark only six, Luke five, Matthew four, and the rest of the New Testament five;[10] that is, John and Acts each use the phrase more than twice as often as all the rest of the New Testament combined.

As to the Law of Moses, John and Acts allude to punishment by stoning (λιθάζειν, John 10:31, 32, 33; 11:8; Acts 5:26; 14:19). The subject is brought up elsewhere in the New Testament only in [John 8:5, 7], 2 Corinthians 11:25, and Hebrews 11:37. Acts has the noun περιτομή three times (7:8; 10:45; 11:2), John twice (7:22, 23), the Synoptics not at all. Luke does use the *verb* περιτεμεῖν with respect to John the Baptist and Jesus; but that is its only mention of the practice, and Matthew and Mark do not have even that. John and Acts, on the contrary, are discussing the regular circumcision of children and adults; and both say explicitly that Moses gave the rite (John 7:22; Acts 7:8; cf. Genesis 17:10–13).

Only in John and Acts do we meet a βασιλικός (John 4:46, 49; Acts 12:20). In all the New Testament, only John and Acts have the word Ῥωμαῖος (John 11:48; Acts 2:10; 16:21, 37 f.; 22:25–27, 29; 23:27; 25:16; 28:17). Στρατιῶται appear in Acts thirteen times, John six, Matthew three, Luke two, Mark one time, and the rest of the New Testament one time. (However, John's occurrences are all in the crucifixion story, 19:2–34.) In John and Acts, but not elsewhere, foes say that Jesus' kingly claim is a direct challenge to Caesar (John 19:12; Acts 17:7).

In the New Testament the Greek language is mentioned in John 19:20, Acts 21:37, and nowhere else. If the Ἕλληνες of John 7:35; 12:20 are Greek men, no other Gospel mentions them, but Acts does (Acts 14:1; 16:1, 3; 17:4; 18:4; 19:10, 17; 20:21; the feminine form Ἑλληνίς does appear in Mark 7:26). If John's Ἕλληνες are Greek-speaking *Jews* (of the Diaspora, 7:35, come to worship at the temple, 12:20), John and Acts are the only books in all the New Testament that refer specifically to them (Acts 6:1; 9:29; 11:20?).

Common expressions. Besides the words examined above, John and Acts share some eighty expressions that Luke's Gospel does not use. Those starred (*) do not occur in Matthew or Mark either, and those double-starred (**) do not occur anywhere else in the New Testament:

*ἁγνίζω, αἰγιαλός, αἰτία of the charge against Jesus, *ἀκούω + παρά, ἀληθής, *ἄλλομαι, **ἄν τις, ἀναγγέλλω, ἀναστρέφω, ἀναχωρέω, ἀνοίγειν ... ὀφθαλμούς, *ἄνω, ἀποκόπτω, ἄρεστος, ἁρπάζω, βῆμα, γεννάω ἐν, *γογγυσμός, *δεκαπέντε, *δέκατος, *διατρίβω, διακόσιοι, **ἐὰν μή τις, **εἴπας partic., ἐκ δευτέρον, **ἑλκύω, ἐμφανίζειν, *ἐντολή .... ἵνα, **ἐξέρχομαι καὶ εἰσέρχομαι, ἐπαύριον, **ἐπιλέγομαι, *ἐρῶ with pers. accus., *ἐχθές, *ζῆλος, *ζήτησις, **ζώννυμι, Ἰησοῦς Χριστός, κακεῖ, *κἄν with indic., κατὰ with num. accus., καταλαμβάνω, κράβαττος, λάθρα, *λαμβάνω ἐκ, λάμπας, *λούω, *μαίνομαι, μάλλον ἤ with gen., *μάχομαι, μεθερμηνεύομαι, μεθύω, **μένειν ἐπί + accus., **νεύω, **ὁμοῦ, **οὕτως .... ὥστε, **παρ' αὐτοῖς, *περιίστημι, περιπατέω metaph., *πιάζω, πιπράσκω, πιστεύω εἰς, πλευρά, πραιτώριον, πρωΐ, *σημαίνω, σημεῖα καὶ τέρατα, σκληρός, σπεῖρα, *σύρω, **σχοινίον, τηρέω, τιμή, *τύπος, ὑγιής, φανερῶς, χειμών, χιλίαρχος, χώριον, *ψῦχος.

The significance of this list will be variously estimated. Sheer chance will of course give, to almost any two books, some words that some other book lacks. Yet the present list can hardly be the result of mere chance. Most of the above expressions are *topical* (nouns and verbs), as though the authors of John and Acts thought often about matters that Luke's own Gospel played down. Further, about half of these terms are absent from Matthew and Mark, too, as though John and Acts really did share some sort of non-Synoptic tradition.

Note, further, that many of the expressions marked **, which are absent also from the Epistles and Revelation, are largely syntactical, as characterizing a narrative style: ἄν τις, ἐὰν μή τις, ἐξέρχομαι καὶ εἰσέρχομαι, κἄν with indicative, μένειν ἐπί with accusative, οὕτως .... ὥστε, παρ' αὐτοῖς. This raises the distinct possibility that their common tradition reached John and Acts in a somewhat fixed, even written form.

Similar stories. Acts has a number of stories about the early church which sound like stories that John tells about Jesus himself.

John 4:53: A nobleman *and all his house* believe. Acts 10:2: A centurion *and all his house* receive the Holy Spirit. If these simply reflect Near Eastern ethos, still they are more sweeping than anything in the Synoptics. Matthew and Mark have nothing of the sort. At Luke 19:9, Jesus says to Zaccheus, "Salvation has come to this house," which does not necessarily take in the entire household. (Cf. Acts 16:14 f., 31.) Further, Zaccheus is positively a Jew; the figures of John 4 and Acts 10 and 16 might, for all John and Acts say, be Gentiles.

John 9:1–41: A beggar in Jerusalem, blind from birth, is healed, to the consternation of the Jewish authorities. Acts 3:1–4:28: A beggar in Jerusalem, lame from birth, is healed, to the consternation of the Jewish authorities. In each story, the healed man appears later in the temple. Also:

John 9:8: The neighbors, therefore, and those who watched him previously, when he was a beggar, said, "Is not this he who sat and begged?"	Acts 3:9 f.: And all the people recognized him, as the one who sat begging for alms . . . and they were filled with wonder and amazement.

John 11:46–51: The Sanhedrin meets and is in a quandary. Acts 4:5–17: The Sanhedrin meets and is in a quandary. Compare particularly:

John 11:47 f.: What do we do? For this man does many signs. If we let him alone thus, all people will believe in him. . . . It is expedient for you that one man should die for the people.	Acts 4:16 f.: What shall we do to these men? For it is manifest to all who dwell in Jerusalem that a notable miracle has indeed been wrought through them. . . . But that it spread no further among the people, let us threaten them.

John 18:18: ". . . having made a fire of coals, for it was cold." Acts 28:2: "They kindled a fire . . . because of the cold." Only in John and Acts does the weather ever get $\psi \hat{v} \chi o s$.

John 18:22 f.: Jesus is struck for insulting the high priest. Acts 23:2 f.: Paul is struck for insulting the high priest.

John 18:31: Pilate tells the Jews that it is a matter for *their* law, not Roman law. Acts 18:15: Gallio tells the Jews that it is a matter for *their* law, not Roman law.

Why? How are we to regard these junctures of John with Acts? There are several possibilities.

a) Discount them, as fortuitous and of little significance. After all, nearly every decade finds John paired with some fresh book or body of literature — the Old Testament, Philo, Mandean writings, Hermetic literature, the Qumran scrolls, the Gospel of Mark, Ignatius of Antioch, and so on and on. Nearly every one of those named has, in its turn, been hailed by somebody as *the* key to the Johannine puzzle. One is tempted to surmise that, with diligence, parallels to John could be found in just about any book that was ever written.

However, the links between John and Acts are impressive for their sheer bulk, and also for their variety. It cannot be too heavily emphasized that John, a Gospel, is constantly closer to Acts than to the other Gospels, and that Acts, a book by Luke, is constantly closer to John than to Luke's other book. Such phenomena are not easily shrugged off.

b) Suppose that Acts was not, after all, written by the Third Evangelist, but by someone closer to the Johannine orbit. This is to fly in the face of nearly all modern scholarship. The description of "the former treatise" (Acts 1:1 f.) fits no known Gospel except Luke. Examination of any good Greek concordance shows how incessantly Acts and Luke correspond, as the works of a single author.

c) Regard Acts as a late development, say in the sequence Mark-Luke-Acts-John, or else Mark-Luke-John-Acts. This theory seems to face insuperable obstacles. Acts and John read not like developments, one from the other, but like independent repositories of similar traditions. These traditions are ensconced, moreover, in books that superficially seem utterly different from each other. Nor is the difference always superficial. Compare, e.g., Acts' overt universalism with the gingerly approach of John: Christ is Savior of the world, yes, but at times in John, "world" means the descendants of Abraham (cf. John 7:14; 12:19; 18:20; also 6:14; 7:7; 11:27). Christ has other sheep, yes, but in the Old Testament the other, scattered sheep are Israel of the Diaspora (cf. Numbers 27:17; 1 Kings 22:17; Psalm 44:11; Jeremiah 23:1–4; 50:6 f.; Micah 2:12; and Ezekiel 34). John speaks of "Greeks" but, as we saw, it might mean Greek-speaking Jews.

A further difficulty, in the foregoing theory, arises when we compare Acts with Mark. The author of Acts writes not as though he would improve on Mark, or refute it, but as though he had never seen it. Indeed, many scholars are now inclined to date Acts comparatively early. Furthermore, canonical Luke is often vague, as we have seen; and often it swings back and forth between the Markan and the John-Acts traditions — quite as though the Third Evangelist were trying, in his *Gospel*, to reconcile two divergent points of view.[11]

d) In a letter to this writer, and in a splendid recent article, Professor Enslin suggests that Acts got most of its information about *Paul* from Paul's own letters.[12] Perhaps so; but Paul can hardly have been its instructor regarding Jesus himself. He says too little, and what he does say sounds rather like the Synoptics — the account of the Last Supper (1 Corinthians 11:23 ff.); "the Lord ordained that those who preach the gospel should live off the gospel" (1 Corinthians 9:14); "If your enemy is hungry, feed him" (Romans 12:20; cf. Proverbs 25:21); a resurrection appearance "to more than five hundred brethren at once" (1 Corinthians 15:6), which might have surprised the writer of Acts 10:40, 41. (Perhaps Paul does *not* contradict Matthew 28:18–20 or Mark 16:7.) *John's theology* may have been informed by Paul. John's and Acts' memories of Jesus surely were not informed by Paul.

e) To the present writer, none of the above recourses appears satisfactory. Rather, these relationships between Acts and John seem greatly to strengthen a series of suggestions that were made elsewhere, and largely on other grounds:[13] The book of Acts was produced *before* our present, canonical Gospel of Luke, and *before* Luke ever saw the Gospel of Mark. The "former treatise" of Acts 1:1 was an earlier, pre-Markan edition of Luke's Gospel. In the final form of his Gospel, then, Luke has tried to reconcile his earlier and, in fact, chiefly Judean traditions with the intensely Galilean traditions he found in Mark. (The Galilean tradition appears also in Matthew, sometimes still more intensely.)

John and Acts enshrine the often highly distinctive Judean tradition. It was Jesus' Judean followers who first got called the sect of the Nazoreans (Acts 24:5) and who, doubtless, thought of Jesus under that rubric. It was they who cared about Samaria, confronted the Sanhedrin, dealt with Greek-speaking converts, strictly kept the Law of Moses, and strictly held to the Jewish concepts of divine will and righteousness and grace and the Spirit. Supremely, they witnessed to their Lord's tragedy and triumph right there in their midst, and to his presence and coming as Lord, Messiah, and King.

Different as John and Acts are in style, and in content, these two books share a grandeur. Whether it be greater or less than the grandeur of Paul, or that of Galilee, one thing seems sure. The traditions that Acts and John share with each other are in a class by themselves.

NOTES

[1] Still less those of the Second. Cf. Pierson Parker, "Mark, Acts, and Galilean Christianity," *NTS*, 16 (1969–1970), pp. 295–304.

[2] And the appendix, and perhaps other Galilean sections, are *addenda* to the original draft of the Gospel. Cf. Pierson Parker, "Two Editions of John," *JBL*, 75 (1956), pp. 303–314.

[3] Perhaps also 4:44, but the text is doubtful.

4 In any case, John and Acts show partiality for the *name* Philip, just as they do for the name John.

5 Unless John 16:21 f. is a parable?

6 The same distinction holds throughout the Epistles, except in Galatians 3:16*b* and, perhaps, Hebrews 2:16.

7 But cf. Matthew 10:16, Luke 10:3, with a different import.

8 Still more decisive would be a rudimentary Logos doctrine if this could be read, e.g., in Acts 10:36; 13:26, 48; 20:32; but such an interpretation is precarious.

9 But Luke and Acts elsewhere have ἔθη, where Jewish customs are obviously meant: Luke 1:9; 2:42; Acts 6:14; 15:1; 21:21; 28:17.

10 Cf. also "Jews" without the article, Acts 20, John 3, Matthew 1, Mark and Luke 0, rest of New Testament 10; "Jew," sing., Acts 10, John 4, Matthew, Mark, and Luke 0, rest of New Testament 11.

11 Cf. the article cited in note 1 above; also Pierson Parker, "The 'Former Treatise' and the Date of Acts," *JBL*, 84 (1965), pp. 52–58.

12 M. S. Enslin, "Once Again, Luke and Paul," *ZNW*, 61 (1970), pp. 253–272.

13 Cf. the articles cited in notes 1 and 11 above.

The Resurrection of Jesus Christ in the Book of Acts and in Early Christian Literature

by Everett F. Harrison

Within the last few years Luke-Acts has become the object of intensive investigation by New Testament scholars, provoked mainly by the work of Dibelius [1] and Conzelmann [2] and pursued by many others.[3] The principal thrust of this research has been to accent Luke's role as a theologian rather than as the historian of the early church, though the historical aspect is not wholly dismissed. Professional historians tend to support the reliability of Acts, while many critical theologians take a negative view. One reason for this is that the two groups are governed by their special interests, the former tending to major on the contacts between Acts and the secular milieu, the latter concentrating largely on the picture of the church, the structuring of the narrative, comparison of Acts with the letters of Paul, and other similar matters.

The chief concern today is not the identity of the author of Acts but his position in the early church and his purpose in writing. Unfortunately the date of composition is elusive, with opinions ranging all the way from early in the sixties of the first century to the middle of the second century. This uncertainty opens the way for students of early church history to look for elements in Acts that seem to tally with developments in the post-apostolic period and thereby to suggest the chronological location of the writer.

So, for example, an attempt has been made to see in Acts the erecting of a bulwark against the menace of Gnosticism. Käsemann ventures to call Luke "the first representative of nascent early catholicism." [4] Charles H. Talbert has written a whole volume citing indications which he deems adequate to demonstrate that Luke-Acts was written as a defense against Gnosticism.[5] He calls attention to the handling of certain themes, such as witness, the interpretation of Scripture, and the succession of tradition as favorable to his conclusion. Naturally his thesis is embarrassed by the failure of Luke to identify the heresy openly, but he tries to meet this problem by noting that Luke does not mention any of the controversies that arose in Paul's churches and that he makes no use of the apostle's letters. According to Talbert, Luke studiously avoided anything which would mar the picture he was trying to paint of the early church as possessing an ideal unity. All that concerns us here is to point out that if Luke is actually countering gnostic ideas as a primary reason for writing, his procedure is quite different from that of Ignatius, who leaves no doubt that docetic teaching, which was a prominent feature of early Gnosticism, is his target, and even from that of the Johannine writings, where the adversary is more delicately but still no less unmistakably delineated. If Talbert is correct in his analysis, it follows that Luke must have counted on a high degree of sophistication on the part of his readers if he hoped to communicate his purpose in such allusive fashion. Perhaps he would reply that his dating of Luke-Acts, roughly a generation after Paul, fits the period of emerging Gnosticism when only the more perceptive were able to detect its subtle danger, and that its author counted on increasing awareness of the value of his work with the passing of time. Even so, a question mark remains over the validity of Talbert's thesis.

If the determination of Luke's position in the development of early church history cannot easily be made on the basis of an alleged anti-gnostic motive, perhaps it will be more profitable to consider something which he places specifically at the very center of the faith and proclamation of the early church, namely, the resurrection of Jesus Christ. A survey of the data in Acts followed by an examination of writings belonging to the post-apostolic period should disclose the extent of agreement and disagreement, opening the way for some conclusion regarding Luke's position in early Christianity. Encouragement for this undertaking has come from at least two sources. W. C. van Unnik writes, "Much work is still to be done with regard to the relation of Luke to later writers such as I Clement and Justin Martyr."[6] Pertinent also is the comment of Leonhard Goppelt that the comparison of Luke with First Clement is a task which has been omitted up to now.[7] To be sure, there are several areas where comparison might be made between Luke and early patristic writers, where indeed observations have been drawn, such as Haenchen's note that Luke's references to the Lord's Supper do not reveal the sacramentalism characteristic of allusions in the early part of the second century and therefore should make one wary of attributing primitive catholicism to him.[8] Along the same line Conzelmann writes, "The concepts νόμος and ἐντολή are not used to describe the Christian faith. This fact needs to be noted, for by the turn of the first century Christianity is coming to be viewed and spoken of as the 'new law'."[9] Some scholars find the situation mixed, feeling that theologically Luke shows traces of later developments, as in awareness of the gnostic peril and in eschatological shift, but not in ecclesiology, since for him the church is not yet an institution.[10] So any light on the Lukan problem should be welcome.

I

The methodology to be followed here is to classify the passages in Acts which deal with the resurrection and note any references from later Christian writers of the post-apostolic period which are similar in nature. In addition to the Apostolic Fathers, the writings of Justin will be used, and this for several reasons: they have copious references to the resurrection, they have some resemblance to Acts in that they are apologetic in nature, and they have been appealed to in recent years as furnishing a basis for dating Acts between 115 and 130.[11]

Appearances of the risen Lord as certifying his resurrection. These are summarized in 1:4, with the added note that they occurred over a forty-day period. Much the same is Paul's allusion in his synagogue sermon at Pisidian Antioch, but the duration is more generally stated in terms of "many days" (13:31). Peter's sermon at Caesarea adds the observation that the appearances were selective, restricted to Peter and his associates as men chosen of God to be witnesses (10:41). Presumably for evidential purposes the apostle states that these men ate and drank with the risen Lord. The appearance to Saul of Tarsus was determinative for revolutionizing his estimate of Jesus and his relation to him (26:13-16). Emphasis falls not alone on the revelation to sight but even more on the communication of the Lord.

This is true also of the other passages with the exception of 13:31.

In a context devoted to refutation of Docetists, Ignatius avers that Jesus "was in the flesh even after the resurrection," citing the fact that Peter and others touched him and that Jesus ate and drank with them (*Smyrnaeans* 3.1). Ignatius agrees with the testimony of Luke 24:39 and Acts 10:41.

Justin has two passages on the appearances (*Apology* 50; 67).[12] In the former, after quoting most of Isaiah 53, he goes on to indicate that after his crucifixion and resurrection Jesus appeared to his own and taught them to read the prophecies aright. After the ascension and their empowering, they went forth to every nation to teach these things. In the latter, a chapter describing Christian worship, Justin notes that on the day of the sun Jesus appeared to his apostles and disciples and taught them.

The apostles as witnesses to the resurrection. This qualification was deemed necessary for Judas's successor (1:22). Four times in the speeches of Peter reference is made to this apostolic witness (2:32; 3:15; 5:32; 10:41). Once it is mentioned in narrative (4:33) and once by Paul (13:31) in addition to his certification for such service (26:16).

This strain seems to be lacking entirely in the early Fathers so far as precise mention is concerned, although implied here and there (e.g., Justin, *Apol.* 50).

The resurrection as the fulfillment of Old Testament prophecy. This is central to Peter's Pentecost sermon (2:25-31; cf. Ps. 16) and to Paul's Pisidian Antioch message (13:33-35; cf. Ps. 2; Isa. 55; Ps. 16) and to his defense before Agrippa (26:22-23, with only a general reference to the prophets and Moses; cf. 17:2-3). Both Peter and Paul avoid this approach when speaking to Gentiles (chaps. 10; 17).

Justin sometimes refers to the resurrection of Jesus as fulfilling Scripture without citing a specific passage (*Apol.* 31; 50). The same is true in part regarding his other major work (*Dialogue* 17; 53), but on most occasions he quotes portions which he deems suitable. At times the reference is more pointedly to the exaltation than to the resurrection (*Dial.* 36, cf. Ps. 24, 110; *Dial.* 85, cf. Ps. 24). The remainder are as follows: *Dialogue* 73, cf. Psalm 96:10; *Dialogue* 100, cf. Psalm 22:3; *Dialogue* 106, cf. Psalm 22:22-23; *Dialogue* 118, cf. Isaiah 57:2. Since the *Dialogue* purports to be a conversation with a Jew, the liberal use of Scripture is understandable.

Jesus' resurrection as a divine reversal of the human verdict registered at the cross. Typical is Peter's strong statement in the Pentecost sermon: "This Jesus . . . you crucified and killed by the hands of lawless men. But God raised him up" (2:23-24). A variation on this theme is the choice of a murderer in preference to Jesus (3:13-15). The guilt belongs to the Sanhedrin in a special way (4:10; cf. 5:30). Other references are 10:39-40; 13:27-30.

A search of early Christian literature fails to disclose a single passage containing this motif.

Resurrection as a stage in the exaltation of Jesus. Peter links closely the raising of Jesus to his exaltation at God's right hand in 2:32-33, again in 3:13-15, where "glorified" is the word used, and finally in 5:30-31. In each case the combination of resurrection and exaltation has resulted in a certain benefit: the gift of the Spirit, a healing miracle, and the granting of repentance and forgiveness of sins to Israel.

Citing Jesus' resurrection and ascension to heaven, Justin seeks in *ad hominem* fashion to relieve the offense of the supernatural by asserting that similar things are claimed by pagans concerning their deities (*Apol.* 21). In another passage, after having quoted Psalm 96:10 in the form, "The Lord hath reigned from the tree" without manuscript authority for the last three words (he accused the Jews of deleting them), Justin speaks of Jesus as fulfilling Scripture by rising from the dead, ascending to heaven, and ruling there (*Apol.* 42). Again, he finds that the action of God in raising Jesus and bringing him to heaven has been anticipated by Psalm 110 (*Apol.* 45). In response to Trypho's objection that Jesus lacked the glory that prophecy attached to the coming Messiah, Justin explains that there are two advents, the first anticipated in Isaiah 53, the second set forth, for example, in Psalm 110 (*Dial.* 32). For this exaltation the resurrection is the necessary prelude. Again, disputing the Jewish claim that Psalm 24 has to do with Solomon's bringing of the ark of testimony into the temple, the apologist finds it fulfilled in the resurrection and ascension of "our Christ" (*Dial.* 36).

The relation of the resurrection to the salvation process. While the book of Acts frequently couples the death and resurrection of our Lord, the death is viewed more from the standpoint of human responsibility and overruling divine purpose than as the crucial item in redemption. Yet there are a few passages that hint at the resurrection as the complement of the death of Jesus, though not with theological precision such as Romans 4:25 exhibits. Peter announces with reference to the one who has been crucified and raised that there is salvation in him alone (Acts 4:12). The raised and exalted one is now both Leader and Savior, through whom God grants repentance and forgiveness of sins (5:30-31; cf. 10:40-43). In 13:37-39 forgiveness and justification are proclaimed as available through the risen one, but without mention of the death as redemptive.

Ignatius shows a tendency to couple the death of Jesus with his resurrection and recognizes that these events benefit believers. "I seek him who died for our sake. I desire him who rose for us" (*Romans* 6.1). He speaks of those who "do not confess that the eucharist is the flesh of our Savior Jesus Christ who suffered for our sins, which [flesh] the Father raised up by his goodness (*Smyrnaeans* 7.1). Justin writes, "For the salvation of those who believe on him, he endured both to be set at nought and to suffer, in order that, by dying and rising again, he might conquer death" (*Apol.* 63.16).

The time of the resurrection. A single passage deals with this, fixing the event on the third day after the crucifixion (10:40; cf. 1 Cor. 15:4).

Besides noting that Jesus predicted his resurrection on the third day (*Dial.* 51), Justin refers to the fact of the resurrection as taking place then (*Dial.* 97; 100; 107). His observation that the event occurred on the eighth day (*Dial.* 41; 138) is intended to indicate that it came after the sabbath (cf. *Barnabas* 15.9).

The resurrection of Jesus as the basis for the resurrection of others. It is not to be expected that the book of Acts would provide anything comparable to 1 Corinthians 15. All the references to this theme come in the closing chapters and relate to Paul's defense. The thrust throughout is that the hope of Israel in terms of resurrection has been sharpened by the raising of Jesus of Nazareth, which Paul had become assured of through personal experience. His compatriots should welcome this new development instead of viewing him with hostility and continuing to reject his Lord (23:6; 24:15, 21; 26:6-8).

Clement begins a rather lengthy exposition of the subject of resurrection by saying, "Let us consider, beloved, how the Master continually proves to us that there will be a future resurrection, of which he has made the first fruits by raising the Lord Jesus Christ from the dead" (*1 Clement* 24.1). In an anti-docetic passage Ignatius refers to Jesus Christ "who also was truly raised from the dead, when his Father raised him up, as in the same manner his Father will raise up in Christ Jesus us who believe in him, without whom we have no true life" (*Trallians* 9.2). A more involved statement appears in *Barnabas* 5. 6-7.

The bearing of Jesus' resurrection on future judgment. Included in Peter's Caesarea sermon is this testimony concerning the risen Lord: "And he commanded us to preach to the people, and to testify that he is the one ordained by God to be judge of the living and the dead" (10:42). A parallel statement is attributed to Paul in his Athenian address, where he indicates that the proof of God's intention to judge the world in righteousness at the appointed time is his action in raising from the dead that man who will be his agent in the judgment (17:31).

With reference to the risen Christ it is said, "He himself will raise the dead and judge the risen" (*Barnabas* 5.7). Justin observes that "Jesus, whom we acknowledge as Christ the Son of God, . . . was crucified, rose from the dead, ascended into heaven, and will come again to judge every man who ever lived, even back to Adam himself" (*Dial.* 132).

Mention of the resurrection followed by warning against unbelief. This emerges most clearly in Paul's Pisidian Antioch sermon (13:40-41) but it is probably to be allowed for also in his conference with Jewish leaders at Rome, since his stern warning contained in 28:25-27 follows the information that he spent a day with these men, "trying to convince them about Jesus both from the law of Moses and from the prophets." The similarity to 17:2-3 as well as to Luke 24:44-47 argues for the inclusion of the resurrection on this occasion.

Somewhat similar are the expostulations and warnings addressed by Justin to Trypho. Despite their possession of the necessary information about Jesus' life, death, and resurrection, the Jews have failed to repent. More than that, they have agitated against the followers of Jesus and have lodged false charges against them. Let them sense their danger and turn in faith to their Messiah (*Dial.* 17; 108).

II

Before drawing any conclusions from the data presented here, we would do well to look for items in the early Fathers which differ from the materials offered by the book of Acts on the theme of our Lord's resurrection.

1. When the resurrection is mentioned, there is a tendency to combine with it a greater number of events than does the book of Acts, so that the resurrection becomes frequently only one item in a series designed to set forth the Christ-event. Justin writes, "He was born as a man of a virgin, was named Jesus, was crucified, died, rose again, and ascended into heaven" (*Apol.* 46. 5). Conversely, Acts provides several examples where the resurrection alone is mentioned (4:2, 33; 17:18, 31; 24:21; 25:19; 26: 8). In addition, there are places where the appearances only are cited (1:4; 9:3ff.; 26:16). This isolation of the resurrection is a rarity among the early Fathers (*Smyrnaeans* 3).

2. Often the allusions to the resurrection have a rather formal and almost creedal character. Justin says with reference to the Lord Jesus, ". . . who is the first-born of every creature, who became man through a virgin, who suffered and was crucified by your people under Pontius Pilate, and died, and rose from the dead, and ascended into heaven" (*Dial.* 85; cf. 132; Polycarp, *Philippians* 2.1).

3. The early Fathers made the death of Christ central, giving the resurrection a less prominent place, which is the reverse of the situation in Acts. Clement has more than twice as many references to the death (or the blood) of Christ as to the resurrection. The proportion is even greater in Ignatius and Barnabas. Whereas the *Epistle to Diognetus* has nothing on the resurrection, it contains a fairly lengthy statement on salvation, including the provision of the Son of God as a ransom (9). With Justin the references to the death, both as matter of history and as redemptive, attain flood proportions. It can truly be said that the death of Christ is his principal doctrinal preoccupation.

4. In the literature of the post-apostolic period more attention is paid to human participation in a future bodily resurrection than in Acts. Although it may have been included in Paul's preaching at Athens (17:18), only after his arrest in Jerusalem does it come clearly to the fore, and then in connection with

his defense, which in its theological aspect turned on the confirmation of the Pharisaic doctrine by means of the resurrection of Jesus of Nazareth (23:6; 24:15, 21).

Clement devotes three chapters to future resurrection (24–26) and shows dependence on Paul rather than on Acts by his reference to Christ as the first fruits and by his illustration of the seed that decays and then yields a harvest (cf. 1 Cor. 15). Furthermore, he introduces the fabled phoenix bird as a kind of parable of resurrection, an approach that is avoided by biblical writers. Other allusions occur in *2 Clement* 19.3; *Didache* 16.6; *Barnabas* 5.6-7; 21.1; Polycarp, *Philippians* 2.2; 5.2; 7.1; and *Martyrdom of Polycarp* 14.2, besides several in Ignatius (*Ephesians* 11.2; *Trallians* 9.2; *Smyrnaeans* 5.3; 7.1; and *Polycarp* 7.1). The apologists, beginning with Justin (*Apol.* 18–19), display a keen interest in this theme, some of them writing whole treatises on it. Emphasis falls heavily on the resurrection of the flesh, which conceivably could go back ultimately to Luke 24:39 for its source.

5. Although the early Fathers made use of some of the passages relied on in the speeches in Acts to present the resurrection as the fulfillment of Scripture (notably Pss. 16, 110), they also employ several which are not found in Acts, as noted earlier, namely, Psalms 22:22-23; 24; 96:10; and Isaiah 57:2. In passing it should be noted that Psalm 24 is utilized also in *The Gospel of Nicodemus* [13] in connection with Christ's harrowing of hell. This strain of thought is completely lacking in Acts.

6. In depicting the risen state of the Lord Jesus, a concern to refute the teaching of the Docetists leads Ignatius to use the word "flesh" for his body. "For I know and believe that he was in the flesh after the resurrection" (*Smyrnaeans* 3.1; cf. 12.2). In Acts the "flesh" is used in this connection only in a quotation (2:26) or in the filling out of a quotation (2:31). Those who find anti-docetism in Acts are obliged to acknowledge that it is virtually absent there and must be ferreted out by indirect means. Luke 24:39 is not restated. There is nothing like the frontal attack of Ignatius.

III

It appears from a survey of the data that there are elements in the Lukan presentation of the resurrection which differ from the treatment in the early Fathers. Some of the more important of these are the stress on the witness element in the apostolic preaching of the resurrection, the viewing of this event as a reversal by God of the human rejection of Jesus, the minor place given to the resurrection of men in relation to that of Jesus, the virtual absence of the word "flesh" in the description of the risen Lord, the refusal to philosophize about the resurrection or to seek analogies in nature, the utilization of fewer Old Testament passages as prophetic of this event in the life of our Lord, and the brevity of the affirmations involving the resurrection, lacking as they do the more confessional, semi-creedal character of those used by the early Fathers. The reader of Acts is caught up in the realization that something exciting and transforming has taken place, so that those who preach the resurrection do so not because it is a duty but because they cannot refrain. Such an atmosphere does not pervade the writings of the early Fathers and indeed could not rightly be expected because of distance from the event and preoccupation with the church.

There is less difficulty, in fact, in seeing Luke's account of the preaching of the resurrection as a faithful report based on contact with early disciples than in according his account of the preaching of the death of Jesus the same evaluation. The problem here is that whereas forgiveness of sins is set forth as a part of the apostolic proclamation, it is not connected with the death of the Savior in direct fashion. Acts 20:28 stands virtually alone, and in this passage nothing is said about the forgiveness of sins. A possible key to the difficulty may be found in the statement of Peter, "God exalted him at his right hand as Leader and Savior, to give repentance to Israel and forgiveness of sins" (5:31). The exaltation, which began with the resurrection and was completed by the ascension and session at the right hand, is so powerfully compelling that it almost appears as the ground of salvation. The redemption of the cross is passed over without specific mention in the same way that the ministry which preceded it is not brought into focus as a part of the salvation process but is simply assumed.

Our immediate concern, however, is Luke's handling of the resurrection. Some scholars may be inclined to acknowledge that his treatment does not reflect the language or the atmosphere of the early second century but prefer to account for this on the basis of a consummate artistry that enabled him by the exercise of historical imagination to create an aura of verisimilitude for the proclamation as he records it. However, with such an approach one would have a hard time explaining Luke's failure to capitalize on many opportunities for the insertion of the resurrection message where it would be altogether fitting to find it. Stephen mentions the betrayal and murder of Jesus but has not a word about resurrection. It fails to appear also in the report of Philip's preaching at Samaria and to the Ethiopian eunuch. The newly converted Saul preaches at Damascus, but in the summary of that preaching nothing is said about the resurrection, despite the fact that the preacher has so recently been confronted with the risen Lord and must have been full of the subject. Nor is anything said about the resurrection in connection with Saul's preaching at Jerusalem, where it would have been eminently appropriate and impressive (9:28-29). A similar silence pervades the report of Peter's ministry in the towns of Judea (9:32-43).

Most of the allusions to the resurrection appear in the speeches, which bear unmistakable marks of Luke's workmanship in terms of style and vocabulary. This being so, it is easy to assume that the content was shaped by him also, in which case we can have no confidence that he is giving us a faithful account of what was said on various occasions. But there are factors which give pause to the acceptance of any such assumption. For example, as C. F. D. Moule has shown, Luke has a discriminating treatment of such terms as Lord, Son of man, prophet, Savior, and Son which is discernible when one compares the Acts with the Gospel of Luke.[14] Moule then goes on to ascribe the contrasts to "the consciousness of the resurrection as marking a decisive vindication of Jesus."[15]

The question that must be raised at this point is whether these delicate nuances are really possible when Luke is thought of as doing his work at the close of the first century or early in the second, separated by over half a century from the rise of the church. As noted above (note 11), O'Neill has proposed a very late dating for Acts, but his viewpoint has not gained acceptance for a variety of reasons.[16] The precision of Luke the historian which so impressed itself on Ramsay that he turned from a second-century to a first-century dating as the only plausible explanation for his accuracy is nowhere taken into account by O'Neill.

C. K. Barrett recognizes that contact with the actual conditions of the primitive church must be recognized in Acts (for example, the equivalence of elder and bishop and the lack of any provision for the transfer of apostolic authority) but is minded nevertheless to put Acts somewhere in the era of Clement and Ignatius.[17] To account for the failure of Luke to reflect the deviations from the apostolic period which appear in these Fathers, he appeals to the guiding and controlling influence of the Spirit.[18] Without questioning that Luke enjoyed such an influence, is it not feasible to hold that he was aided also by proximity to the tradition of the early church at a point fairly close to its source, of which contact his treatment of the resurrection is a notable example?

NOTES

[1] Martin Dibelius, *Aufsätze zur Apostelgeschichte*, ed. H. Greeven (Göttingen: Vandenhoeck & Ruprecht, 1951), Eng. tr. by Mary Ling, *Studies in the Acts of the Apostles* (London: SCM, 1956).

[2] Hans Conzelmann, *Die Mitte der Zeit* (Tübingen: J. C. B. Mohr, 1954), Eng. tr. by G. Buswell, *The Theology of St. Luke* (New York: Harper & Row, Publishers, 1960).

[3] See the surveys by C. K. Barrett, *Luke the Historian in Recent Study* (London: Epworth Press, 1961); new edition with select bibliography, Facet Books, Biblical Series, 24 (Philadelphia: Fortress Press, 1970); and R. H. Fuller, *The New Testament in Current Study* (New York: Charles Scribner's Sons, 1962).

[4] E. Käsemann, *New Testament Questions of Today*, trans. W. J. Montague (Philadelphia: Fortress Press, 1969), p. 21.

[5] Charles H. Talbert, *Luke and the Gnostics* (Nashville: Abingdon Press, 1966).

[6] W. C. Van Unnik, "Luke-Acts, a Storm Center in Contemporary Scholarship," in *Studies in Luke-Acts: Essays Presented in Honor of Paul Schubert . . .*, ed. L. E. Keck and J. L. Martyn (Nashville: Abingdon Press, 1966), p. 29.

[7] L. Goppelt, *Apostolic and Post-Apostolic Times*, trans. Robert A. Guelich (New York: Harper & Row, Publishers, 1970), p. 141.

[8] E. Haenchen, *Die Apostelgeschichte*, Meyer Kommentar (5th ed.) (Göttingen: Vandenhoeck & Ruprecht, 1965), p. 84.

[9] Conzelmann, *The Theology of St. Luke*, p. 159.

[10] So C. K. Barrett, *Luke the Historian in Recent Study*, pp. 70-71.

[11] J. C. O'Neill, *The Theology of Acts in Its Historical Setting* (London: S.P.C.K. Press, 1961, rev. ed., 1971).

[12] All references are to the *First Apology of Justin* (*Apol.* hereafter).

[13] See Part II of this work, *The Descent into Hell*, 5, in *E. Hennecke, New*

Testament Apocrypha, ed. W. Schneemelcher, trans. and ed. R. McL. Wilson (Philadelphia: The Westminster Press), vol. 1, *Gospels and Related Writings* (1963), pp. 473f., citing Psalm 23 LXX.

[14] C. F. D. Moule, "The Christology of Acts," in *Studies in Luke-Acts* (Schubert festschrift, cited above, note 6), pp. 159-185.

[15] *Ibid.,* p. 165.

[16] H. F. D. Sparks, review in *JTS,* n.s. 14 (1963), pp. 457-466; W. G. Kümmel, *Introduction to the New Testament,* trans. A. J. Mattill, Jr. (Nashville: Abingdon Press, 1966), pp. 132-133; Hans Conzelmann, "Luke's Place in the Development of Early Christianity," in *Studies in Luke-Acts* (Schubert festschrift, *op. cit.*), p. 304.

[17] Barrett, *op. cit.,* p. 75, note 91.

[18] *Ibid.,* p. 76.

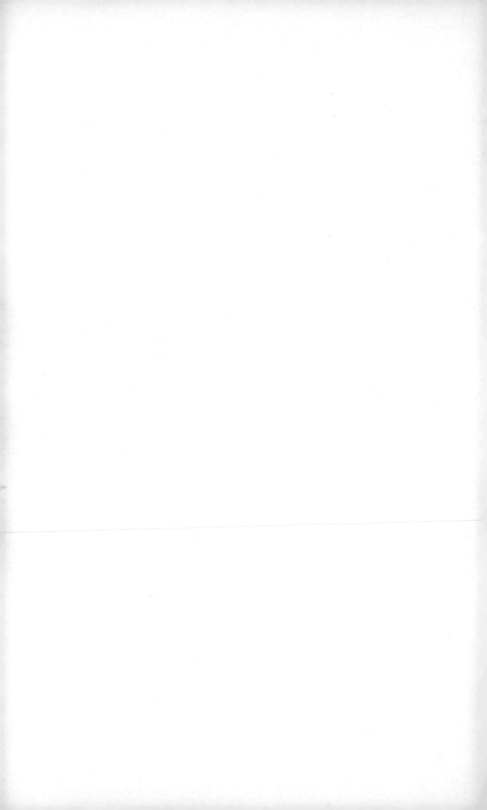

Eusebius
and His
Church History

by Robert M. Grant

In ancient and modern times Eusebius of Caesarea has found severe critics of his historical reliability, but there is a question whether or not these critics have gone as far as they should go. It seems highly probable that under the influence of his apologetic purposes Eusebius suppressed, neglected, or falsified a good deal of the historical information available to him. Sometimes he made mistakes which can be explained as due to simple ignorance. There are key points, however, in regard to which a pattern or a group of patterns emerges and suggests that what looked like ignorance is due to intention.

A study of this kind is appropriately dedicated to Morton Scott Enslin, indefatigable searcher for truth in the obscure Christian history of the early centuries. It involves both Christian beginnings and an ethical question or two — though hardly "the ethics of Paul"!

We shall consider two aspects of Eusebius's work and the purposes lying behind what he did. These are (1) his picture of apocalyptic eschatology, especially as expressed in "chiliasm," and (2) his picture of the Antonine emperors as related to Christianity.

I

The essential points of Eusebius's outlook in regard to eschatology are indicated in the theological preface to his work (1.2–5), largely a reply to objections against Christianity levied by Porphyry a generation earlier. The answers, like the objections, deal with past history, not with expectations for the future. In 1.2.23 Eusebius lists some events predicted by the prophets: the miraculous birth, new teaching, and miracles of the Logos; his death, his resurrection, and finally "his divine restoration (ἀποκατάστασις) to the heavens." This use of ἀποκατάστασις is surprising (cf. *Demonstratio Evangelica* 4.16.41 [Oxford Patristic Greek Lexicon, ed. G. W. H.

Lampe, p. 195a]). Even more surprising is the fact that Eusebius says not one word about the expectation of Christ's second coming and the establishment of God's kingdom. For him the ascension of Christ brought an era of human history to an end (1.13.4, 10–11, 20; 2.1.3, 2.1, 13.3; 3.5.2.), and he says nothing about a future return. The mysterious "weeks" of the Book of Daniel had been fulfilled at the time of Jesus' birth (1.6.11). The grandsons of Jude, brother of the Lord "after the flesh," must have spoken the truth when they said that the kingdom of Christ was "not worldly or earthly but heavenly and angelic, to come at the end of the age when, coming in glory he will judge living and dead and will repay each one in accordance with his pursuits" (3.20.4; cf. John 18:36; 2 Tim. 4:1, 18; Matt. 16:27; 24:3). This interpretation of the kingdom of Christ still retains an eschatological note in spite of the words "heavenly" and "angelic," but the note — as in most patristic thought — is muted.[1]

It is worth noting that in Eusebius's view, based on Irenaeus, the Apocalypse of John was written at just the time the grandsons of Jude were giving their testimony (3.18.3 = 5.8.6). In discussing John he concentrates almost exclusively on the Gospel and on the tradition that the apostle died in the reign of Trajan, thus provided with enough time to write his most important work (3.23–24). Eusebius never discusses the content of the Apocalypse, except when much later in the *Church History* he quotes from the attack made on it by Dionysius of Alexandria (7.25.1–3). Writing about heretics under Trajan, he manages to describe the book by quoting from Gaius of Rome and Dionysius and claiming that they were attacking the heresy of Cerinthus (3.28.1–5). Irenaeus's account of Cerinthus then remains to be discussed. What to do with it? Irenaeus referred neither to Cerinthus's eschatology nor to his possible authorship of the Apocalypse. What Eusebius does is to state that Irenaeus described the "more secret" doctrine of Cerinthus; he then passes on to tell a piquant anecdote from Irenaeus about Cerinthus and Polycarp of Smyrna (3.28.6 = 4.14.6).

Since Irenaeus discussed first Cerinthus, then the Nicolaitans, Eusebius follows suit, relying first on Irenaeus's account of these heretics mentioned in the Apocalypse, then on Clement of Alexandria for another anecdote (3.29).

This is all he says at this point. Later on, however, he speaks of Papias as a hearer of John (3.39.1) but refrains from reporting (from Irenaeus) what it was that Papias heard.[2] Irenaeus was wrong when he supposed that Papias was "a man of antiquity" (3.39.13). We shall return to this point. In notes on the content of Justin's *Dialogue with Trypho* he refers to the presence of "prophetic gifts" among Christians (*Dial.* 82.1) and to the apostolic authorship of the Apocalypse (81.4). Eusebius obviously was acquainted with this part of the *Dialogue* (4.18.8). But he has managed to suppress any mention of the chiliastic doctrine held by both Justin and John (*Dial.* 80.5; 81.4). Similarly, in quoting (5.8.5) a brief passage from Irenaeus on the number of the beast in Revelation 13:18, he adroitly omits reference to Irenaeus's appeal to those who had seen John face to face and to the number itself (*Adv. haer.* 5.30.1 [*Sources . . .*, p. 370]). Naturally he leaves out any detailed discussion of Irenaeus's own chiliastic views (*Adv. haer.* 5.32–36 [*Sources . . .*, pp. 396–466]).

We are not surprised, then, to find him providing a discussion of Dionysius's criticism of the Apocalypse (7.24–25) while placing no emphasis on the fact that in a letter Dionysius referred Revelation 13:5 to the emperor Valerian (7.10.2).

The foundation of Eusebius's attitude, therefore, lies in a downgrading of apocalyptic eschatology, and this is reflected in his attitude toward the Apocalypse of John.

In other instances he meets apocalyptic eschatologists head on, or nearly so. First, let us consider Papias. By quoting from Papias's own book he convinces himself that this author, who in Irenaeus's opinion was early, actually belonged to the second generation after the apostles. Papias wrote about marvels as if from tradition. Eusebius again refrains from saying what they were (cf. note 2 above). Papias obtained stories from the (unreliable?) daughters of Philip. He told strange parables of, or unrelated to, the Savior. He included highly mythical (chiliastic) traditions. He failed to understand that the apostles spoke μυστικῶς. In short, he was highly limited in intelligence (3.39.1–13). Second, let us look at the Montanists. Why bother to state that one of their principal concerns was the advent of the new Jerusalem from heaven? All that Eusebius says, following "an ecclesiastical writer called Apollonius," is that Montanus "named Pepuza and Tymion (small towns in Phrygia) Jerusalem, in his desire to gather to them people from everywhere" (5.18.2). He offers no hint that there the heavenly Jerusalem was expected to descend. His discussion of Montanism makes one wonder about his use of Tertullian. After all, he could read Latin; at least he says that he could.[3] Could he not have found more about Tertullian? Could he not have used something beyond the *Apology* (see Part II)? Did he simply prefer not to discuss Montanism any further? Third, a certain Judas, writing in the tenth year of Septimius Severus (= 201/202), studied the seventy weeks in Daniel (cf. 1.6.11) and concluded that the Antichrist was near. Eusebius explains his ideas away. "Thus strongly the impetus of the persecution against us at the time disturbed the thoughts of *the many*" (6.7; italics mine).

We have seen how Eusebius suppresses the mention of various aspects of the thought of writers he discusses, as he presses on toward his non-apocalyptic eschatological goal. We now turn to what seems to be the suppression of whole works. One could hold that it is a matter of ignorance or neglect (as perhaps in the case of Tertullian) rather than one of suppression. The results for Eusebius's viewpoint are so favorable, however, that it appears that a pattern continues to be involved. Our witnesses will be two Roman writers of the early third century. First there is Gaius, whose *Dialogue* with the Montanist Proclus Eusebius certainly knew — though oddly enough he never used it for information about Montanism (2.25.6–7; 3.28.1–2, 31.4; 6.20.3). What Eusebius tells us about Gaius himself is that he did not accept the Epistle to the Hebrews as canonical "when curbing the recklessness and audacity of his opponents in composing new scriptures" (6.20.3). Eusebius does not consider it appropriate to say that the "new scriptures" consisted of the Gospel and Apocalypse of John, or to say, as is clear from 3.28.2, that he ascribed the Apocalypse (and the Gospel) to the heretic Cerinthus. In addition he does not mention the work of Hippolytus "On Behalf of the Gospel and Apocalypse According to John" or his "Chapters Against Gaius."[4] In fact, he is remarkably vague about Hippolytus. He mentions neither his commentary on Daniel (which could have been noted at the point where he refers to the apocalypticist Judas) nor his treatise on the Antichrist. He prefers to say only that Hippolytus presided over a church "somewhere" (6.20.2) and to list his treatise *On Easter* ($\pi\epsilon\rho\grave{\iota}\ \tau o\hat{\upsilon}\ \pi\acute{\alpha}\sigma\chi\alpha$), precisely datable in the first year of Alexander Severus, and other exegetical and antiheretical writings.

In 5.28 Eusebius provides quotations from "a certain narrative" describing the activities of heretics in the time of Zephyrinus. Theodoret later made use of Eusebius's selections and perhaps knew the document itself; he calls it "the *Little Labyrinth*," denies that it was written by Origen, but does not say who he thinks wrote it (*Haereticarum fabularum compendium* 2.5 [Migne PG 83, 392B-C]). Presumably its author was Hippolytus. The tenth book of Hippolytus's *Refutatio* begins with the words, "The labyrinth of the heresies" (*Refutatio* 10.5.1, p. 265, 7, ed. Wendland, GCS 26 [1916]), and R. H. Connolly provided vocabulary parallels which make the case highly probable.[5] Perhaps it is to be identified with Hippolytus's treatise *Against All the Heresies*, mentioned in Eusebius's list (6.22). It is unlikely that Eusebius actually knew the *Refutatio* — the larger *Labyrinth* — though he would have found most unedifying Hippolytus's criticisms of Zephyrinus and Callistus. He did not know, for he would have found it relevant, Hippolytus's προσομιλία *de laude domini salvatoris*, in which he indicated that he was speaking in Origen's presence (Jerome, *De viris illustribus*). But Hippolytus was not one of Eusebius's favorite authors.

Three more early Christian writers are passed over in complete silence. (1) Eusebius never mentions the apologist Athenagoras or the treatise *On the Resurrection* ascribed to him. The reason for this silence seems fairly clear: in his anti-Origenist treatise *De resurrectione* (to which the *Apology for Origen* by Pamphilus and Eusebius was a reply) Methodius had cited Athenagoras as his authority for a rather extensive discussion of the devil.[6] Eusebius was not going to look up an author quoted approvingly by his enemy. If the tradition (if, indeed, it was a tradition) that Athenagoras was the first head of the school at Alexandria was in circulation,[7] this would have conflicted with Pamphilus's view that the school was founded by Pantaenus, the predecessor of Clement and Origen (PG 103, 397A). (2) Methodius himself was certainly not to be mentioned. As we have just pointed out, Eusebius had joined Pamphilus in producing a defense of Origen directed against him (Jerome, *Contra Rufinum* 1.11 [PL 23, 423C]). Indeed, he went to considerable lengths in obliterating Methodius's memory. In his later *Praeparatio Evangelica* (7.22) he quoted from a certain Maximus, Περὶ τῆς ὕλης, a passage which indubitably comes from Methodius (*De autexusio*, 5.1–12.8). In the *Church History* (5.27) he dated the same work in the reign of Septimius Severus, thus placing his opponent's efforts about a century in the past. Since Eusebius evidently knew the treatise *De autexusio*, we may wonder if there was not a trace of irony in his words about Papias's failure to understand what the apostles said μυστικῶς (3.39.12). Methodius used the same expression about their teaching and its interpretation at the beginning of this treatise (*De autexusio* 1.5). (3) In the Alexandrian school, Eusebius made no mention of the teacher Theognostus.[8] Perhaps he was ill-informed about the history of the school after Origen's removal to Caesarea; perhaps he preferred not to discuss it. There is reason to suppose that the latter explanation is correct. Eusebius knew that Heraclas was Origen's successor (6.26) and was followed by Dionysius (6.29.4). We find nothing more about teachers at Alexandria, except for quotations from Dionysius on the Apocalypse, until we come to Anatolius, head of the Aristotelian school (7.32.6), the presbyter Pierius, famous for asceticism and philosophy (26–27), and Achillas, a presbyter "along with Pierius" and head of "the school of the sacred faith" under Theonas, bishop at the end of the third century (30). It is likely that Theognostus taught around the middle of the century; Athanasius called both him and Origen παλαιοὶ ἄνδρες.[9] The unreliable Philip of Side described the Alexandrian succession as running from Heraclas through Dionysius to Pierius and then to Theognostus,[10] but this notion is certainly wrong as regards Pierius. What Theognostus did was to continue living at Alexandria after Origen left there; he taught a doctrine essentially the same as Origen's,[11] but not under Origen's auspices. Eusebius refrained from mentioning him because he had taken Origen's place at Alexandria.

We should also explain why Eusebius said so little about Pierius. According to Photius, some said this Alexandrian died as a martyr under Diocletian, while others held that after the persecution he spent the rest of his life at Rome.[12] We now know that in 307 the prefect of Egypt was able to tell Christians that by obeying the order to sacrifice, Pierius had "saved many."[13] Presumably he was not a martyr.

All these inclusions, exclusions, and distortions are related to one main purpose. They were intended to rid Christian history of any suspicion that Christian leaders were chiliastic enthusiasts, eagerly awaiting the coming of the kingdom of God on earth. The true Christian doctrine was best interpreted by Origen and his loyal disciples, who had to be defended and exalted. Their opponents had to be criticized, reinterpreted, or passed over in silence. One can hold that in many respects Eusebius's picture was right without finding anything to commend in his method.

II

Eusebius's anti-chiliastic bias was not the only factor that led him to write fiction. He also went wrong when discussing the Antonine emperors, as we shall show. First we shall set forth the evidence, then proceed to conclusions. According to Eusebius (4.11.11) Justin wrote a treatise *Against the Greeks* and also "addressed other discourses [plural] containing an apology for our faith to the emperor Antoninus (the same who was called Pius) and the senate of the Romans." It is not really clear whether or not Eusebius has two works in view, for he goes on to quote the opening words of "the Apology." These show that it was addressed to "the emperor Titus Aelius Hadrianus Antoninus Pius Caesar Augustus and to Verissimus his son the philosopher and to Lucius, by birth son of Caesar the philosopher and by adoption son of Pius, and a lover of learning, and to the holy senate of the Romans." This address has occasioned considerable controversy, partly because the one manuscript of Justin's *Apology* makes Lucius not "son of Caesar the philosopher" but "the philosopher, son of Caesar." It is an odd preface. The titles of Antoninus Pius are correct, but they are in the wrong order; they should have read "the emperor Titus Aelius Caesar Hadrianus Antoninus Augustus Pius" or "the emperor Caesar Titus Aelius Hadrianus Augustus Pius." We may assume that Justin was aiming at correctness but missed. Beyond that, it is strange to find the full name of Antoninus Pius followed by the nickname of Marcus Aurelius and the *praenomen* of Lucius Verus (*Scriptores Historiae Augustae, Vita Marci* 1.10 [cf. Dio 69.21.2]). In addition, only the fourth-century *Historia Augusta* suggests that Marcus Aurelius can possibly have adopted Lucius Verus (*Historia Augusta* 5.1), and even that is not exactly what Justin says. E. Schwartz has suggested various emendations to the text.[14]

Here we suggest only that Justin wrote φιλοσόφῳ and that Eusebius changed the word to φιλοσόφου, for reasons which will appear later.

Before proceeding further with Justin, Eusebius says that "the same emperor" (i.e., Antoninus Pius) wrote a letter to the Koinon (Council) of Asia in favor of the Christians. This is then quoted (13.1–7) and turns out to have been written by "the emperor Caesar Marcus Aurelius Antoninus Augustus, Armenius [!]," etc. A cross-reference to Melito of Sardis (13.8) leads us either to "Antoninus" (26.2) or to Antoninus Pius (cf. 26.10). It must be that one of Eusebius's research assistants supplied the wrong forgery for insertion at this point; the right forgery seems to have survived in the manuscript of Justin's works.

At this point (4.14) Eusebius inserts a discussion of Polycarp (continued from 3.36), perhaps because he is aware that Polycarp really belongs in the reign of Antoninus Pius. In 4.14.10 we learn of the death of Pius and the succession of "his son Marcus Aurelius Verus, also called Antoninus, together with his brother Lucius." It was "at this time," according to Eusebius, that Polycarp became a martyr. He provides extensive paraphrases and quotations of the *Martyrdom* (15.1–46), wrongly synchronizing martyrdoms under Decius with these events (15.47–48).

Now we hear of Justin again, this time as a martyr (16). But since Eusebius does not possess the *Martyrdom of Justin*, he has to show that Justin at least foresaw a martyr's death. It must have been occasioned by a second book "to the aforesaid rulers" (16.1; i.e., Marcus Aurelius and Lucius) and by conflicts at Rome. A citation from "the aforesaid *Apology*" — not the "second book"[15] — provides evidence for the conflicts (16.2–6), as do notes from Tatian (16.7–8). Eusebius wrongly states that Tatian's words prove that Justin was "perfected." A further quotation from Justin ἐν τῇ προτέρᾳ ἀπολογίᾳ (=τῇ δεδηλωμένῃ ἀπολογίᾳ) shows that there were other martyrs at Rome before him (17).

Then Eusebius turns to his catalogue of books in the library at Caesarea and lists the ὑπομνήματα of Justin. They include (*a*) a λόγος προσφωνητικός to Antoninus Pius and his sons [!] and the senate of the Romans, and (*b*) another λόγος containing a second apology addressed to τὸν τοῦ δεδηλωμένου αὐτοκράτορος [Antoninus Pius] διάδοχόν τε καὶ ὁμώνυμον ᾿Αντωνῖνον Οὐῆρον, "the events of whose reign we are now discussing" (18.2). We shall later try to discover what emperor Eusebius had in mind. Here we simply state our agreement with Schwartz (*loc. cit.*): there is no reason to suppose that there are any traces of the second λόγος in Eusebius's work.

To round out our discussion of the literary materials related to the Antonines, we note that Melito of Sardis also wrote a βιβλίδιον πρὸς ᾿Αντωνῖνον (26.2), already described by Eusebius (13.8) as an apology "to the emperor Verus" (13.8). Apollinaris of Hierapolis also wrote to "the aforesaid emperor" (27). This work must have included a description of "the thundering legion" (5.5.4).

Finally, in the preface to Book 5 Eusebius carefully dates the accession of Eleutherus, bishop of Rome, and the martyrdoms in Gaul in "the seventeenth year of the emperor Antoninus Verus," who, one would suppose, was the emperor who imposed the death penalty on Roman Christians in Gaul (5.1.44, 46). It is to be noted, however, that the emperor is called "Caesar" in the account of the event. This fact gave Eusebius the opportunity of stating that "these events took place under Antoninus" and of going on to differentiate him from "his brother Marcus Aurelius Caesar" (5.5.1).

Marcus Aurelius was the emperor under whom the "thundering legion" served, as Eusebius goes on to say with an appeal to the witness of Apollinaris and Tertullian. In his *Apology* (5.6–7) Tertullian had actually spoken of a pro-Christian letter written by Marcus Aurelius and had gone on to praise the emperors Vespasian, Trajan, Hadrian, Pius, and Verus for not enforcing the laws against Christians. Eusebius quotes from Tertullian but drops the name of Verus. Mention of him would not have fitted into his theory of Antonine attitudes. The discussion ends with Eusebius's remark, "Let each one view these matters as he pleases." We accept this invitation to critics.

To some extent Eusebius's confused and confusing picture of the Antonines is due to simple error. It is true that both Antoninus Pius and Marcus Aurelius were often called by the same name, Antoninus. The *Apology* of Justin, written about 150,[16] can have been addressed to Pius and to the Caesar, Marcus Aurelius, who held tribunician power after 146.[17] An address to Lucius (Verus) is unlikely,[18] though barely possible. As Caesar, Marcus Aurelius did bear the name Verus, but it was transferred to Lucius in 161. Eusebius should have known, however, that the term "Antoninus and Verus" occurs repeatedly in documents of the years 161–169, with reference to two emperors,[19] while the name Antoninus Verus never existed except in the imagination of the fourth-century author of the *Historia Augusta* (*Vita Antonini Pii* 4.5 [Verus Antoninus]; cf. 6.10; *Vita Marci* 7.7; *Vita Veri* 1.2). Eusebius's notion that either Marcus or Lucius bore this name is quite wrong, or wrongheaded.

Something more than error, however, is involved in Eusebius's dating of various events in the Antonine period. What may possibly have begun as error led to a thorough and complex revision of the history of the later second century. To be sure, Eusebius's collection of martyr-acts may have contained few dates. This would explain why he placed Decian martyrs in the Antonine period (4.15.47–48). But something more has taken place in regard to the martyrdoms of Polycarp and the Gallicans.

Modern scholars have sometimes supposed that Polycarp was martyred in 167 (so Eusebius's *Chronicle*, to which we shall later turn) or at least in the period 161–169.[20] It has been thought that perhaps he did not possess the *Martyrdom* with chapter 21, which could have told him that Statius Quadratus was proconsul of Asia,[21] although, as W. R. Schoedel points out, "it is possible that he did not know enough about the details to be able to make use of it."[22] Statius Quadratus, consul in 142, could have been proconsul only in the reign of Antoninus Pius, not under Marcus Aurelius and/or Lucius Verus.[23] The true date would not have suited Eusebius's scheme. Antoninus Pius, in his view, was no persecutor.

Similarly, Marcus Aurelius cannot have persecuted Christians. In defiance of the exact date given in the preface to Book 5 — A.D. 177, Eusebius ascribes the Gallican martyrdoms to "Antoninus" in order to show that Verus, not Marcus Aurelius, put Christians to death. This is why Eusebius put the date of Polycarp's martyrdom in the time of Verus and why, against himself and all the historical evidence, he ascribed the Gallican martyrdoms to this emperor. For this reason we should claim that he wrongly supposed that Melito addressed his apology to Lucius Verus; a persecution was in progress (4.26.5–6).

One may claim that it was Tertullian who was responsible for misleading Eusebius. His was the theory, anticipated by Melito, that bad emperors persecuted Christians, while good ones did not.[24] Tertullian, indeed, had said that Verus did not persecute. But if he did not, Marcus Aurelius must have done so; and Marcus was a hero for Dio Cassius and Herodian, for Philostratus, and for the circles in which the *Historia Augusta* was to be read. Waiting for the coming of another philosopher-king,[25] Eusebius could not use the reign of Marcus as a precedent if he persecuted Christians; he therefore (*a*) kept Justin from speaking of Lucius Verus as a philosopher, (*b*) indicated that Polycarp and the Gallican martyrs suffered under Verus and that Melito knew of persecution under him, (*c*) refrained from saying when Verus died, and (*d*) deleted mention of him when quoting from Tertullian. He adjusted the past in relation to the future. In other words, he falsified his account.

We may now ask when precisely it was that Eusebius undertook this venture of changing the past (a feat which according to Greco-Roman philosophers and theologians God himself could not perform).[26] Before beginning the *Church History*, he had completed the first edition of the *Chronicle*,[27] and in it we find the following dates (adjusted to the Christian era):[28]

> 161: Accession of Marcus Aurelius, *qui et Verus*, and Lucius Aurelius Commodus (reign of 19 years)
> 167: Deaths of Polycarp, Pionius, Gallican martyrs
> 169: "some," 171, Latin; 170, Armenian: Death of the emperor Lucius
> 170 (Latin only): Melito of Sardis
> 170, Latin; 171, Armenian: Apollinaris of Hierapolis
> 173–175, Latin; 172, Armenian: Rain miracle under Antoninus; mention of "king Marcus" (Armenian) or Marcus Aurelius (Latin)

This table shows that Eusebius had already begun work on his theory when he wrote the *Chronicle* — in which there are references to Tertullian's *Apology*. (a) He had placed the deaths of Polycarp, Pionius, and the Gallicans under Marcus Aurelius and Lucius Verus, but had not as yet noticed that the Gallicans' relation to Eleutherus made such a date impossible.[29] (b) If "some" in the Latin version refers to a version of the *Chronicle* (one would like to think so, in spite of the further difficulties involved), he had recognized that Melito should have written before the death of Lucius Verus if he was going to address him. Perhaps, however, "some" comes from a later version in which the difficulty was recognized. (c) An unfaced problem arises from his placing Apollinaris before the rain miracle which he discussed.

This tangle had to be sorted out, and when Eusebius reached Books 4 and 5 of the *Church History*, he (a) set Polycarp and Pionius close to the beginning of the joint reign of Marcus Aurelius and Lucius Verus, (b) made sure to have Melito write to (Lucius) Verus, (c) placed the Gallican martyrs in 177, though perversely stating that they were put to death by the orders of Antoninus = Lucius Verus, and (d) necessarily refrained from mentioning the death of Lucius Verus. He had also discovered that Apollinaris referred to the rain miracle and therefore did not mention it at all in Book 4 (the chronological problems were too complicated), reserving discussion of it for 5.5.4.

What, then, of the true course of human events under the Antonines? Negatively, it must be said that there is no reason to assign the martyrdom of Polycarp to the period 161–169, and when this objection to *Martyrdom of Polycarp* 21 falls, no reason for rejecting the last years of Antoninus Pius as its setting. At this point we may add that Eusebius also errs when he places the career of Bardesanes in Book 4 (chap. 30). He has been misled by his own theory that "Antoninus" means Marcus Aurelius. Actually, in this case it means Elagabalus — about whom he knows practically nothing (6.21.1–2).[30] Positively, we learn that the documents quoted by Eusebius must be dated with extreme caution, since when under the spell of political-theological theory he does not hesitate to arrange them as he pleases, to reinterpret (i.e., misinterpret) them, and even to alter their text. Such activities, rather surprising in a relatively "neutral" section of the *Church History*, are reflected even more strongly in other books, especially in Book 6 (chapters 1–39), where he is writing a defense of his hero Origen and, indeed, relying upon a similar document written earlier. They pervade Books 7–10.

We should also point out that modern historians or theologians who scorn "mere" chronology have not, perhaps, recognized what can be done with it, given strong enough presuppositions on the part of a historian.

NOTES

[1] Cf. G. W. H. Lampe, "Some Notes on the Significance of ΒΑΣΙΛΕΙΑ ΤΟΥ ΘΕΟΥ, ΒΑΣΙΛΕΙΑ ΧΡΙΣΤΟΥ in the Greek Fathers," *JTS*, 49 (1948), pp. 58–73.

[2] What Papias heard was apocalyptic-eschatological tradition; cf. Irenaeus, *Adversus haereses* 5.33.3–4 (in the ed. of Rousseau–Doutreleau–Mercier, *Sources chrétiennes* 153 [Paris: Éditions du Cerf, 1969], pp. 414–416).

[3] See H. J. Lawlor and J. E. L. Oulton, *Eusebius* (London: S.P.C.K., 1928), vol. 2, pp. 36–37.

[4] Cf., e.g., J. Quasten, *Patrology*, vol. 2 (Westminster, Md.: Newman Press, 1953), p. 197.

[5] R. H. Connolly, "Eusebius, *H.E.*, v. 28," *JTS*, 49 (1948), pp. 73–79.

[6] Athenagoras, *The Supplication for the Christians* (*Libellus pro Christianis*) 24, ed. E. Schwartz, *TU*, 4, 2 (Leipzig: 1891), p. 32; Methodius, *De resurrectione* 1.37.1–3.

[7] Cf. Gustave Bardy, "Pour l'histoire d'école d'alexandrie," *RevBib.*, 51 (1942) (= *Vivre et Penser* 2), pp. 81–82.

[8] Cf. A. Harnack, *Die Hypotyposen des Theognost, TU*, 24,3 (Leipzig: 1903); R. M. Grant, *After The New Testament* (Philadelphia: Fortress Press, 1967), pp. 78–80.

[9] A. Harnack, *op. cit.*, pp. 74–75.

[10] See note 7.

[11] Cf. PG, 103, 373C–76C.

[12] *Ibid.*, 401A.

[13] V. Martin, *Papyrus Bodmer* XX (Coligny: 1964), p. 26, lines 5–8.

[14] E. Schwartz, *Eusebius: Kirchengeschichte* III (Leipzig: J. C. Hinrichs, 1909), p. cliv, note 3.

[15] *Ibid.*, p. clvi.

[16] Cf. Justin, *Apol.* 1.29.2 (L. Munatius Felix was prefect of Egypt not later than 154); O. W. Reinmuth in *Bulletin of the American Society of Papyrologists* 4 (1967), p. 97; Justin, *Apol.* 46.1 (Christ born 150 years earlier).

[17] *Inscriptiones Italiae* XIII, 1 (Rome, 1947), pp. 206–207.

[18] So E. Schwartz, *op. cit.*, p. clv.

[19] P. Bureth, *Les titulatures impériales* (Brussels, 1964), pp. 65–72, 77–81.

[20] Cf. H.-I. Marrou, "La date du martyre de S. Polycarpe," in *Analecta Bollandiana* 71 (1953), pp. 5–20.

[21] H. von Campenhausen, "Bearbeitungen und Interpolationen des Polykarpmartyriums," *Sitzungsberichte der Heidelberger Akademie der Wissenschaften, Philosophisch-Historische Klasse* (Heidelberg: C. Winter, 1957), no. 3, 31.

[22] W. R. Schoedel, *Polycarp, Martyrdom of Polycarp, Fragments of Papias,* in The Apostolic Fathers: A New Translation and Commentary, ed. Robert M. Grant (Camden: Thomas Nelson & Sons, 1967), p. 77.

[23] Cf. T. D. Barnes, "A Note on Polycarp," *JTS*, 18 (1967), pp. 433–437.

[24] Tertullian, *Apol.* 5, largely reproduced in Eusebius, *Church History* 2. 2. 5–6, 25.4; 3. 20.7; 5. 6–7; see also Melito as cited in 4. 26.9 (Nero and Domitian). Obviously Tertullian, who knew something of Melito's writings (Jerome, *De viris illustribus* 24), relied on his idea.

[25] Cf. N. H. Baynes, *Byzantine Studies and Other Essays* (London: Athlone Press, 1955), pp. 168–172.

[26] R. M. Grant, *Miracle and Natural Law in Graeco-Roman and Early Christian Thought* (Amsterdam: North-Holland Publishing Co., 1952), pp. 129, 131.

[27] D. S. Wallace-Hadrill, "The Eusebian Chronicle," *JTS*, n.s. 6 (1955), pp. 248–253.

[28] Armenian *Chronicle*, p. 222, tr. Karst, GCS, 20 (1911); Latin *Chronicle*, pp. 204–207, ed. Rudolf Helm, GCS, 47 (1956).

[29] The Gallican martyrs themselves wrote a letter to Eleutherus (5. 3.4; 4.2), who was bishop only in 177 (5. preface 1).

[30] Cf. H. J. W. Drijvers, *Bardaisan of Edessa* (Assen, 1966), pp. 178, 208, 214, 218. The true date is indicated by Julius Africanus. Cf. J.-R. Vieillefond, *Jules Africain: Fragments des Cestes* (Paris, 1932), pp. 49–50.

Tabula
Gratulatoria

Frank F. Adler, Pastor, Messiah Ev. Lutheran Church, Sea Isle City, New Jersey

Paul W. Allison, Executive, BSA, Inc., Collegeville, Pennsylvania

Bernhard W. Anderson, Professor of Old Testament Theology, Princeton Theological Seminary, Princeton, New Jersey

Donald P. Austin, Pastor, Bethel United Methodist Church, Camden, New Jersey

Robert and Muriel Back, Rector, St. Luke's Parish, Darien, Connecticut

Anastasius C. Bandy, Assoc. Professor of Classics, University of California, Riverside, California

Clifford E. Barbour Library, Pittsburgh Theological Seminary, Pittsburgh, Pennsylvania

Cyril Blackman, Emmanuel College, Toronto, Ontario, Canada

William Boggs, Chicago, Illinois

Robert E. Bornemann, Professor of Old Testament, Lutheran Theological Seminary, Philadelphia, Pennsylvania

John Renville Bowering, Pastor, United Methodist Church of Manasquan, New Jersey

Paul Hoover Bowman, Executive Director, Institute for Community Studies, Kansas City, Missouri

Crawford F. Bright, Jr., Dean, Bishop O. T. Jones School of Christian Education, Philadelphia, Pennsylvania

Jesse H. Brown, Colgate-Rochester/Bexley Hall/Crozer Seminaries, Rochester, New York

F. F. Bruce, Rylands Professor of Biblical Criticism & Exegesis, University of Manchester, England

T. A. Burkill, Head of the Dept. of Theology, The University of Rhodesia, Salisbury, Rhodesia

Robert E. Burns, Chicago, Illinois

Henry J. Cadbury, Hollis Professor of Divinity, Emeritus, Harvard University

Alexander B. Cairns, Co-ordinator of Pastor Services, The Counseling Center, Bangor, Maine

Louis Cardarelli, School Social Worker, Pittsburgh Public Schools, Pittsburgh, Pennsylvania

Percy C. Carter, Pastor, St. Michael United Methodist Church, Bennettsville, South Carolina

Thomas H. Caulkins, Pastor, Murfreesboro Baptist Church, Murfreesboro, North Carolina

Ernest Cadman Colwell, Visiting Professor, Stetson University, Deland, Florida

Wallace J. Cook, Pastor, Ebenezer Baptist Church, Richmond, Virginia

Gordon N. Craig, Jr., Minister, Main Street United Methodist Church, Jacksonville, Florida

G. Wayne Cuff, Supt. Dover District, Peninsula Conference, The United Methodist Church, Dover, Delaware

Oscar Cullmann, Professor at the Sorbonne, Paris, and the University of Basle

Charles and Isabelle Cunningham, Brookhaven, Pennsylvania

Frederick W. Danker, Concordia Seminary, St. Louis, Missouri

Harold B. Dilker, Pastor, Woodland Baptist Church, Philadelphia, Pennsylvania

William G. Doty, Douglass College of Rutgers University, New Brunswick, New Jersey

Walther Eltester, Professor Emeritus, Tübingen, Germany

Earl Eugene Eminhizen, Youngstown State University, Youngstown, Ohio

Eldon Jay Epp, Professor of Religion, Case Western Reserve University, Cleveland, Ohio

Floyd V. Filson, Dean Emeritus and Professor Emeritus of New Testament, McCormick Theological Seminary, Chicago, Illinois

Joseph A. Fitzmyer, S. J., Fordham University, Bronx, New York

Edwin D. Freed, Professor of Religion, Gettysburg College, Gettysburg, Pennsylvania

Reginald H. Fuller, Baldwin Professor of Sacred Literature, Union Theological Seminary, New York, New York

Robert W. Funk, Executive Secretary, Society of Biblical Literature, Dept. of Religious Studies, University of Montana, Missoula, Montana

Paul Leslie Garber, Professor of Bible, Agnes Scott College, Decatur, Georgia

Albutt L. Gardner, Rector, St. Paul's Episcopal Church, Elkins Park, Pennsylvania

Kenneth Lloyd Garrison, Division of Parish Ministries, American Baptist Churches of Massachusetts

John P. Gates, Pastor, Bethesda First Baptist Church, Bethesda, Maryland

F. W. Gingrich, Professor of Greek, Albright College, Reading, Pennsylvania

Elmer Q. Gleim, Special Teacher, William Penn Senior High School, York, Pennsylvania

Arthur W. Greeley, Minister, Plymouth Congregational Church, Kenosha, Wisconsin

Earl R. Grose, Baltimore, Maryland

Leon Wade Hampton, Frederick, Maryland

Charles E. Harlow, La Jolla, California

Walter Harrelson, Dean, Divinity School, Vanderbilt University, Nashville, Tennessee

Edward G. Harris, Dean, Philadelphia Divinity School, Philadelphia, Pennsylvania

Howard G. Hartzell, Pastor, First Baptist Church, Philadelphia, Pennsylvania

James M. Harvey, Rector, Episcopal Church of the Resurrection, Mayfair, Philadelphia, Pennsylvania

Raymond L. Hightower, Professor of Sociology, Kalamazoo College, Kalamazoo, Michigan

Robert C. Hill, Chaplain and Chairman of Science Dept., The Annie Wright School, Tacoma, Washington

Sidney B. Hoenig, Chairman of the Faculty, Bernard Revel Graduate School, Yeshiva University, New York

Maurice L. Holder, Minister, First Baptist Church, Baltimore, Maryland

Paul M. Humphreys, Minister, First Baptist Church, Waterbury, Connecticut

John C. Hurd, Jr., Professor of New Testament, Trinity College, Toronto, Ontario, Canada

Judy and Durham Ipock, Minister, Orange Baptist Church, Orange, Virginia

Illie L. Jefferson, Windsor, Connecticut

Louis B. Jennings, Professor and Chairman, Dept. of Bible and Religion, Marshall University, Huntington, West Virginia

William O. Johnson, Pastor, First Baptist Church, Stratford, Connecticut

George Johnston, Dean, Faculty of Religious Studies, McGill University, Montreal, Canada

W. Randolph Keefe, Pastor, Grace Baptist Church, Cumberland, Maryland

Robert G. Kelly, Sr., Minister, United Methodist Church, Lincoln, Delaware

Glenn A. Koch, Eastern Baptist Theological Seminary, Philadelphia, Pennsylvania

Charles F. Kraft, Professor of Old Testament Interpretation, Garrett Theological Seminary, Northwestern University Campus, Evanston, Illinois

Robert A. Kraft, Associate Professor of Religious Thought, University of Pennsylvania

Nancy E. Krody, United Church Board for Homeland Ministries

George Eldon Ladd, Fuller Theological Seminary, Pasadena, California

G. W. H. Lampe, Regius Professor of Divinity, University of Cambridge, Cambridge, England

Mark H. Langford, Assistant to the President, Upsala College, E. Orange, New Jersey

George W. Lawrence, Jr., Minister, First Congregational Church, Burlington, Vermont

Mrs. H. E. Lawson, Pastor, Chester, Pennsylvania

Charles R. Leech, Associate Rector, Trinity Episcopal Church, Tulsa, Oklahoma

Gösta Lindeskog, Professor, Swedish University, Abo/Turku, Finland

Mrs. Irene E. Lovett, Career Counselor, The American Baptist Center for the Ministry, Wellesley Hills, Massachusetts

O. Edwyn Luttrell, Minister, First Baptist Church, Columbia, Missouri

Harvey K. McArthur, Hartford Seminary Foundation, Hartford, Connecticut

Walter R. McCall, Pastor, Providence Baptist Church, Atlanta, Georgia

Randall E. McCaskill, Pastor, New Hope Baptist Church, Niagara Falls, New York

William C. McDermott, Professor of Classical Studies, University of Pennsylvania

Bruce G. McGraw, Public Relations Counselor, American Baptist Board of Education and Publication

Clinton D. McNair, Pastor, Garfield Park Baptist Church, Chicago, Illinois

Malcolm J. MacQueen, Pastor, Second Baptist Church, Wilmington, Delaware

George W. MacRae, Professor of New Testament, Weston College, Cambridge, Massachusetts

Reese A. Mahoney, Pastor, First Baptist Church, Lakewood, New Jersey

Ira Jay Martin, III, The Henry Mixter Penniman Professorship, Berea College, Berea, Kentucky

M. Theodore Mason, Jr., Mental Health Administrator, Mercer County, Trenton, New Jersey

Peter Mellette, Virginia Director, National Conference of Christians and Jews

C. F. D. Moule, Lady Margaret's Professor of Divinity, University of Cambridge, Cambridge, England

Lucetta Mowry, Wellesley College, Wellesley, Massachusetts

James Muilenburg, Professor Emeritus of Old Testament, San Francisco Theological Seminary and Graduate Theological Union

Russell R. Myers, Greeley, Colorado

H. Clarke Nabrit, Pastor, Third Baptist Church, Toledo, Ohio

Harry V. Newkirk, School Psychologist, Binghamton School District, Binghamton, New York

Herbert N. F. G. Nurse, Minister, Easton, Maryland

John J. O'Rourke, St. Charles Seminary, Overbrook, Pennsylvania

William Russell Pankey, Minister and Author, Richmond, Virginia

R. Carrington Paulette, Pastor, East Washington Heights Baptist Church, Washington, D.C.

Lindsey P. Pherigo, Saint Paul School of Theology Methodist, Kansas City, Missouri

Willard R. Pierce, President and Executive Director, Virginia Social Research and Re-Hab. Clinic, Inc.

Otto A. Piper, Princeton Theological Seminary, Princeton, New Jersey

Petr Pokorny, Associate Professor at the Comenius Faculty of Protestant Theology, Prague, Czechoslovakia

Samuel D. Proctor, Professor, Graduate School of Education, Rutgers University, New Brunswick, New Jersey

Harold A. Rantz, Chicago, Illinois

Otto Reimherr, Susquehanna University, Selinsgrove, Pennsylvania

Karl Heinrich Rengstorf, Professor, Westf. Wilhelms-Universität, Münster (Westf.), Germany

B. Rigaux, Professeur à l'Université Catholíque de Louvain, Belgium

L. Edward Robbins, Social Worker, Ohio Youth Commission

Clarence A. Robinson, Pastor, Macedonia Baptist Church, Arlington, Virginia

Donald F. Robinson, Minister, Second Parish in Hingham, Massachusetts

Jack Fay Robinson, Minister, Waveland Avenue Congregational Church, Chicago, Illinois

W. Harold Row, Director Inter-Church Relations, Church of the Brethren, Washington (office) Representative, Washington, D.C.

Donald Rowlingson, Professor of New Testament Literature, Boston University School of Theology

Dr. and Mrs. James B. Sadler, Professor of Psychology, Sioux Falls College, Sioux Falls, South Dakota

Robert L. Salmons, Pastor, First Baptist Church, Glenside, Pennsylvania

Daniel A. Scott, Pastor, Bethany Baptist Church, Chester, Pennsylvania

R. B. Y. Scott, Professor of Religion, Emeritus, Princeton University, Princeton, New Jersey

Leroy General Seals, Associate Professor, Division of Social Science, Bishop College, Dallas, Texas

Wilbur Spenser Sheriff, Minister, First Baptist Church of Williamsport, Williamsport, Pennsylvania

Wilbur M. Sims, Director, Martinsville Memorial Public Library, Martinsville, Virginia

Charles W. F. Smith, Rousmaniere Professor of the New Testament, Episcopal Theological School, Cambridge, Massachusetts

William A. Smith, Professor, University of South Florida, Tampa, Florida

Eugene W. Spradling, Pastor, First Christian Church, Walnut, Illinois

Merle E. Spring, Pastor, Old Mystic Baptist Church, Mystic, Connecticut

Krister Stendahl, Dean, Harvard Divinity School

Georg Strecker, Professor, Vereinigte Theologische Seminare der Universität Göttingen, Göttingen, W. Germany

Albert C. Sundberg, Jr., Professor of New Testament Interpretation, Garrett Theological Seminary; Professor of Religion, The Graduate School, Northwestern University, Evanston, Illinois

William R. Tasker, Pastor, The Prospect Hill Baptist Church, Prospect Park, Pennsylvania

Herbert C. Taylor, Pastor, First Baptist Church, Cordova, Illinois

Warren F. Taylor, Jr., Minister, Etiwanda United Church of Christ, Etiwanda, California.

Howard M. Teeple, Head, Reference Dept., Chicago State University Library

Teologiska institutionerna, Lund, Sweden

Burton H. Throckmorton, Jr., Hayes Professor of New Testament, Bangor Theological Seminary, Bangor, Maine

Aubrey S. Tomlinson, Pastor, Louisburg Baptist Church, Louisburg, North Carolina

Etienne Trocmél, Professor, Faculté de Théologie Protestante, Université des Sciences Humaines, Strasbourg, France

The United Methodist Church, Manasquan, New Jersey
Franklin J. Upthegrove, Utica, New York

Philipp Vielhauer, Professor an der Universität, Bonn, W. Germany

Murray L. Wagner, Pastor, Church of the Brethren, Quarryville, Pennsylvania
Archibald Ward, Division of Training and Research, Saint Elizabeth Hospital NIMH, Washington, D.C.
Mr. and Mrs. Edwin F. Weeks, Teacher of Special Education, Thornwood, New York
Dennis A. Westbrooks, Councilman of Central Ward, Newark, New Jersey
Jesse M. Wester, Pittsburgh, Pennsylvania
Milton C. Westphal, Lansdowne, Pennsylvania
H. Edward Whitaker, Area Representative for New England, M & M Board of ABC
Allen Wikgren, University of Chicago
Amos N. Wilder, Harvard Divinity School
Albert E. Wilkerson, Associate Professor of Social Administration, Temple University, Philadelphia, Pennsylvania
Fred V. Winnett, Dept. of Near Eastern Studies, University of Toronto, Toronto, Canada
Chester T. Winters, Minister, The Baptist Church in the Great Valley, Devon, Pennsylvania
Charles R. Woodson, Pastor, First Baptist Church, Waukegan, Illinois

Franklin W. Young, Duke University, Durham, North Carolina

Solomon Zeitlin, Distinguished Professor of Post-Biblical Literature and Institutions, Dropsie University, Philadelphia, Pennsylvania